B&T
$14.00

S0-BAG-095

THE URGE TO THE SEA

THE URGE TO THE SEA

The Course of Russian History

~~~~~~~~~~~~~~~~~~~~~~~~~~~~~~~~~~~~

THE ROLE OF RIVERS
PORTAGES, OSTROGS
MONASTERIES, AND FURS

BY ROBERT J. KERNER

SATHER PROFESSOR OF HISTORY IN THE UNIVERSITY OF CALIFORNIA

Wingate College Library

~~~~~~~~~~~~~~~~~~~~~~~~~~~~~~~~~~~~

NEW YORK / RUSSELL & RUSSELL

TO THE MEMORY OF

Sergei Mikhailovich Solov'ev

BRILLIANT RUSSIAN HISTORIAN, WHO FIRST
EMPHASIZED THE HISTORICAL IMPORTANCE
OF THE FACTORS DISCUSSED IN THIS STUDY

PUBLICATION OF THE NORTHEASTERN ASIA SEMINAR
OF THE UNIVERSITY OF CALIFORNIA

COPYRIGHT, 1942, BY
THE REGENTS OF THE UNIVERSITY OF CALIFORNIA
COPYRIGHT RENEWED, 1970, BY FRANCES KERNER
REISSUED, 1971, BY RUSSELL & RUSSELL
A DIVISION OF ATHENEUM PUBLISHERS, INC.
BY ARRANGEMENT WITH
THE UNIVERSITY OF CALIFORNIA PRESS Oct. 21, 1974
L. C. CATALOG CARD NO: 72-102511   77-102511
PRINTED IN THE UNITED STATES OF AMERICA

Preface

~~~~~~~~~~~~~~~~~~~~~~~~~~~~~~~~

FOR HISTORIANS, *and in fact for most social scientists, the expansion of Russia and the building by the Russian people of a vast Eurasian empire is a story of major importance. What forces, geographic or economic, political or social, material or spiritual, became active in that urge to the sea which was a prime factor of Russian expansion into three continents? Through what instruments and in what ways did these forces act? And what do they imply for the future as their activity gains direction? These and many other questions are raised, if we view this problem in the long perspective. Adequate answers would give fuller meaning not only to the entire sweep of Russian history, but possibly also to the history of Europe and Asia. In this monograph the role of rivers, portages, ostrogs, monasteries, and furs is analyzed with a view to indicating their respective parts in this absorbing story. Here geography and history, economics and politics, religion and social life were but components, or adjuncts, of one powerful force which carried a people from the innermost sources of great rivers to the majestic seas into which they flow.*

My interest in this subject was first aroused seven years ago by work on a monographic and documentary history of Russian eastward expansion. The role of the factors enumerated above indicated that they constituted the driving power and the mechanics of the expansion. A study of these factors in

62958

PREFACE

Russian history from early times indicated that they were at work in the whole course of Russia's historical development and in all directions to the seas. A preliminary statement was given to the press on February 10, 1937 (*see* New York Times, *February 23, 1937*).

I have no desire to emphasize any deterministic interpretation, nor to lay claim to the complete working out of this set of factors in every detail of every epoch and region of Russian history. That would represent the task of a lifetime. All that I have endeavored to do has been to indicate the chief factors at work, the main direction and character of their action, and the results of their activity.[1] The rest I must leave to other scholars as they work through the history of the Russian people and have an opportunity through detailed research to confirm or to reject the indicated influence of rivers, portages, ostrogs, monasteries, and furs on the course of Russian history.

For those who would pursue this subject farther the numerous footnotes will give ample opportunity. A critical analysis of the bibliography thus offered will indicate that Z. Khodakovskii ("Puti soobshcheniia v drevnei Rossii,"* Russkii istoricheskii sbornik, Moscow, 1837, I, 1–50) first thoroughly studied the means of communication in ancient Russia. He offered many valuable observations on his personal investigations and on materials which he collected about trade routes, rivers, and portages. He did not perceive the interrelations of the factors he studied so far as they pertain to this study.*

---

[1] The groundwork of a new synthesis of Russian history, as well as of the Russian eastward movement, based on heretofore undigested and uncorrelated sources, as well as on unrelated studies, has been laid in the personal researches of the author and in the series of studies of his graduate students at the University of California. This monograph is a brief preliminary exposition of only a part of the work.

PREFACE

Apparently without knowledge of Khodakovskii's contribution, the eminent Russian historian, Sergei Mikhailovich Solov'ev—to whom this study is dedicated—first clearly pointed out the historical importance of the factors involved, in the first chapter of the first volume of his History of Russia from the Earliest Times (Istoriia Rossii s drevneishikh vremen, *first published in 1851). He confined his penetrating observations, brief but brilliant, chiefly to the early and medieval period. N. P. Barsov, using Nestor's chronicle as a basis, turned his attention to the ancient and early medieval periods and cast much light on the subject from the point of view of the historical geographer.*

The distinguished Russian historian, V. O. Kliuchevskii, whose main thesis is that "the history of Russia is the history of a country in the process of colonization" (Kurs russkoi istorii, *I, 24), necessarily touches on the influence of the factors emphasized in the present study, but chiefly in a more general way than would be expected; when he is confronted with the possibility of a "river policy" on the part of the early Muscovite princes, we find him asking himself whether expansion was the result of "some plan [or policy] which evolved of itself"* (Kurs, *II, 16). We shall look more closely at that evolution, and may find more than self-evolvement there.*

ROBERT J. KERNER

Acknowledgments

IN THE PREPARATION *of this study since its inception seven years ago, I have been assisted by a number of my former students. I am especially in debt to Dr. George V. Lantzeff, Research Fellow in History, who acted as my research assistant during the last three years and who relieved me of much drudgery in the verification of numberless clues in the many chronicles and extensive documentary publications from which this study emerged. For their unfailing help in the earlier phases of the work, I desire to thank Dr. Anatole G. Mazour, now Associate Professor of History in the University of Nevada, Oleg Maslenikov, Lecturer in Russian, and Andrew Malozemoff, now concluding his preparation for the doctorate in history. For the attractive maps and illustrations I am grateful to George W. Noia.*

Martine Emert efficiently prepared the typewritten manuscript and assisted in many other ways.

I am sincerely grateful for financial assistance from the Institute of Social Sciences of the University of California and the Works Progress Administration of the United States Government.

R. J. K.

Contents

〜〜〜〜〜〜〜〜〜〜〜〜〜〜

CHAPTER   PAGE

  I. Introduction: The Valdai Hills Region . . .   1

 II. The "Road from the Varangians to the
       Greeks"—The Kievan State 11

III. Novgorod, Gateway to Europe and the Urals . 25

 IV. Moscow, Pivot of Eurasian Empire 35

      Moscow's Strategic Position 35

      The Rise of Moscow to the Domination of the
         Upper and Middle Volga Basin 36

      Moscow's Domination of the Caspian–Baltic Sea
         Axis. 41

      The Expansion of Muscovite Russia to World
         Empire 54

         Expansion to the Black Sea 54

         Expansion to the Pacific. 66

  V. Waterways, Railroads, and Land Highways . . 89

 VI. General Observations and Conclusions . . . 103

APPENDIX

  1. Portages and the Important Russian River Sys-
     tems 107

  2. Extracts from the Smolensk Trade Codes of 1229
     and 1274, Illustrating the Regulations in Re-
     gard to the Portage from the Western Dvina to
     the Dnieper 153

CONTENTS

APPENDIX   PAGE

3. Extracts from Documents and Other Sources Illustrating the Fortified Line of 1571 and Its Successors 155

4. Seventeenth-Century Descriptions of Portages and Ostrogs, and River and Land Transportation in Siberia 165

5. A List of the More Important Monasteries in Their Relation to the River Systems and the Ostrogs 177

6. A List of Important Siberian Ostrogs 185

Index 193

ILLUSTRATIONS

Outer Walls of the Ostrog of Iakutsk 78

A View of Iakutsk in the Eighteenth Century . . 79

Fur Tribute (Iasak) Paid at a Siberian Ostrog . . 85

A Siberian Village in the Seventeenth Century . . 87

An Ostrog (Blockhouse) and Portage in Siberia 104

MAPS

PAGE

1. Key Map. Russian River and Portage System 4–5

2. The Valdai Hills. Russia's Grand Portage System . . . 6–7

3. The Road from the Varangians to the Greeks (from the Baltic to the Black Sea) 12

4. The Eastward Expansion and Trade of Novgorod . . . . following 26

5. The Struggle for the Dvina Region—Rivalry of Novgorod and Volga Princes (13th–16th Centuries) . . following 28

6. The Strategic Position of Moscow 37

7. Moscow: Northern and Eastward Expansion (15th–17th Centuries) 40

8. Russo-Swedish-Finnish Frontiers (1618–1940) 48

9. The Advance to the Black Sea: Line of 1571 55

10. The Advance to the Black Sea: End of the 16th Century 57

11. The Advance to the Black Sea: The Advance of the Frontier to 1687 59

12. Moscow: Eastward Expansion and Trade in the Ob' Basin . . . . following 66

13. Conquest of the Ob' River System (Western Siberia) . 70–71

14. Russian Eastward Expansion: The Enisei Basin (1618–1647) 74

15. Russian Eastward Expansion: The Lena Basin (1630–1648) 76–77

16. Russian Eastward Expansion: The Amur Basin (1648–1689) 80

17. Moscow, Port of Five Seas 90–91

18. Russia in Asia: (1) Western Siberia 94

19. Russia in Asia: (2) Central Siberia 96

20. Russia in Asia: (3) Northeastern Siberia 98

TRANSLITERATION

A MODIFIED FORM of the Library of Congress system has been used. In titles of works in the footnotes and in the text the apostrophe (') is inserted for the soft sign wherever it can help in the pronunciation of the word, but its excessive use has been avoided in the interest of economy.

Chapter I ◄ Introduction: The Valdai Hills Region

~~~~~~~~~~~~~~~~~~~~~

THERE IS a small upland region in northwestern Russia, less than one hundred miles square and not much more than one thousand feet above sea level at its highest point, from which rise great rivers that, either by themselves or by easy portages to others, lead through two continents to give access to all the seas in the world. The Valdai Hills,[1] the name by which this region is known, may be described as embracing the most strategic and important portages of Europe and Asia. In fact, the region may be regarded as a single grand portage in itself and hence the key portage of the world. (See map 1.) Early in their history the Russian Slavs penetrated into the region of the upper reaches of the Western Dvina, Lake Ilmen, the Volga, and the Dnieper.[2] And it is the expansion of the Russians down the rivers in all directions from this portage region that created the "Russian urge to the sea"—as will be explained and illustrated in the pages which follow.

---

[1] See V. Kamenetskii, "Valdaiskaia vozvyshennost'," Bol'shaia sovetskaia entsiklopediia (65 vols. planned, Moscow, 1926–; hereafter cited as Bol'shaia sov. entsik.), VIII, 629–630; D. N. Anuchin, "Rel'ef poverkhnosti Evropeiskoi Rossii v posledovatel'nom razvitii o nem prestavlenii," Zemlevedenie, No. 1 (Moscow, 1895), 77–126, No. 4, 65–124; idem, Verkhnevolzhskiia ozera i verkhov'ia Zap. Dviny (Moscow, 1897); S. Nikitin, Bassein Volgi (St. Petersburg, 1899); G. I. Tanfil'ev, Geografiia Rossii, Ukrainy i primykaiushchikh k nim s zapada territorii (Odessa, 1922), part 2, issue 1; V. P. Semenov-Tian'-Shanskii, Putevoditel' "Povolzh'e" (Leningrad, 1925); N. P. Barsov, Ocherki russkoi istoricheskoi geografii (Warsaw, 1885). The Valdai Hills region was also called by the chroniclers the Okovskii (Vokovskii, Volokovskii) Forest. The last of these names, "Volokovskii," indicates that it was the "Portage Forest." Barsov, op. cit., pp. 16–17.

[2] A. A. Shakhmatov, Drevneishiia sud'by russkogo plemeni (Petrograd, 1919), pp. 10, 28–52.

[1]

Neither the ancient Near Eastern portage of Naharina, situated between the Euphrates and the Orontes and linking the Persian Gulf and the Mediterranean, nor the Lake Winnipeg district in North America can approach the Valdai Hills country in the range of its access to two continents, and only Naharina can compare in historical importance with the Valdai Hills.

Of the portage of Naharina, Moret and Davy give the following testimony:[3]

The Plain of Naharina [is] . . . the keystone of the arch of the Fertile Crescent.

To insure the security of Egypt in the face of a threatening or restless Asia Minor, only one tactic could be effective—the military occupation of the branch of the Fertile Crescent which leads from the Euphrates to the Isthmus [of Egypt], and the establishment of a bridgehead at the extremity of the corridor of invasion—i.e. in this region of Naharina which is the glacis upon which the routes through Cilicia, Anatolia and the Euphrates Valley converge. . . . It is always in Syria that great captains have defended the gates of Egypt.

Naharina [is] a strategic position of the utmost importance at the junction of the roads which lead from Mesopotamia to the Black Sea, the Mediterranean, and Egypt, and in the inverse direction.

Of the Lake Winnipeg center of North America's river and portage system, Lawrence J. Burpee writes as follows:[4]

It is not merely theoretically possible to travel in a canoe across the continent, east and west, north and south, with an occasional portage, but the fact has been demonstrated over and over again by explorers and fur traders. From Lake Winnipeg, in the heart of the continent, one may paddle east up Winnipeg River to the Lake of the Woods, thence by Rainy River, Rainy Lake, and a series of

---

[3] See, for suggestive material, Alexandre Moret and Charles Davy, *From Tribe to Empire* (New York, 1926), pp. 240, 264, 303; Alexandre Moret, *The Nile and Egyptian Civilization* (New York, 1927); Richard Thoumin, *Géographie humaine de la Syrie Centrale* (Paris, 1936).

[4] See Lawrence J. Burpee, "Highways of the Fur Trade," *Transactions of the Royal Society of Canada*, Ser. III, Sec. II, Vol. VIII (September, 1914), pp. 183–192; Archer B. Hulbert, *Portage Paths, the Keys of the Continent* (Cleveland, 1903) and *Waterways of Westward Expansion: The Ohio River and Its Tributaries* (Cleveland, 1903).

smaller waterways over the almost imperceptible height of land and down to Lake Superior, coast along the shore of that inland sea, descend the St. Mary's River to Lake Huron, and from there either follow the Great Lakes down to the St. Lawrence, or take the old route by way of Georgian Bay, French River, Lake Nipissing, and the Ottawa to Montreal. From Lake Winnipeg, again, one may take either the Hayes route or the Nelson to Hudson Bay. From the same central lake, one may ascend the Saskatchewan to the Rocky Mountains and descend the Columbia to the Pacific; or, leaving the Saskatchewan at Cumberland Lake, paddle through a series of small waterways to the Churchill, ascend that river to Lake LaLoche, descend the Clearwater to the Athabaska, the latter to Lake Athabaska, ascend Peace River to one of its sources at the headwaters of the Parsnip, portage to the Fraser, and descend that wild stream to the ocean. Again, following the last route to the Athabaska, one may descend Slave River to Great Slave Lake, and follow the mighty Mackenzie to the Arctic. Finally, returning once more to Lake Winnipeg, one may ascend the Red River to its upper waters, portage to the Mississippi and descend the Father of Waters to the Gulf of Mexico. And these are but a few of many possible routes from Lake Winnipeg to the shores of the three oceans. The fur traders did not need any gift of shrewdness to lead them to the adoption of water routes. Water routes were practically thrust upon them. Wherever they went they found some river flowing to or from the place they sought, and that river was generally the easiest and often the only road to follow.

It was the Valdai Hills region, some hundred miles south of Novgorod, two hundred miles northwest of Moscow, and about five hundred miles north of Kiev, that the Scandinavian Varangians, usually known as the Vikings, utilized in order to trade from the Baltic to the Black and Caspian seas. (See map 2.) It was the nerve center of the first Russian state based on Kiev and Novgorod, which never relaxed its grip on this portage system until the Kievan state went to pieces. It was this region that held the key to the empire built up by Novgorod the Great after the fall of Kiev. It controlled Novgorod's access to food in the south and the southeast, and her fur empire to the north and northeast, without which the empire could not

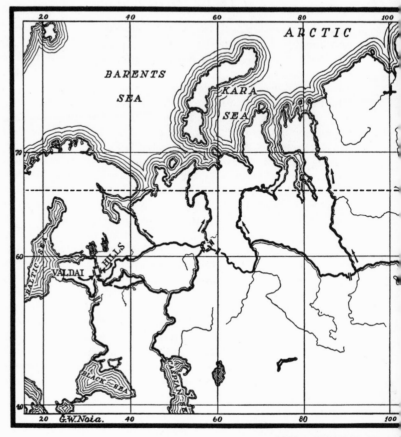

MAP 1. KEY MAP. RUSSIA

exist. It was this region that Moscow wrested from Novgorod
late in the fifteenth century in its drive for markets and natural
resources. The acquisition at that time of the necessary part of
this portage region for a Baltic–Caspian trade route, and of the
rest of it in the sixteenth and seventeenth centuries, made it
possible for Moscow to dominate the whole of the eastern European plain and to expand to the five seas: westward to the Baltic, southward to the Black and the Caspian, northward to the
Arctic, and eastward to the Pacific.

[4]

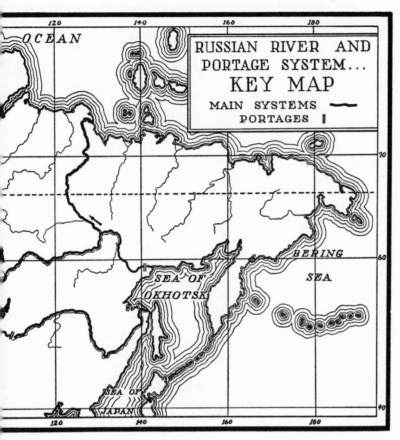

RUSSIAN RIVER AND
PORTAGE SYSTEM...
KEY MAP

MAIN SYSTEMS ——
PORTAGES |

ER AND PORTAGE SYSTEM

The successive overlordship of this region, which embraces the sources of the Volga, the Dnieper, the Western Dvina, and the Lovat', by the Swedes, by the early Russians of Kiev and Novgorod, and by the Muscovites, taught its possessors the secret of the mastery of eastern Europe. In brief, this secret lay in the domination of river systems and the control of portages between them by means of ostrogs (blockhouses) or of fortified monasteries. Smolensk, Torzhok, and Moscow were originally ostrogs. Smolensk was the key ostrog of the main highway of

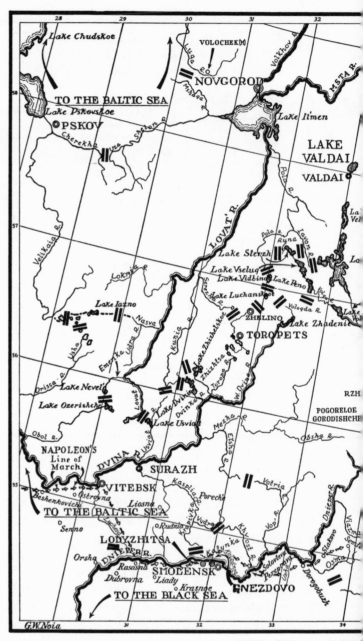

MAP 2. THE VALDAI HILL

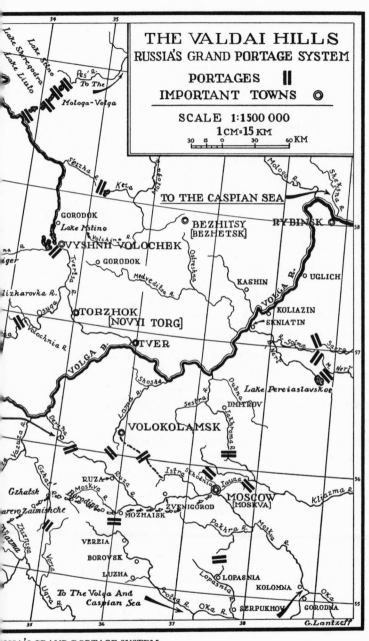

THE VALDAI HILLS
RUSSIA'S GRAND PORTAGE SYSTEM

PORTAGES ‖

IMPORTANT TOWNS ◎

SCALE 1:1500 000

1 CM = 15 KM

30 15 0 30 60 KM

Lake Shegodna
Lake Liuto
Lake Voldno

Pes' R.
To The
Mologa-Volga

Serzha R.
Keza R.

TO THE CASPIAN SEA

Mologa R.
Sheksna R.

GORODOK
Lake Mstino
Volchina R.
VYSHNII VOLOCHEK

BEZHITSY
[BEZHETSK]

RYBINSK ◎ 58

Tvertsa R.
Osuga R.
Medveditsa R.
Ostreshna R.

GORODOK

KASHIN

UGLICH

Tzharovka R.
Volochnia R.
Osuga R.

TORZHOK
[NOVYI TORG]

VOLGA R.

KOLIAZIN
SKNIATIN

TVER

R. Solma
Sara R.
Nerl R.
M. Nerl' 57

Shosha R.
Lama R.
Sestra R.
Dubna R.

Lake Pereiaslavskoe

DMITROV

VOLOKOLAMSK

Yakhroma R.

Vazuza R.
Derzha R.

Gzhat R.
Ruza R.
Istra R.
Skhodnia R.
Iauza R. 56

RUZA
Moskva R.

MOSCOW
[MOSKVA]

Kliazma R.

Gzhatsk
Borodino
arevo Zaimishche
Zhizdra

MOZHAISK
ZVENIGOROD

Moskva R.
Pakhra R.

VEREIA

BOROVSK

Vorya R.
Ugra R.

LUZHA

To The Volga And
Caspian Sea

Lopasnia R.
LOPASNIA

KOLOMNA ◎

Protva R.
Oka R.
SERPUKHOV ◎

Oka R.
GORODNA 55

G. Lantzeff

the Dnieper. The grand portage of the Valdai Hills region (see map 2) controlled in all four directions the trade routes and the movements of population, and determined as well the high strategy of interstate politics. It was a dominant factor in the history of Russia.

In the historical perspective over the centuries, one item in the trade which this and other portages in Russia controlled stands out as a permanent and usually the most important feature. That item was furs. Slaves, amber, forest products, and other commodities played their several parts at one time or another; but furs were always the most valuable single item of trade from the very earliest beginnings to the eighteenth century and beyond.

The Western Dvina, rising from the Valdai Hills upland basin, flows into the Baltic. The Lovat' joins Lake Ilmen, on which Novgorod stands. From Lake Ilmen the route passes along rivers and through lakes to the Baltic and even to the White Sea and the Pacific. The Dnieper flows into the Black Sea and gives access by portages through the Volga system at several places to the Caspian. The Western Dvina and the Dnieper lead by portages into the Niemen, the ancient axis of Lithuania, and into the Vistula, the vital nerve chord of Poland, and from them into the rivers of central and western Europe, which empty into the North Sea and the Atlantic Ocean.[5] The Volga flows into the Caspian. By portages to the east it opens the way over the Ural Mountains into that remarkable series of Siberian river systems which finally reaches the Pacific, and by portages to the north the Volga leads to the White and Barents seas and the Arctic Ocean.

These fundamentals, buttressed hereafter by conclusive evidence from the sources, indicate that the Valdai Hills region, in which these great rivers take their origin, has played a role beyond all imagination in the destiny of eastern Europe and

---

[5] Lucien Febvre, *A Geographical Introduction to History* (London, 1925), pp. 316 ff.; also E. Romer, "Problèmes territoriaux de la Pologne," *Scientia* (1920), T. XXVIII, num. CII, pp. 288–301.

Asia.* From it came the Russian urge to the sea. From it sprang the Russian motive to colonial expansion. Out of it came the Russian empire, which at one time spread over three continents.

* For suggestions relative to China see Ch'ao-ting Chi, *Key Economic Areas in Chinese History as Revealed in the Development of Public Works for Water Control* (London, 1936); K. A. Wittfogel, *Wirtschaft und Gesellschaft Chinas* (Leipzig, 1931), I.

Chapter II ⚜ "The Road from the Varangians to the Greeks"—The Kievan State

~~~~~~

THE RICHEST and most important city in Europe from the eighth to the thirteenth century was Constantinople. It was the focal point of trade routes from Asia and Europe. Among the most important of these trade routes in Europe—if not the most important—was that which connected the Black and the Baltic seas. "There is a road," so explains the chronicle, "from the Varangians to the Greeks. From the Greeks it runs along the Dnieper and up the Dnieper by portage to the Lovat'. The Lovat' flows into the great Lake Ilmer [Ilmen], and from that lake there flows the Volkhov which descends into the great Lake Nevo [Ladoga]. That lake empties into the Varangian Sea [the Baltic]. On that sea it is possible to go to Rome, and from Rome by that same sea to Tsargorod [Constantinople] and from Tsargorod into the Sea of Pontus [the Black Sea], into which flows the Dnieper. The Dnieper takes its source in the forest of Okov, and flows to the south; the Dvina takes its source in the same forest and flows to the north, emptying into the Varangian Sea; from the same forest the Volga takes its source on the east and flows through a delta with seventy branches into the Sea of Khvalin [the Caspian]."[1] (See map 3.) It was the

---

[1] Arkheograficheskaia Kommissiia, *Polnoe sobranie russkikh letopisei* (24 vols., St. Petersburg, 1846–1914; hereafter cited as *P.S.R.L.*), I, 3; V. A. Brim, "Put' iz Variag v Greki," *Izvestiia akademii nauk S.S.S.R.*, Ser. VII, Otdelenie obshchestvennykh nauk, No. 2 (1931), pp. 201–249.

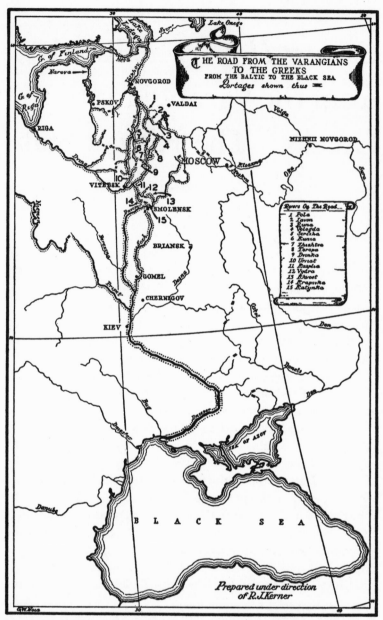

MAP 3. THE ROAD FROM THE VARANGIANS TO THE GREEKS (FROM THE
BALTIC TO THE BLACK SEA)

domination of this road from the Varangians to the Greeks through the grand portage system which became the basis of the first Russian state, known as Kievan Russia. Four centuries of Russian history gain a meaning by virtue of foreign trade and the strategic significance of this highway. When this basis was undermined the Kievan state disintegrated.

From the Baltic the grand portage basin of the Valdai Hills region may be reached by water by at least two well-marked routes: first, by the Baltic–Novgorod route, which lay up the Neva River, Lake Ladoga, the Volkhov River and its tributaries, and Lake Ilmen; and second, by the Western Dvina route. Once in the Valdai Hills region, portages lead from Lake Ilmen up the Lovat' and its tributaries to the Western Dvina and from that river to the Dnieper, which empties into the Black Sea, or from the Lovat' and its tributaries to the Volga system. (See map 2 and App. 1.)

The western part of this system may have been used by the Goths when they left their northern homeland and reached the shores of the Black Sea. It is entirely likely that they even lived along this highway for some time and built settlements, perhaps even large towns, on it. At any rate, the Russian Slavs and the Scandinavian Varangians or Vikings fell heir to whatever was accomplished or left behind by these peoples.[2]

The Varangians, if we are to trust the little evidence that remains, appear first to have used the Western Dvina route, and only later what became known as the Baltic–Novgorod route.[3] The hardy adventurers and traders of Sweden began penetrating these regions—already in part occupied by the Slavs in the seventh and eighth centuries—in order to dominate the trade

[2] M. Rostovtsev, "The Origin of the Russian State on the Dnieper," *Annual Report of the American Historical Association for the Year 1920* (Washington, 1925), pp. 163–171.

[3] Birger Nerman, "Swedish Viking Colonies on the Baltic," *Eurasia Septentrionalis Antiqua* (Helsinki, 1934) (Minns Volume), IX, 364–377; and T. J. Arne, "La Suède et l'Orient. Etudes archéologiques sur les relations de la Suède et de l'Orient pendant l'âge des Vikings," *Archives d'Etudes Orientales*, VIII (Uppsala, 1914), 14 ff.

Wingate College Library

to the south and east, especially to tap first the trade of Baghdad, through the realm of the Khazars along the Volga, and then that of Constantinople. Already, about the year 800, the town of Hedeby (just south of the present Schleswig in the peninsula of Jutland) had been built to dominate the portage between the Gulf of Slien on the Baltic and the river Treene, a branch of the river Eider, which flows into the North Sea.[4] This route from the Baltic to the North Sea across the Jutland peninsula gave the Vikings direct access to western Europe. Thus the Vikings came to dominate an east–west commercial route which began in the Near East at Constantinople, led through Russia by the Dnieper–Western Dvina–Lovat' route to the Baltic, and then into the North Sea and western Europe. It is in the light of this sweeping view that we must conceive the impact of the Vikings on Europe during the ninth century.[5]

It was, therefore, no accident that the first Russian state was consolidated during the ninth century under the leadership of the Scandinavian Varangians at Novgorod in the north and at Kiev on the Dnieper in the south. The numerous expeditions to the Black Sea and Constantinople indicate that the Varangian leaders and their Slavic comrades already dominated the entire waterway from the Baltic to the Black Sea in that century. By the end of the next century we find the Varangian groups Slavicized.

From the earliest times it is evident that the rivers determined the direction of colonization, as well as the creation of the four ancient political divisions in Russia: the Novgorodian or lake region, centered on Lake Ilmen and the rivers flowing into it; the Polotsk region on the middle Western Dvina; the Dnieper region, with Kiev as its key—ancient Russia proper;— and the region of Rostov along the upper Volga.[6] The portages

---

[4] Nerman, *op. cit.*, pp. 377–380.

[5] See T. D. Kendrik, *A History of the Vikings* (London, 1930), pp. 143–178, and Sven Axel Anderson, *Viking Enterprise* (New York, 1936), pp. 82–98.

[6] S. M. Solov'ev, *Istoriia Rossii s drevneishikh vremen* (29 vols. in 7, St. Petersburg, 1894–), I, 11–15. This is one of the best accounts of the influence of rivers, portages, and ostrogs on early Russian history.

(called *voloki* in Russian)[7] between these rivers and lakes served usually as territorial and state boundaries—they were, so to speak, the mountains in the vast plains of Russia. The early chronicles and treaties, reread in the light of the present interpretation, give us hints of the significance of these portages.

In the early history of Russia the portages naturally became sources of dispute between various principalities the boundaries of which they formed. As a result they were often divided between the two states concerned, each holding only one side of the portage. The boundaries between Novgorod and Tver were the portages, or the towns which controlled the portages, between them. There was Torzhok (Novyi Torg), which guarded Vyshnii Volochek, the chief portage between the Msta and the Tvertsa, the main water route from Novgorod to Tver. There was the portage of the Lama River, called Volok Lamskii with the town, Volokolamsk, between the Lama-Shosha tributaries of the Volga, and the Istra and Ruza tributaries of the Moskva, on which Moscow was built. This was Novgorod's main route to the lower Volga. (See map 2.)

From the treaties of 1265 and 1270 between Novgorod and Tver we see that the ruler of Tver is to keep his Bailiffs of the Portages (*Tiuny*) in his half of Torzhok and Volokolamsk, and Novgorod in its half of both portage controls. This is expressed more pungently in a document which runs as follows: "and you, Prince [of Tver], keep the Bailiffs of the Portage in your part of Volokolamsk and Torzhok, and Novgorod will keep its Bailiffs in its part."[8]

---

[7] The Russian word for portage, *volok*, by derivation means the place between two rivers or bodies of water over which boats were "dragged" or "pulled," rather than "carried" as indicated in the word *portage*. *Perevolakivat'* and *peretaskivat'*, the Russian verbs used in this connection, definitely point to this practice. See *Century Dictionary;* also I. I. Sreznevskii, *Materialy dlia slovaria drevnerusskago iazyka po pis'mennym pamiatnikam*, I, 291, and *Bol'shaia sov. entsik.*, XII, 777–778. Apparently, Russian river boats were dragged, while light Indian canoes were carried over the portage. On the other hand, the goods in Russian boats were often taken out of the boats and carried by the men over the portage.

[8] See *Sobranie gosudarstvennykh gramot i dogovorov* (5 vols., Moscow, 1813–1894; hereafter cited as *S.G.G. i D.*), I, 1, 2, 3, 6–8, 27–28; Solov'ev, *op. cit.*, I, 14.

The strategic region on this Baltic–Black Sea water road, guarded at the north by Novgorod with its outpost Torzhok, and at the south by Kiev, was the southwestern part of the grand portage system of the Valdai Hills region, with the principality and town of Smolensk and its dependency, the principality of Toropets, as its core. Smolensk stood at the portage from the Dnieper to the Western Dvina, and Toropets in the midst of several portages from the Western Dvina to the Lovat', and from the Dnieper to the Volga. (See App. 1, C. Dnieper, x–xiii; D. Western Dvina, xi–xviii; A. Volga, xx–xxx.)

The portage most commonly used from the Lovat' to the Western Dvina is in dispute. We do not know whether it was that of the Lovat'–Serezha–Toropa–Western Dvina or the Lovat'–Kunia–Lake Dvin'e–Western Dvina or the Lovat'–Kunia–Usviat–Western Dvina routes. Any one of the routes may have been used, possibly one more than the others at different times.

There were several routes and hence a number of portages from the Western Dvina to the Dnieper. The best known of these appears to have been that up the river and Lake Kasplia, a tributary of the Western Dvina, up its tributary, the Vydra, Lake Kuprino, the Krapivka (or Lelekva), then by portage to the River Katynka (a tributary of the Dnieper) to the village of Lodyzhnitsa (or Lodenitsa) near Gnezdovo on the Dnieper, and then up that river to Smolensk.[9] (See map 2 and App. 1, A. Volga, xx–xxv; C. Dnieper, iv, viii–xiii; D. Western Dvina, xviii; G. Lovat', i–x.)

This Lovat'–Western Dvina–Dnieper portage section of the grand portage of the Valdai Hills region appears to have emerged historically as belonging chiefly to the principality of Smolensk. This principality in the eleventh and twelfth centuries was kept within the family of the Grand Prince of Kiev,

---

[9] Brim, op. cit., pp. 230–232; N. P. Barsov, op. cit., pp. 16–26; and Z. Khodakovskii, "Puti soobshcheniia v drevnei Rossii," Russkii istoricheskii sbornik (Moscow, 1838), I, 1–50; S. M. Seredonin, Istoricheskaia geografiia (Petrograd, 1916), pp. 228–230; Arne, op. cit., p. 15.

who ruled both at Kiev and Novgorod; that is, it was included in the famous rotation system whereby at the death of the Grand Prince the six great principalities rotated to male members of the family as a whole in order of their seniority. Smolensk was assigned by Iaroslav the Great (1054) to his fifth son—or the fourth then alive, as Vladimir, the eldest, had died before his father.

TABLE 1
THE PRINCES OF SMOLENSK

After the death of Iaroslav, Grand Prince of Kiev, 1054, Smolensk was ruled by:

1) Viacheslav, the fifth (then the fourth living) son of Iaroslav, 1054–1057
2) Igor, the sixth son of Iaroslav, 1057–1060
3) Iziaslav (the second son of Iaroslav)
4) Sviatoslav (the third son of Iaroslav)
5) Vsevolod (the fourth son of Iaroslav)
   (Iziaslav, Sviatoslav, and Vsevolod divided the income from Smolensk, 1060–1073)
5) Vsevolod (the fourth son of Iaroslav) alone, after Sviatoslav (4) moved to Kiev, as Grand Prince. Vsevolod remained in Chernigov and sent to Smolensk
6) Vladimir Monomakh, son of Vsevolod (5), 1073–1078
7) Mstislav, the first son of Vladimir Monomakh (6)
8) Iziaslav, the second son of Vladimir Monomakh (6)
9) David, son of Sviatoslav (4), 1095–1097, who seized Smolensk

After the Liubech Convention (1097), awarding Smolensk to the family of Vladimir Monomakh—

10) Sviatoslav, the third son of Vladimir Monomakh (6) until 1116
11) Mstislav (7), the first son of Vladimir Monomakh (6), 1125–1128, or his son, Rostislav Mstislavovich (12), 1125–?
12) Rostislav, the sixth son of Mstislav (7), 1128–1160

Hereafter, Smolensk remained in the hands of the Mstislavoviches, the descendants of Rostislav Mstislavovich, until its seizure by the Lithuanians in 1935.[a]

[a] *P.S.R.L.*, I, 70, 72, 98, 103, II, 4, 14, 269, 275, 295, V, 139, 148, VII, 2–3, 232–235, 333, IX, 129; Solov'ev, *op. cit.*, I, 286, 290, 300–302, 305, 322, 327, 339, 361; P. V.

Under this system Smolensk was not allowed to fall into the hands of a prince outside of the succession in the family, nor to become an independent principality as did some other parts of Russia. For instance, it was never in the hands of the princes of Polotsk, who ruled lower down on the Western Dvina and carved out for themselves a virtually independent state in the Russian system.[10] Furthermore, the prince of Polotsk was not allowed to rule in Novgorod.[11] As a minor principality under the dominion of Smolensk, Toropets gradually grew more and more independent of Smolensk and became more closely connected with Novgorod, which was especially interested in the Lovat'–Western Dvina portage. In the thirteenth century the branch of the family of the Mstislavoviches who ruled at Toropets played a role in Russian history out of all proportion to its possessions.[12]

Thus it may be seen that Smolensk was the chief connecting link between Novgorod and Kiev along the great water road. Smolensk kept Novgorod and Kiev in touch with each other and vitally influenced the fate of both, as the details of this period amply testify. But it was not only on the road that ran north and south. It was also on the road that ran east and west, namely the Western Dvina–Dnieper–Moskva–Volga route. It was the pivot of the two great roads. (See maps 2 and 3.) Endowed with splendid forest resources and a key river and portage position, Smolensk became the center of the ancient Russian river-shipbuilding industry. Its boats were used at Novgorod and at Kiev and on the Black Sea. The greater part of the revenues of the princes of Smolensk came from the os-

---

Golubovskii, *Istoriia Smolenskoi zemli do nachala XV stoletiia* (Kiev, 1895), pp. 205–206, 261–263, 266; V. E. Rudakov, "Smolenskaia zemlia," *Entsiklopedicheskii slovar'* (41 vols. in 82, St. Petersburg, 1890–1904; hereafter cited as *Entsik. slovar'*), XXX:2, 554.

[10] V. Kliuchevskii, *Kurs Russkoi istorii* (5 vols., Moscow, 1908–1921; hereafter cited as *Kurs*), I, 208–209; Hogarth translation, *History of Russia* (5 vols., London, 1911–1931; hereafter cited as Hogarth tr.), I, 97–98.

[11] *P.S.R.L.*, I, 72.

[12] Solov'ev, *op. cit.*, I, 18.

trogs and fortified towns which guarded the portages and trade routes that ran through the principality.[13]

The first Russian state based on Kiev-Novgorod, or the water road and its portages, came into existence late in the ninth century. From the tenth to the thirteenth century the water road remained the dominant artery of commerce in eastern Europe. This was in part the result of the decline, in the tenth century, of Baghdad and of the Khazar state in southern Russia, and hence of the trade route dependent upon them (the Caspian–Volga–Baltic axis); but of almost equal importance was the energetic action of such princes as Sviatoslav, who in 966 took Sarkel (Belaia Vezha) from the Greeks of Constantinople and opened the way through the lands of the Viatichi to the domination of the middle Volga, then under the Bulgars. The expeditions of the Varangian princes against Constantinople late in the ninth century, and in the tenth, testify to their policy of keeping Constantinople from dominating the main trade routes of Russia, the western Dnieper route as well as the eastern Volga route.[14]

As early as the twelfth and early thirteenth centuries events were taking place which heralded profound changes along the great water road. The Normans, and after them the Italians, had, during the eleventh and twelfth centuries, advanced steadily by way of the Mediterranean into the commercial domain of Constantinople, completing the process with the sack of that city by the Venetians in the Fourth Crusade (1204). Constantinople never recovered its commercial preëminence after this catastrophe and soon ceased to play its former role of middle-

---

[13] I. M. Krasnoperova, "Ocherk promyshlennosti i torgovli Smolenskago kniazhestva s drevneishikh vremen do XV veka," *Istoricheskoe obozrenie* (St. Petersburg, 1894), pp. 102–104.

[14] See N. Znoiko, "O pokhodakh Sviatoslava na vostok," *Zhurnal ministerstva narodnago prosveshcheniia* (hereafter cited as *Zhurnal M.N.P.*), ser. 2, Vol. XVIII (December, 1908), pp. 258–299; and A. A. Spitsyn, "Istoriko-arkheologicheskiia razyskaniia," *ibid.*, ser. 2, Vol. XIX (January, 1909), pp. 67–98; A. L. Pogodin, "Kievskii Vyshgorod i Gardariki," *Izvestiia otdeleniia russkago iazyka i slovesnosti imperatorskoi akademii nauk*, XIX (1914), bk. 1.

man between Asia and Europe. That function passed to the
Italian cities, and the road from the Varangians to the Greeks
declined as an international highway of commerce and was
reduced more and more to its local possibilities. The victorious
advance of Novgorod and Pskov against the Germans, who
built Riga at the mouth of the Western Dvina in 1201 and
who were beginning to penetrate the upper Western Dvina
commercially, was checked[15] by the Russian national disaster at
the hands of the Mongols and Tatars on the Kalka River in 1223.
In 1239 the Tatars ". . . came [from Rostov and Suzdal] and
captured Moscow, Pereiaslavl', Iuriev, Dmitrov, Volok [Lam-
skii], Tver; . . . [they] besieged Torzhok . . . there was no help
from Novgorod . . . and the pagans took Torzhok. . . . Then the
godless pagans rushed by the Seliger route . . . killing people
like grass, [stopping] within a hundred versts from Novgorod.
But God saved Novgorod . . ."[16] The fall of Kiev to the same
invaders in 1240 sealed the fate of the southern half of the water road. The north–south trade route was thereby almost destroyed.

Two new elements now appeared on the scene, which changed
the flow of commerce from its original north–south direction
to an east–west orientation. The Valdai portage system was being increasingly used by Germans from Riga and the Hanseatic
League; and the Lithuanians began to conduct a series of raids
into the region of the portages. (See map 2.)

In 1229 Smolensk made with the Germans a treaty (also
known as the Smolensk Trade Code) by which German merchants especially were to be safeguarded in making the portage
from the Western Dvina to the Dnieper. (See App. 2.) The
Bailiff of the Portage (to use the code after 1274), on the arrival
of German merchants in the portage, was "to send his man
without delay to the Portagers (*Volochane*) so that they might
transport the German merchants and the men of Smolensk
with [their] goods [across the portage]. No one should cause

---

15 Krasnoperova, *op. cit.*, p. 84.   16 *P.S.R.L.*, III, 52.

them any hindrance, because . . . it may lead to a great deal of damage to the men of Smolensk and to the Germans at the hands of the pagans [i.e., the bandits and the Lithuanians]." For the purpose of crossing the portage there existed a commune or artel of portagers (*perevozchiki* or *volochane*) who bound themselves under the collective guaranty of all members to be responsible for the property and wares of the merchants in transit through the portage. When the merchants arrived in Smolensk, the Bailiff of the Portage received gauntlets (*ruka-vitsy perstaty—perchatki*) and the Princess of Smolensk a roll of cloth (*postav polotna*).[17] Novgorod and Smolensk became members of the Hanseatic League, which now took the place of Constantinople in the trade carried on by Russia.

The Lithuanian raiders increased their activity in the region of the Valdai portages in the first half of the thirteenth century. According to the chronicles (1223–1226), the following took place: "This winter the Novgorodians came to Iaroslav of Pe-reiaslavl' asking him to accept the authority (*stol*) over Nov-gorod. . . ." Before he dismissed the ambassadors, he received the news: "The Lithuanians, seven thousand strong, are plan-ning to raid in the vicinity of Novgorod, Torzhok, Toropets, Smolensk, and Polotsk." Upon hearing that, Iaroslav marched upon them with his army from Pereiaslavl' and caught up with them in the land of Polotsk at the small town of Osviacha. "They [the Lithuanians] made a stand . . . and fought him at the lake. Iaroslav defeated them, took prisoners, and destroyed them. The prisoners included two thousand men; their prince also was seized. In this battle David, Prince of Toropets, and Vasilii, page of Iaroslav, were killed. From there, Iaroslav pro-ceeded to Novgorod and occupied the prince's seat (*stol*)."[18]

Many other incidents may be cited from the chronicles. The situation, in fact, became so serious later that Novgorod on several occasions had to drive the Lithuanians out of Toropets, where they wished to settle, since that place controlled the por-

---

[17] Krasnoperova, *op. cit.*, pp. 87–88.   [18] *P.S.R.L.*, XX, 154, I, 190, III, 39.

tages in which the great city of the north was especially interested. Under the Lithuanian prince Olgerd (1345–1377), Toropets was finally taken; and Smolensk in 1404, by the Lithuanian ruler Witovt.[19] Nearly a century later both were recovered for the Russians by the Muscovite princes, who in 1471 had annexed Novgorod. However, Smolensk passed under Polish rule in 1611 and was not really recovered until 1686. Thus the grand portage system had been under Lithuanian or Polish rule for nearly three centuries. By the Treaty of Nystadt (1721) Peter the Great gained access to the Baltic; under Catherine II, by the First and Second Partitions of Poland and the Russo-Turkish War of 1768–1774, the road was once more Russian in its entirety from the Baltic to the Black Sea. The north–south road, however, never recovered from the catastrophes of the thirteenth and fourteenth centuries. The economic axis of Russia had shifted farther to the east, to the Baltic–Volga–Caspian water road, and the east–west route remained an important branch of that highway.

An illustration of the military significance of the portage system of the Valdai Hills and the crossroads represented by Smolensk may be found in Napoleon's line of march to Moscow in 1812.[20] (See map 2.) If any attention is paid to portages, one finds that after the Russian armies failed to meet at Minsk, their further retreat and Napoleon's advance found them facing each other on a series of seven successive portages, three to

[19] *Ibid.*, V, 182, III, 54–55, VIII, 17, XVI, 94, XV, 430, XI, 14, XX, 161, IV, 107, XI, 190.

[20] See esp. M. I. Bogdanovich, *Istoriia tsarstvovaniia imperatora Aleksandra I i Rossii v ego vremia* (6 vols., St. Petersburg, 1869–1871), III, 203–258; N. P. Ermolov (ed.), "Zapiski generala Ermolova," *Chteniia v imperatorskom obshchestve istorii i drevnostei rossiiskikh pri moskovskom universitete* (Moscow, 1864; hereafter cited as *Chteniia . . . pri moskovskom universitete*), IV, 115–282; "Zapiski grafa E. F. Komarovskago," *Istoricheskii vestnik*, LXX (1897), 43–69; and E. Foord, *Napoleon's Campaign of 1812* (London, 1914), pp. 194–197. For maps of the line of march see those copied from the originals belonging to the French Quartermaster General's Department in John Philippart, *Northern Campaigns from the Commencement of the War in 1812 to the Armistice Signed and Ratified June 4, 1813* (2 vols., London, 1813).

the west and three to the east of Smolensk, until at last at Borodino—at the entrance to the seventh portage on the road to Moscow—a battle of some magnitude was fought. The first portage
was between the Ushacha (tributary of the Western Dvina) and
the Berezina just east of Glubokoe. The second portage was between the Luchesa (tributary of the Western Dvina) and the
Dnieper just east of Senno. The first Russian army retreated to
Porech'e and Rudnia; the latter is at the portage (the third in
the series) between the Rutoveha (tributary of the Kasplia,
tributary of the Western Dvina) and the *small* Berezina (tributary of the Dnieper). Napoleon, after crossing the Dnieper between the second and third portages, engaged the Russians in
a battle for Smolensk near the portage between the Krapivka
(tributary of the Lake Kuprino—river Vydra—Kasplia Lake
and River system, a tributary of the Western Dvina) and the
Katynka (tributary of the Dnieper), the French attacking along
the northern bank of the Dnieper. This was the fourth portage. The retreating Russians left Dorogobuzh and retired to
Viazma, where there is a portage (the fifth in the series) between the Viazma (tributary of the Dnieper) and the tributaries
of the Ugra (tributary of the Oka). The Russians thereupon
retreated through a series of minor portages from Viazma to
Tsarevo-Zaimishche (between the tributaries of the upper Volga
and the Oka) until they reached the significant portage (the
sixth in the series) between the Gzhat' (a tributary of the Vazuza,
a tributary of the Volga) and the Voria (a tributary of the Ugra,
a tributary of the Oka). Further retreat brought them past
Gridnevo, a village, and the Kolotskii monastery on the Kolotsa
to Borodino (ten versts from Mozhaisk), where there is an important portage (the seventh in the series) between the Moskva
(tributary of the Oka) and the Protva (also tributary of the Oka)
and where the battle which gave Napoleon access to Moscow
was won by him.

It was also significant that the Russian staff established its
military food base at Vyshnii Volochek, one of the most im-

portant portages in the entire Valdai system, and that in its retreat from Moscow the Russian army stationed itself at various
portages to the south of the capital city.

From this account it is evident that within the portage system of the Baltic–Black Sea water road Smolensk and Toropets
had been the key positions. They were equally important on
the east–west route. Originally they both were ostrogs, just as
were Novgorod to the north and Kiev to the south. From the
earliest beginnings the records indicate that the continuously
important commodities of commerce were furs from the Russian side and textiles and metallic products from the other side.
The life of Kievan Russia was bound up in these portages,
ostrogs, and the fur trade. When the Russians lost the grand
portage system in the thirteenth and fourteenth centuries, the
main axis of the first Russian state was broken and the Kievan
state on which it was founded disappeared.

Chapter III ✍ Novgorod, Gateway to Europe and the Urals

〰〰〰〰〰〰〰〰

WITH THE FALL of Kiev in 1240, Novgorod became the leading Russian city, and in spite of its distant location in the extreme northwest of Russia it retained that primacy for nearly two centuries. Other Russian cities and principalities looked up to or envied it, for reasons which will be explained, while the greater part of the Russian population—under the Mongol-Tatar yoke—was gradually finding a new center for itself in the upper Volga basin. Novgorod suffered least from the Tatar depredations and financial exploitation. The Tatars advanced into the portage region, but whether on account of the swamps and the bad weather, or for some other reason, they never took Novgorod. The first Novgorod Chronicle states that in 1238 "the Tatars followed the Seliger route from Torzhok and stopped at a distance of one hundred versts from Novgorod."[1] Almost at the same time (1236–1240) that Kiev succumbed to the Tatars, Novgorod had to withstand the attack of the Swedes on the Neva. That the Swedes knew what they aimed at is to be seen from the following passage in the first Novgorod Chronicle:[2] "The Swedes came with large forces in ships, also the Murmans and Sum' and Em'. . . . [They]

---

[1] *P.S.R.L.*, III, 52. For the history of Novgorod in general see A. I. Nikitskii, *Istoriia ekonomicheskago byta velikago Novgoroda* (Moscow, 1893).

[2] *P.S.R.L.*, III, 52–53; confirmed for 1241, *ibid.*, XXIII, Ermolin Chronicle, 78; see also (in 1253) *ibid.*, III, 55.

stopped on the river Neva, at the mouth of the Izhora. They wanted to seize Ladoga, then the river [Volkhov], then Novgorod and all the lands of Novgorod. . . . Prince Alexander went against them with the men of Novgorod and Ladoga and defeated them."

The Baltic Germans had to be stopped on Lake Peipus in 1242. This was not to be the last of the attacks from the Swedes and the Baltic Germans, but, once past this crisis, Novgorod grew into an empire as Kiev declined and as the Russian nation licked its wounds and reorganized in the Volga basin.³

Novgorod was a great colonizing center even in the days of the Kievan state. In the ninth, tenth, eleventh, and twelfth centuries its wealthy boiars, hardy traders, and peasants began penetrating the regions around them in two directions: to the northeast, and to the southeast. "Rurik in Novgorod," states the chronicle under the year 862, "distributed the towns among his men; to one he gave Polotsk, to another Rostov, to [still] another Beloozero . . . and the power of Rurik extended over all these." This would indicate that at this early date Novgorod dominated the most important portages to the north, southeast, and west.⁴ The region toward the northeast—the basin of the Northern Dvina, which lay beyond the portages and forests of the Valdai Hills—was called Zavolochie, the "Country-beyond-the-Portage," a word the meaning of which one must bear in mind if he is to understand the history of Novgorod's empire. The motive for the advance of traders and peasants to the north and northeast was chiefly the acquisition of furs by tribute or by trapping, and the domination of the fur trade. Tusks from the seacoast and silver from the Ural country were also important commodities. As a consequence of Novgorod's expansion in this direction, that city became the center of the fur trade of Europe. It held a virtual monopoly of furs both within its own territory and over those coming from any other part of

---

³ *Ibid.*, III, First Novgorod Chronicle, 53–54.
⁴ *Ibid.*, I, Laurentian Chronicle, 9.

Russia. It is no exaggeration to say that, after the fall of Kiev, Novgorod built up an empire on furs and that this empire, loose and extensive as it was, was dependent upon the rivers and portages of the northeast which made possible the fur trade in the region to the south which in turn gave food to the capital. (See maps 2, 3, 4, 5, 6.)

To the southeast the people of Novgorod crossed the Valdai Hills portages, in the region which they called the "uplands," to the upper Volga country, which they called the "lowlands." Here they not only guarded certain portages, thereby controlling their grain supply, but also founded towns which later became independent of the mother city.

In the west, from early times the river boatmen of Novgorod, though inhabiting an inland region, attempted to establish themselves on the Baltic where pirate ships and seamen roved at will. In 1188, states one among many such references in the chronicles, "the men of Novgorod were plundered by the Varangians in Gothland and by the Nemtsy [Germans] in Khoruzhk and in Novyi Torg [Torzhok], and in the spring they let no man of their own go beyond the sea from Novgorod, and gave no envoy to the Varangians, but sent them away without peace."[5] The Novgorodians were generally unsuccessful in this unequal struggle. In fact, it may be said that if they traveled at all they usually sailed as merchants and traders on foreign ships on the Baltic. Participation in their own river boats was on a very small scale. This helps to explain why foreign-merchant quarters, especially those of the Hanseatic League (after its formation in the middle of the thirteenth century), played so important a role in the external commercial history of Novgorod. The Hansas monopolized the trade of the Baltic; Novgorod controlled that of Russia. The two met in the markets of Novgorod.

But if Novgorod had many advantages on her side, there were also some disadvantages. Among these was weather, which

---

[5] *Ibid.*, III, 19–20.

was generally unfavorable to agriculture. This led to the pre-
dominance of fur trading and fishing. The heart of the empire
which Novgorod built up, as well as the city itself, was dependent on grain chiefly from the Dnieper region in the south
during the Kievan period, and from the Volga country to the
southeast during the period which followed. The vast supply
of animals to the north and northeast gave meat in abundance,
but agriculture did not yield enough grain and what harvest
there was depended upon frosts which were frequently so severe
that the price of bread went up by leaps and bounds and often
Novgorod was on the verge of hunger, or even starvation. (See
maps 2, 4, 6.)

It has already been pointed out that the portages in the power
of Smolensk between the Lovat', the Western Dvina, and the
Dnieper controlled the bread supply in Novgorod during the
time of the Kievan state. The portages from the Pola (an eastern branch of the Lovat') and the Msta were to play a leading
role in bread supply in the period that followed. Together with
the portages that made possible Novgorod's expansion to the
north and northeast, they were vital to its existence at this
period. After creating a series of defensive rings of monasteries[6]
around Novgorod at a distance of from two to twelve kilometers, the Novgorodians made it a fundamental policy to
dominate the above-mentioned portages or at least to secure
free passage for their traders and merchants over them and the
trade routes leading from them. This was historically the sub-
stance of their relations with other Russian principalities. (See
App. 1, A. Volga, xxiv–xxv, xxvii–xxxii.)

The route to the northern sea was wholly in the regions
which were to become Novgorodian. It followed down the

---

[6] See A. Rado, *Guide Book of the Soviet Union* (New York, 1928), p. 337; I.
Pushkarev, *Opisanie rossiiskoi imperii* (St. Petersburg, 1844), I, 27–28; A. G.
Slezskinskii, "Khutynskii monastyr'," *Istoricheskii vestnik*, XCIV (1903), 926;
ibid., "Savvo-Visherskii monastyr'," LXXXVI (1901), 270. The role of monasteries
in Russian history other than in their religious functions offers a wide opportunity for research. Here the purpose has been merely to indicate their military
functions as ostrogs, i.e., as fortifications. See App. 5, below.

Volkhov from Novgorod into Lake Ladoga and from that lake to Lake Onego on the Svir' River. (See App. 1, I. Onega, i, vii.) From Lake Onego the fur trader or trapper went up the Vodlia, across the portage to Lake Kenozero, then along the Kena and Onega rivers to Lake Emetskoe, then down the river Emtsa into the lower Northern Dvina. From there one could descend to the White Sea or continue eastward along the Pinega and portage to the Kuloi and then reach the sea once more. Thereafter he could ascend the river Mezen, then its tributary the Peza, portage to the Chirka, and then go down the Tsilma, a tributary of the Pechora. (See App. 1, K. Pechora, i, vii.) One could then sail up the Pechora to the Usa, up the Usa to its tributary the Elets, portage across the Urals, and sail down the river Sob', a tributary of the Ob' in Siberia. A sea route to the Ob' beginning at the mouths of either the Northern Dvina, the Mezen, or the Pechora led through the channel between Vaigach Island and the mainland to the Ial-Mal peninsula. Here the river Mutnaia was ascended; a portage crossed to the river Zelenaia before the Ob' was reached. Thus it may be seen that not only all the north coastal region, but even Siberia, was accessible by lake, river, and portage. (See maps 4, 5.)

To reach Siberia, however, the more inland route doubtless became the desirable one because it was physically less difficult. This inland route to Siberia was reached by turning south from Lake Onego up the Vytegra River and portaging to the Kovzha, which flows into Lake Beloe (Beloozero). From this lake the road lay down the Sheksna and by portage and lakes near by into the Porozovitsa and then into Lake Kubenskoe. Here the Sukhona, a tributary of the Northern Dvina, takes its origin. Flowing east, the Sukhona empties into the Northern Dvina at a point near where the Vychegda empties into the same river. By following eastward up the Vychegda and then up its tributary, the Nem, a portage to the Visherka is reached. The latter is a tributary of the Kolva, which in turn is a tributary of the Kama. A portage from the Visherka leads to the Volosnitsa, a tributary of the Pechora. The road then leads down the Pechora and up its tributary the Shchugor. Here there is a portage across the Urals which leads by the Vol'ia or Iatriia tributaries of the Sosva to the Ob' in Siberia. (See App. 1, A. Volga, xxxii, xxxiv, lii, liii; K. Pechora, vi.)

Thus we see the northern route divided into the lateral west–east routes along the coast and inland.

It has been indicated that the inland route to Zavolochie, the "Country-beyond-the-Portage," turned south from Lake Onego to the Sheksna and then east through Lake Kubenskoe and down the Sukhona. It was at this point that the portages over the Valdai Hills joined it. This region of the Sheksna, Lake Beloe (Beloozero), and Lake Kubenskoe, dominated by the town of Vologda, was a crossroads of great significance since streams of immigrants and traders moving north and east from the Volga country met here with those moving northeast and east from Novgorod. (See map 5.) Another route, the one along the Volga and the Kama—the great highway to Siberia,—was then in the hands of the Tatars. This route to Siberia from the upper Volga region was closed to the Russians until the sixteenth century. (See map 4.)

Such indeed were the main river highways and portages which the merchants, fur-tribute collectors, and trappers of Novgorod used either singly or in companies (vatagi). The process of gaining domination over this vast territory with such small groups of men was much the same in this region as in the one previously studied: the domination of successive river basins by the control of the portages between them, the speed of the expansion being determined by the exhaustion of fur-bearing animals in each successive basin. In each case, however, the raiding of a basin preceded this development until its strategic control was established. In the district of the Urals (which came to be known as Iugria) the raiding policy never ended, because the Novgorodians never succeeded in securing domination there.

From the middle of the thirteenth century it is possible to state positively just what constituted the Novgorod empire, because beginning in 1265 treaties with Tver enumerate its territories as including Vologda, Zavolochie, Tre, Perm, Pechora, and Iugria.[7] Beginning about this time and for nearly two hundred years thereafter Novgorod probably enjoyed, even if at times precariously, its greatest prosperity.

We are now ready to turn our attention to the portages from the Novgorod–Ilmen Lake region into the Volga basin. These were decisive in Novgorod's existence: they had become keys to the routes bringing grain to the city, and at the same time were a challenge to Novgorod's northern fur empire from the Volga region along the inland route described above. Illustrations of this are very frequent in the chronicles. In 1272 a brother, Vasilii, and a son, Dmitrii, of Alexander Nevskii competed for the princely throne of Novgorod. ". . . Prince Vasilii came to Torzhok and burned the dwellings and installed his own Bailiff of the Portage (*Tiun*) and went back to Kostroma. And Sviatoslav with the men of Tver began to ravage the Novgorod districts: Volokolamsk, Bezhitsy, and Vologda. Bread was dear in Novgorod. . . ."[8] And again in 1312, "Prince Mikhail of Tver quarreled with Novgorod and withdrew his officials and cut off the grain from Novgorod. . . . he occupied Torzhok and Bezhitsy and the entire district. And in the spring when the roads were bad, the Vladyka [bishop] David went to Tver and concluded a peace; the Prince opened the gates and sent his officials into Novgorod. . . ."[9]

In 1445, Prince Boris of Tver seized fifty Novgorod districts, ravaging Bezhitsy and the country about Torzhok, and he took

---

[7] *S.G.G. i D.*, I, 1; see also I. V. Shcheglov, *Khronologicheskii perechen' vazhneishikh dannykh iz istorii Sibiri, 1032–1882* (Irkutsk, 1883), p. 7.

[8] *P.S.R.L.*, III, 62–63; *The Chronicle of Novgorod, 1016–1471* (London, 1914, translated from the Russian by Robert Michell and Nevill Forbes; hereafter cited as Michell and Forbes), p. 106; A. E. Presniakov, *Obrazovanie velikorusskago gosudarstva* (Petrograd, 1918), pp. 78–79.

[9] *P.S.R.L.*, III, 70; Michell and Forbes, p. 118.

Torzhok. ". . . Bread was dear in Novgorod, and not only this year but during ten whole years. . . ."[10]

To those who lived in the Volga basin the control of these portages meant access to the Baltic and to the Arctic—to commerce with Europe and to the fur empire.

The two portages of outstanding importance in this connection for Novgorod were: first, Vyshnii Volochek (Upper Little Portage), between the Msta, which flowed into Lake Ilmen, and the Tvertsa, which flowed into the Volga; and second, the Portage of the Lama (Volok Lamskii), also known as *The Portage* (*Volok*). (See maps 2 and 6.) The former gave access to the upper Volga, the latter to the lower Volga. The latter could be reached from Novgorod by several routes; its chief advantage was that it could be reached, if Tver blocked the Msta-Tvertsa route, by going up the Pola from Lake Ilmen, portaging to Lake Seliger, and sailing down the Selizharovka to the Volga or from the Pola directly by portage to the source lakes of the Volga and then down the Volga to the Derzha, portaging to the Ruza near Volokolamsk and following that river to the Moskva River and on to the Oka and again to the Volga. Alternately, the Portage of the Lama could be reached from the Msta by portaging eastward to the Mologa—on which stood the important ostrog or fortified center of Bezhitsy—and then up the Volga to the Shosha, up the Shosha to the Lama, from which the portage takes its name, and then to the Ruza or Istra into the Moskva. the Oka, and the Volga again. (See App. 1, A. Volga, x–xii. xx–xxxiii.)

These two routes through the Valdai Hills avoid the mouth of the Tvertsa (at the Volga) where, in 1137, the town of Tver was built. This town became the northern outpost of the region south of the Valdai Hills portages. After crossing the Msta-Tvertsa portage from the north, the ostrog of Torzhok is reached. (See map 2.) This became Novgorod's guaranty that the portage should belong to her. Before the town of Tver was

---

[10] *P.S.R.L.*, IV, 124; Michell and Forbes, pp. 201–204.

built, the passage into the Volga from this portage was open; after that, good relations between Novgorod and the princes of the Volga, especially those of Tver, determined whether access to the Volga along this route would be easy. On the other hand, there were numerous attacks by the Volga princes on Torzhok, which the Novgorodians regarded almost as sacred as their own city. It was burned or destroyed many times, but as long as Novgorod was independent, Novgorod always rebuilt it and reëstablished its control there.

Novgorod could expect to maintain itself only so long as Smolensk and Suzdal, and Tver and Moscow, were at odds with each other long enough to allow her grain supply to come through, or as long as Suzdal, Rostov, and Moscow in the Volga basin did not take it upon themselves to extend their territories north into the fur empire after their inhabitants began to emigrate into that region. Once either of these matters should become a point of policy, Novgorod's doom would be sealed. The routes would be cut, the portages seized, and Novgorod annexed. If it was true that Novgorod had to be on good terms with Smolensk in the Kievan period, it was now true that that city had to be on good terms first with Suzdal (before Tver dominated the Tvertsa region), then with Tver, and finally with Moscow.

When Moscow emerged as the dominant power in the Volga region in the fifteenth century, it could not avoid an interest in the direct trade with Europe, which passed through Novgorod and its portages to the Baltic, nor in the chief raw materials of that trade in the fur empire to the north and northeast. Moscow also looked forward to the end of Tatar domination of the lower Volga–Caspian trade route and the markets of central Asia and beyond. It was this Baltic–Volga–Caspian trade route that was to form the axis of the new Muscovite state. Landlocked Moscow's future on the middle course of this route was either suffocation or domination of the rivers and portages from sea to sea.

It must not be supposed that the fur empire of Novgorod was a closely knit, firm state organization. Stretching out over a vast area, with points of defense and domination chiefly at strategic localities amidst hostile Finnish tribes, it was thinly populated by Novgorodians and Volga Russians. This was also a population in motion most of the time. The empire consisted of ostrogs and monasteries at portages and key points of the river basins. (See Apps. 1, 5.) The Novgorodians levied a tribute of furs on the inhabitants. The raids of the Novgorodians became a regular policy, both for the exaction of tribute and for keeping interlopers from the Volga and the Kama country from approaching the northeast.[11] Because Novgorod lacked mass population with which to settle intensively the country thus opened up, and because of the raiding policy, no solid imperialism could be established over this region. Iugria, or the Ural country, was never held as a country, but was a territory into which raids were made and where tribute was collected from inhabitants living in the fear of raids. But there were expeditions sent out by Novgorod that did not return victorious from these raids.[12] Over most of the distant northeast country Novgorod exercised rather a sphere of influence than the actual sovereignty of a state.

---

[11] P.S.R.L., III, 79 (1340), 81–82 (1342), 88 (1366), IV, 66 (1369), 71–72 (1375), XI, 126 (1390), IV, 102–103 (1398); also III, 98–100, 110; see also M. Berezhkov, "O torgovle Rusi s Ganzoi do kontsa XV veka," Zapiski istoriko-filologicheskago fakul'teta imperatorskago s.-peterburgskago universiteta, Part III (St. Petersburg, 1878), p. 44, who indicates that the river raids from 1359 to 1409 were often large-scale enterprises.

[12] See P.S.R.L., III, 21–22; Michell and Forbes, op. cit., pp. 36–37; P.S.R.L., III, 73, 74, IV, 124.

Chapter IV ᴁ Moscow, Pivot of Eurasian Empire

~~~~~~

THE HISTORY of Moscow is the story of how an insignificant ostrog became the capital of a Eurasian empire. This insignificant ostrog, built in the first half of the twelfth century, on an insignificant river by an insignificant princeling, became, in the course of time, the pivot of an empire extending into two, and even three, continents.

Moscow's strategic position.—As the Kievan state declined and finally collapsed, a large part of the Russian population migrated into the Mezhduriechie—the Russian Mesopotamia—formed by the upper Volga and the Oka, which flows into the Volga lower down. Moscow found itself on the Moskva River, which flows into the Oka. It was, therefore, in the heart of the Russian Mesopotamia. (See maps 2 and 6.) It was at the center of the portages and rivers in this upper Volga basin, with direct access to the Volga on the north, east, and south, and to the Dnieper and Western Dvina on the west. To the north, portages from the Moskva and its tributaries led to the Lama through Volokolamsk and down that river and the Shosha to the Volga and to the Derzha, a tributary of the Volga. To the east, portages from the Skhodnia and Iauza, tributaries of the Moskva, led the boatmen to the Kliazma, a tributary of the Oka, in turn a tributary of the Volga. This led to the Caspian. It should be noted here that from the Volga one could reach Zavolochie to the north and Siberia to the east. A more southern route led by portage from the Moskva to the Protva, or from the Pakhra tributary of the Moskva to the Lopasnia, both

of which joined the Oka; and that in turn by other portages led
to the Don, the Dnieper, and the Black Sea. To the west, portages from the Moskva opened the road through the Volga tributaries, the Gzhat' and Vazuza, to the Dnieper and the Western
Dvina. These in turn connected Moscow by water with the
grand portage system of the Valdai Hills and hence gave access
to the Baltic as well as the Black Sea. Moscow, therefore, could
reach by portage all the river systems of the vast territory that
became the Russian empire.[1] It was the crossroads of two great
waterways and trunk lines of trade, the Caspian–Baltic axis of
rivers and portages, and the west–east route from the Western
Dvina to the Volga. It was more centrally situated than any
capital of a Russian state before or after—Kievan, Novgorodian,
or Petrine—and hence it was the natural pivot of the Eurasian
empire which the Russians founded. The transfer of the capital
from St. Petersburg (Leningrad) to Moscow under the Soviet
rule was, among other things, a recognition of this fundamental
fact. (See App. 1, A. Volga, v–xxviii.)

*The rise of Moscow to domination of the upper and middle
Volga basin.*—The feudal or appanage period in the Volga system which followed the decline and collapse of the Kievan
state in the thirteenth century was, in large part, a struggle
to dominate the basins and portages of that river and its tributaries. To bring these together meant political unity and domination. A glimpse of what such a development might mean is
given when, in 1469, "Grand Prince Ivan [III, of Moscow] sent
his army on boats into the Kazan region. . . . [Some Muscovites]
went on the Moskva River to Nizhnii Novgorod; other [Mus-
covites] went by way of the Kliazma. The men of Kolomna,
and all those living along the Oka above them, went down the
Oka. Those from Murom did likewise. The men from Vladimir
and Suzdal went down the Kliazma. Those from Dmitrov and

---

[1] For some observations on this subject see Ivan Zabelin, *Istoriia goroda
Moskvy* (Moscow, 1904), pp. 1–21; Khodakovskii, *op. cit., passim;* and Barsov,
op. cit., pp. 23, 29–30, 43, 51, 171–172, 188–189, 196, 252, 258–262.

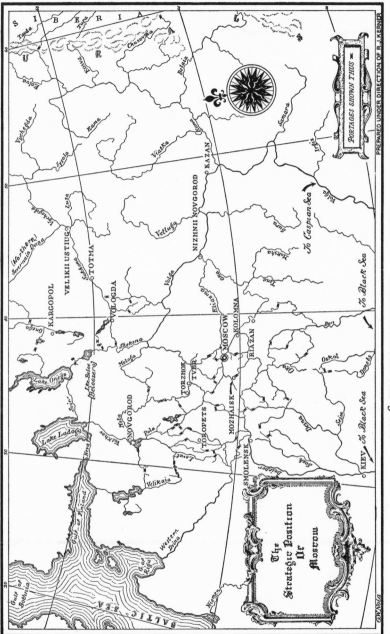

PREPARED UNDER DIRECTION OF R. J. KERNER

MAP 6. THE STRATEGIC POSITION OF MOSCOW

The
Strategic Position
Of
Moscow

Mozhaisk and Uglich, from Iaroslavl and Rostov, from Kostroma and the others in the Volga region, came down the Volga, arriving at [Nizhnii] Novgorod at the same time."[2]

Moscow was founded certainly by the last quarter of the twelfth century by the princes of Suzdal-Vladimir, in all probability as a military base or outpost against the south. Soon it began to acquire another significance.[3] Like others in this region, the minor principality of Moscow engaged in the business of "gathering together" pieces of territory here and there. Not long after it began to rise in importance, a "definite plan," so to speak, emerges.[4] First, it appears, the entire Moskva River was dominated in 1301 by the seizure of Mozhaisk at its source, and Kolomna, where it empties into the Oka. These "in the future served as bases for Muscovite expeditions against Smolensk on one side and toward the Oka and Volga regions on the other."[5] It soon became evident that the acquisition of the Moskva River, with its customs duties at Mozhaisk and Kolomna, had a real commercial and financial significance.[6] Next, the Kliazma was obtained by the absorption of the suzerain province of Vladimir. There followed other accretions of territory on the upper Volga and Oka until Tver[7] on the Volga and Riazan on the Oka were almost surrounded. When Nizhnii Novgorod on the middle Volga was acquired in 1394, Moscow virtually dominated the trade of that river. (See map 6.)

---

[2] Nikon's Chronicle, *P.S.R.L.*, XII, 121.

[3] S. F. Platonov, "O nachale Moskvy," *Bibliograf* (1890), bks. 5–6, argues, and A. E. Presniakov, *op. cit.*, p. 115, accepts the view, that Moscow was not originally a commercial center, but the outpost or base of operations of the Prince of Suzdal-Vladimir against the south. The weight of evidence is in that direction, and this view is accepted by the present writer.

[4] Kliuchevskii, *Kurs*, II, 16–17 (Hogarth tr., I, 283), asks if this is not a definite policy—a river policy. The answer appears clearly to be in the affirmative. Illustrations are to be found in the wills of the princes of Moscow. Presniakov, *op. cit.*, pp. 165, 170–171, 172, 175–176.

[5] Presniakov, *op. cit.*, pp. 118–119.

[6] *S.G.G. i D.*, I, 39, 59–61.

[7] *P.S.R.L.*, VII, 188, illustrates how Prince Iurii of Moscow summoned Novgorod, which had sufficient reasons to oppose Tver, to assemble at Torzhok, while he established his camp at Volokolamsk. Iurii, however, was not successful in this campaign.

The northern affluent of the Volga, the Kostroma, gave access by portage to Zavolochie, the Northern Dvina country, the already mentioned "Country-beyond-the-Portage," including especially Vologda and Totma, formerly Novgorodian colonies, now fast becoming independent, and Velikii Ustiug. They, in turn, opened up a road to raw materials of great wealth for that day, furs and silver, then in the domain of Novgorod. In the thirteenth and fourteenth centuries minor princes, their retainers, and peasants from the upper 'Volga country made their way up the Mologa and Sheksna, northern tributaries of the Volga, and into the Lake Beloe (Beloozero) country. At the same time, monasteries in that locality were founded by monks from the Volga region. In this strategic triangle (see maps 5, 4, 7), cutting across the inland Novgorod route into the Northern Dvina country, a long and bitter struggle was waged over access to the Vologda country and the Sukhona, a tributary of the Northern Dvina, one of the highways to the Arctic Ocean and Siberia, as indicated above. (See App. 1, J. Northern Dvina, i–xxiv.) Here the Novgorod and Volga governments (which meant Moscow in the first half of the fifteenth century), the Novgorod and Volga monasteries and churches, and the Novgorod and Volga populations fought it out.[8] The chronicles give much testimony on the subject. Novgorod's canoe men (*ushkuiniki*), sometimes called the "Braves of Novgorod," raided along the Volga, especially from 1369 to 1450, in an attempt to prevent the supremacy of the Volga country along this great inland highway—the Northern Dvina. Slowly, stubbornly, and with decisive force when Moscow assumed the leadership, the line advanced from the portages between the Kostroma and the Sukhona to the next watershed northward, between the Sukhona and the Vaga. In this way Vologda, Totma, and Velikii Ustiug, gradually filled by Volga immigrants, became, first, independent of Novgorod, and then,

---

[8] For the pre-Tatar and Tatar period see Presniakov, *op. cit.*, pp. 36–39, 48–51, 80–81, 138–139. The Tatars opposed the union of the Volga countries and Novgorod.

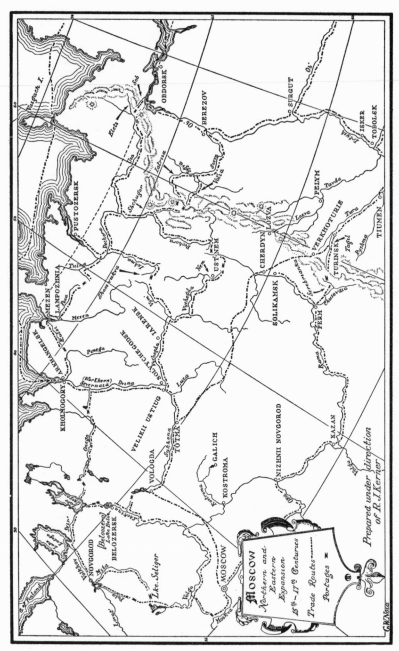

MAP 7. MOSCOW: NORTHWARD AND EASTWARD EXPANSION (15TH–17TH CENTURIES)

in the first half of the fifteenth century, allies of Moscow. Thus Moscow opened up the road to the fur empire, to the Arctic, and to Siberia.[9]

Moscow's domination of the Caspian–Baltic sea axis.—Moscow held the gateway to the lower Volga and the trade of Asia, particularly in silk, at Nizhnii-Novgorod from the time of its acquisition in 1394. After the disintegration of the Golden Horde, the Tatar Khanate of Kazan, which dominated the lower Volga, proved a new and powerful factor.[10] Barred from the Caspian by Kazan and from the Baltic by Novgorod, Moscow, the ruler of the middle and upper Volga, was faced with the alternative of suffocation or of forging her way out to both seas. Should she make her way out, she would dominate a part of the silk trade of Asia and obtain a virtual monopoly of the fur trade of Europe.[11]

It is not difficult to see in which direction Moscow would act first, since a breach had already been made into the fur empire of Novgorod.[12] Acquisition of the northeastern part of the Valdai Hills portage would give access to the Baltic. Long had the princes of the Volga region yearned to do this! As far back as the twelfth century and in the two centuries which followed, the aspiration was there and frequent attempts were made to bring Novgorod under the domination of the Volga princes. The chronicles are full of these incidents.[13] Lithuania was in control of the southwestern half of the Valdai Hills portage

---

[9] S. F. Platonov, *Proshloe russkogo severa* (St. Petersburg, 1923), pp. 7–10; A. A. Kizevetter, *Russkii sever* (Vologda, 1919), pp. 12–40; Kliuchevskii, *Kurs*, II, 313–315.

[10] See Presniakov, *op. cit.*, pp. 397–399, which ably describes the effect upon Moscow of the establishment of the Khanate of Kazan. It caused Moscow to hurry the subjugation of Novgorod the Great.

[11] S. F. Platonov, *op. cit.*, pp. 20–36; Theodor Schiemann, *Russland, Polen und Livland bis ins 17. Jahrhundert* (Berlin, 1886–1887), I, 285; Presniakov, *op. cit.*, pp. 277–282.

[12] L. K. Goetz, *Deutsch-russische Handelsgeschichte des Mittelalters* (Lübeck, 1922), p. 9.

[13] *P.S.R.L.*, III, 91–92, 98–102, 106–107, 113, IV, 91–94, 99–103, 115–116, XI, 155; also Presniakov, *op. cit.*, pp. 143–146.

system. As already indicated, it held Smolensk, Toropets, and all portages from the Western Dvina to the Dnieper and from the Dnieper to the Volga system. In the past, Novgorod could always lean on Lithuania if the Volga princes became too aggressive, and on the Volga princes if Lithuania threatened, as she did on numerous occasions, to absorb Novgorod. Actually the latter at times paid tribute to both sides. But it was a dangerous game, which she finally lost.

The struggle between Moscow and Novgorod, which culminated in 1471–1478, was fundamentally one of raw materials and highways, that is, furs, river systems, and portages. For Moscow it meant empire and a new Russian national development, or disintegration. For Novgorod it meant either Muscovite or Lithuanian domination.

When Orthodox Novgorod signed a treaty acknowledging as her overlord Roman Christian Lithuania, which held Smolensk and Toropets and hoped to acquire Torzhok, Bezhitsy, and the remaining strategic points in the Valdai Hills portage system (see map 2), the able but unscrupulous Muscovite princes could rouse up Russian national feeling in its religious and racial aspects throughout all Russia. And this is what Ivan (III) the Great did when he suddenly carried out the subjugation of Novgorod in 1471 and effected its complete absorption by 1478. Otherwise, Lithuania would have blocked Moscow from these regions and possibly even conquered Moscow, for the control of the entire Valdai Hills portage system would have given Lithuania decisive advantages over Moscow.

For our purposes it is interesting to note that the Muscovite campaign of 1471 included certain river and portage factors. (See map 2.) The main army of Ivan III, concentrating at Volokolamsk, proceeded by way of Torzhok and Vyshnii Volochek into the Novgorod country; in other words, through two portages and on connecting rivers. Next, we hear of the army near Lake Valdai (at the village of Iazholbitse), although we do not know how it got there, whether by land or water. From there it went to Rusa. One of the Muscovite armies was sent originally against Rusa (by what route we do not know), and finally it was ordered to join the army of Pskov on the Shelon' River (probably at or near the portage from the Cherekha to the Uza, a tributary of the Shelon'). Here on the Shelon' River was fought the battle which decided the fate of Novgorod proper.[14]

At the same time that this campaign in Novgorod proper took place, Ivan III ordered his military commanders *(voevodas)* Obrastsov and Slepets at Ustiug to take the forces stationed there and at Viatka and proceed by boat to the Northern Dvina country. (See map 5.) "On the River Shilenga," so reports the chronicle, "they were met by Prince Vasilii Vasilievich Shuiskii with the military commander of the Dvina and a strong force of men from the Dvina country. There followed a terrible battle . . . ; the Novgorodians were defeated and fled to Novgorod."[15] Thus, in this medieval blitzkrieg, Moscow first starved Novgorod (by seizing Torzhok) and then with lightning strokes subdued her on the Shelon' and Northern Dvina. A rising of the Novgorod population followed the cutting off of grain supplies and completed the military victory.[16] With one stroke Moscow won access to the Baltic and White seas and the entire fur empire to the north and east. In 1485 Tver, now wholly surrounded by Muscovite territory, was absorbed by Moscow.[17]

The Baltic–Caspian axis of the new Muscovite state was advanced a step farther when Kazan and the lower Volga were annexed in 1552 by Ivan (IV) the Terrible, who had previously occupied the important fords across the rivers which led to Kazan,[18] and built the ostrog of Sviiazhsk in 1551 as a base against that strategic stronghold.

---

[14] Solov'ev, *op. cit.*, I, 1361–1364.

[15] A. A. Titov (ed.), *Letopis' velikoustiuzhskaia, po Braginskomu spisku* (Moscow, 1902), p. 4.

[16] Kliuchevskii, *Kurs*, I, 364.

[17] *P.S.R.L.*, VIII, 216–217.

[18] *Ibid.*, XIII, 166, 177, 198–203; see esp. the Kazan Chronicle, *ibid.*, XIX, 34–36, 62, 71, 104, 114, 126, 304, 325.

The Livonian War (1558–1583) of Ivan the Terrible was an attempt to acquire for Muscovite Russia a foothold on the Baltic, in other words, direct access to the sea. It was a continuation of the struggle between the Swedes and Germans (as well as the Lithuanians) on one side, and the Russians on the other—a struggle which, so far as it pertains to the Swedes, began in 1240 when Prince Alexander of Novgorod defeated them on the Neva and ended in 1721 when Peter the Great concluded in triumph the Peace of Nystadt.[19]

In this struggle the Swedes, seeking at least the commercial, if not always the political, control of the Baltic Sea and northern Russia, aimed to eliminate Russia from the Baltic and to secure themselves against the rising power of Russia by obtaining certain strategic points and rivers. Among these was the fortified city of Narva, which, subject to one condition, commanded the road to Pskov up the Narova River, and the way up the Luga River with a portage to the Mshaga River, which empties into Lake Ilmen, on which Novgorod is to be found. That condition was Swedish command of Ivangorod,[20] which the Russians had built in 1491. The way into the Valdai portage system from the northwest would thus be opened up.

Then there was the Neva River, which flowed from Lake Ladoga to the Gulf of Finland. The river itself was controlled at Lake Ladoga by the ostrog of Oreshek, built by the Russians

---

[19] For the best accounts of this see esp. G. V. Forsten, "Bor'ba iz-za gospodstva na Baltiiskom more v XV i XVI stoletiiakh," *Zapiski istoriko-filologicheskago fakul'teta s.-peterburgskago universiteta* (St. Petersburg, 1884), XIV; *idem*, "Baltiiskii vopros v XVI i XVII stoletiiakh (1544–1648)," 2 vols., in *Zapiski*, XXXIII–XXXIV (St. Petersburg, 1893–1894); *idem*, "Akty i pisma k istorii baltiiskago voprosa v XVI i XVII stoletiiakh," 2 vols., in *Zapiski* (St. Petersburg, 1889–1893); also *idem*, "Politika Shvetsii v smutnoe vremia," *Zhurnal M.N.P.* (St. Petersburg, 1889), CCLXI, 325–349, CCLXV, 185–213, CCLXVI, 17–65; H. Almquist, *Sverge och Ryssland, 1595–1611* (Uppsala, 1907); *idem*, "Die Carenwahl des Jahres 1613," *Zeitschrift für osteuropäische Geschichte*, III (Berlin, 1913), 161–202; Generalstaben, *Sveriges krig (1611–1632)*, I, *Dansk och Ryska Krigen* (Stockholm, 1936); C. G. Styffe (ed.), *Konung Gustaf II Adolfs Skrifter* (Stockholm, 1861); J. Hallenberg, *Svea rikes historia under konung Gustaf Adolf den Stores regering* (4 vols., Stockholm, 1790–1796).

[20] Forsten, "Bor'ba . . . ," pp. 151–153.

in 1322,[21] which later was called Noteburg by the Swedes and Schlüsselburg by Peter I, and at the place where it emptied into the Gulf of Finland by Nienshants,[22] virtually on the site of St. Petersburg. Nienshants was built by the Swedes in 1300, seized and destroyed by the Russians in 1301, and rebuilt by the Swedes in 1609. The Neva River was for the Russians their direct way of access to the sea; for the Swedes it was a highway into all northern Russia. The Volkhov River flows from Lake Ilmen, on which Novgorod stands, into Lake Ladoga; at its mouth was built the ostrog of Ladoga. The Volkhov, Lake Ladoga, and the Neva together constituted the chief highway of Novgorod to the sea. (See map 4.) Lake Ladoga, in addition, gave access by river, lake, and portage to all northern and northeastern Russia, as has already been pointed out. Viborg, in which the Swedes first established themselves at the end of the thirteenth century, was probably useful for two reasons: (1) as a base for the control of the eastern end of the Gulf of Finland, and (2) for access to Lake Ladoga through the Karelian Lakes system in the period when the Swedes did not dominate the Neva. In the hands of the Swedes it also blocked a possible Russian advance into Finland.

In the fourteenth, fifteenth, and sixteenth centuries the Swedes tried to gain possession of Oreshek, the Russians to acquire Viborg.[23] The Livonian War ended in 1583 to the disadvantage of the Russians, with the acceptance of Swedish domination of Baltic Esthonia and Swedish possession of Narva, in Esthonia, and Ivangorod, Iama (later called Iamburg), and Kopor'e, as well as Kexholm on Lake Ladoga in Karelia, all in Novgorod territory. Kexholm probably assured Swedish access from the Gulf of Finland through the Karelian Lakes to Lake

---

[21] "Russko-shvedskiia voiny," *Entsik. slovar'*, XXVII:1, 343–344.

[22] Also called Nishants, Shants-Ter'nien, Landeskron, Nyenskans, Nyenshantz, or Neivaschanze, Nevalinna, Skanz ter Nyen, Kantsve, Novyi Kantsy. See A. Shchekatov, *Slovar' geograficheskii rossiiskago gosudarstva*, IV, 663–664, and *Entsik. slovar'*, XIII:1, 213.

[23] *Entsik. slovar'*, XXVII:1, 343–344; Forsten, "Bor'ba . . . ," pp. 156–161; *idem, Baltiiskii vopros . . .* , I, *passim.*

Ladoga. With Narva, Ivangorod, Iama, Kopor'e, Viborg, and Kexholm in Swedish hands, the rising power of the north was closing in on Russia.[24]

There remained the control of the easiest line of communication between the Gulf of Finland and Lake Ladoga—the river Neva. Opportunity for the Swedes to gain this control (i.e., through Nienshants and Oreshek) came with Russia's "Time of Troubles," especially after 1604, when the Poles sought to dominate Russia. The Swedes intervened as allies, prompted by their fear of Polish domination of Russia. They took advantage of the virtual collapse of that country and of its desire for aid from Sweden against Poland by demanding occupation of these important river bases as guaranties of future payment for their services. In one or two instances they obtained these advantages by fraud, became involved in war with the Russians over them, and obtained a peace (1617) which gave them all that they had demanded for their services with the exception of Novgorod.

To show that the Swedes had a keen sense of the value and significance of the rivers, portages, ostrogs, and fur trade it is only necessary to mention a few details. In 1609 the Swedes rebuilt Nienshants[25] at the mouth of the Neva. That same year, in a treaty between Skopin-Shuiskii and the Swedes, the Russians surrendered Kexholm in return for the sending of Swedish troops from Torzhok to Koliazin at the junction of the Volga and the Zhabka;[26] this actually put the Swedes in domination of the northern half of the Valdai portage system, while the Polish king, Sigismund III, was demanding the surrender of Smolensk, the key to the southern half of this system.[27] Two years later, the Novgorodians, by treaty with Jacob de la Gardie, commander of the Swedish troops, or by the strategem of the latter, surrendered the key fortifications of Novgorod and the

[24] Solov'ev, op. cit., VI, 282–292; Forsten, Baltiiskii vopros . . . , I, 699–715.
[25] Entsik. slovar', XIII:1, 53.
[26] S.G.G. i D., II, 374, 375–383.
[27] Ibid., II, 504–506.

ostrogs of Oreshek and Ladoga.[28] In 1611, therefore, the Swedes actually dominated the Russian north—they had all the keys in their hands. As a result of hostilities which broke out between the Swedes and the Russians in 1613 in the region of Tikhvin and of Bezhitsy—strategic centers of great importance for access to the northern regions—the fictitious relationship of Swedish "allies" became that of Swedish enemies.[29] In 1617 at Stolbovo a peace was signed giving Sweden all she had demanded with the exception of Novgorod, to which from the north the Swedes held all the points of access. (See map 8.)

All this is best described in the words of Gustavus Adolphus, who, in his speech before the Riksdag at Örebro on January 28, 1617, said:[30]

The chief reason for the slowness of procedure [i.e., in making peace with the Russians] has been that they have been unwilling to grant us our rights and an indemnity. It was absolutely impossible to obtain the seventy barrels of gold we asked for at Dedrina [Dederin]. The [Russian] offer of forty barrels, which the mediators considered reasonable, was regarded [by the Swedes] as intolerable. Iwanogrod [Ivangorod], Jama [Iama], Copori [Kopor'e], Nöteborg [Oreshek], and Kexholm, with their land and provinces, were very dear to the Russians, but no peace could be established without the fulfillment of one of the two demands. Otherwise a settlement would have been altogether too far removed from the suggestion given me by Your Highnesses [lords] and you [commons] at the last meeting of the Estates. If the offer had been accepted, it would have brought shame and dishonor upon our fatherland and myself, and would have led to the greatest insecurity in the future. For what could have been more humiliating than to have accepted 110,000 riksdaler, which would not have been enough to pay even half of the soldiers' wages, and then return nine well-fortified cities and

[28] *Ibid.*, II, 553–555. See also Almquist, *Sverge och Ryssland*, pp. 105–268; *idem*, "Die Carenwahl des Jahres 1613," pp. 161–202.

[29] *P.S.R.L.*, III, 307–308; also see *Entsik. slovar'* for Borovitskii monastery (IV:1, 429) and Vvedenskii monastery (XXXIII:1, 280); Generalstaben, *Sveriges krig (1611–1632)*, I, 318–572.

[30] See Styffe, *op. cit.*, pp. 140–143, 179–187, as translated by Peter Gulbrandsen and revised by Albin T. Anderson. This has been paraphrased and quoted by Forsten, "Politika Shvetsii ...," pp. 31–33.

castles, together with the land and fiefs belonging to them, which
I now rightfully own? For it would then have seemed as if we Swedes
had been subdued by the Russians, or that we were exhausted, or
that I, as Sweden's king, had been so pusillanimous that I was afraid

MAP 8. RUSSO-SWEDISH-FINNISH FRONTIERS (1618–1940)

of trusting God to lead and help my just cause to a successful conclusion. All that would have been no little humiliation. And besides, what guaranties would we have had from the enemy, who
rarely keeps his word and whose recent acts have amply testified to
his lack of reliability? Even in times of peace Swedish subjects in
Finland and Estland [Esthonia] have not been safe against Russian
invasion, because the Russian has us so close to his frontier. Now

that he has already inflicted injury upon us, should we present him an opportunity to do so again when he is actually in our hands? No man in his senses, and least of all one who loves his country, could ever agree to that. Why, merely for the sake of three or four years of peace, should we Swedes be such thoughtless fools as to let the Russians come to our very doorsteps in Lijfland [Livonia] and Finland, when we can separate ourselves from them with Lake Laduga [Ladoga], with the extensive, thirty-miles-wide swamp and the turbulent Narfweske [Narova] River, and when it is not their custom to remain at peace? Moreover, these territories are not to be esteemed too lightly, as they are of great value and also of extensive area—so large, in fact, that they themselves can defray the expenses connected with holding them. For these reasons it would not have been advisable to return these territories to Russia.

Thus our position has made things more difficult for the Russians, in this, that they have been cut off from the shores of the Baltic. Henceforth they are forbidden entrance to the Baltic at any point, and cannot use it for their ships for their own accommodation, either for war purposes or for trade, without our special permission, as Narwen [Narva] and Ivanogrod [Ivangorod] block their outlet through the Narviske [Narova], and Nöteborg through the Nyen [Neva], and only by these routes could they reach the Baltic Sea. They have also seen in the past the benefit to ourselves of the control of these rivers, and how this control enabled us to inflict injury upon the enemy, for, making use of these rivers, we have swept across most of their territories which border upon our country. This has given the Russians so much the more reason to hesitate about ceding these territories for all time.

At the opening of the Riksdag in Stockholm, on August 26, 1617, after the conclusion of the Peace of Stolbovo, Gustavus Adolphus made the following remarks:

This victory is indeed not the least favor that God has bestowed upon the government of our fatherland in the course of our reign and the reigns of our predecessors. It should be treasured highly, because nothing could be better and more glorious than our depriving our enemy the Russian, in a just cause, of many mighty castles and provinces; yes, we have taken them away from our enemy the Russian, who has always boasted of the extensive provinces over which he rules. . . . He could justly boast that he was lord and master over a large part of Europe and Asia, the most prominent regions of the world. His power is not to be belittled, for these countries are filled with a numerous nobility, many peasants, and many populous cities, and this might he has often demonstrated by the inordinately large armies he has led into the field. Boris Gudanow [Godunov] first made this apparent when he came into power in Russia; it is said that he collected an army of 1,500,000 men in order to frighten the Tatars, so that he could win honor by defeating them and making them beg for peace. It is not necessary to describe the appallingly large armies he has led in the field against us, as there are many living today who have seen them with their own eyes. This great power of his swells the strength of the naturally well-situated lakes and rivers which cover his country, for in a short while he could easily transport his forces on the Caspian Sea up the Volga and down the Welock [Volkhov] River to the Baltic; and along the Dvina and the Thanniam [Niemen?], he could easily gather his forces from all corners of his empire. . . . What is still better, as an eternal reminder of this triumph of ours, they have had to turn over to us the fortresses of Ivanogord [Ivangorod], Jama [Iama], Coporie [Kopor'e], Nöteborg [Oreshek], and Kexholm, together with their widely scattered lands and fiefs, according to the peace treaty which has just now, thank God, been concluded.

Yes, it is not less appreciated that because of the location of these fortresses we may now live safe and secure in Finland and Estland [Esthonia], and be protected against Russian invasions not only in times of peace, but also in times of war. Finland is now separated from Russia by the large Laduga [Ladoga] Lake, which is probably as wide as the ocean between Sweden and the Åland Islands, or the distance between Estland [Esthonia] and Nyland [Newland], which till now no Pole has ventured to cross. Thus I trust God that henceforth it will be difficult for the Russians to leap this water barrier. However, should they manage to get across—and may God prevent it,—the forts of Kexholm and Nöteborg, well fortified both by nature and by construction, may well, next to the power of God, halt them for some time and prevent them from entering Finland. Narfwen [Narva] and Iwanogrod [Ivangorod] are shielded by Estland [Esthonia] and are also protected by the wide and turbulent Narfwiske [Narova], which rises in the beautiful Lake Peibas [Peipus] and which it is not easy to cross. Neither are Narfwen [Narva] and Iwanogrod [Ivangorod] easy to take, and no warrior would care to cross the Narfwiske [Narova] River without the protection of these fortresses. Through this victory, and the peace which has followed, not only have the boundaries of Old Sweden been protected, but protection has also been given to the sections recently acquired by the help of God, for on three sides the Wotskepetiniske country [Votskaia Piatina] is bordered by the Baltic and Lakes Laduga [Ladoga] and Peibas [Peipus], and where the country joins Russia it is made secure by enormously large and swampy marshes which separate Swedish and Russian territory. The Kexholm province or Carelen [Karelia] is also somewhat protected by Lake Laduga [Ladoga], while the remaining part spreads into high mountains through which no one can take an army. Thus it seems as if God Himself, through nature, has wanted to shield us by this victory from our treacherous neighbors, the Russians. God has actually given us a better opportunity to wage war upon our enemy, if we—and God forbid—have to fight him once more. The way has now been opened for us to take ships and lighters up the River Nyen [Neva] to Lake Laduga [Ladoga], and by means of the Wolck [Volkhov] River take them to the very gates of Novgorod. Likewise, by means of the Sweri [Svir'] River we have access to Lake Ognega [Onego], and may enter into the Anegiske [Onega] territory and conquer all the region about Novgorod, which is one of the best in Russia, and then later on conquer all of Russia's northland. . . . The enemy has previously held these positions, and has been able to sail back and forth along the aforementioned rivers with lighters, and sweep over the entire Finnish archipelago. It would have been difficult to prevent him from doing that, as he had many thousands of lighters at his disposal, and all Finland might have been in danger had he ventured to make use of this opportunity. But, by the mercy of God, he is now prevented from doing it, since he can no longer show himself in the Baltic with a single boat (to say nothing of several boats) without our permission. Nöteborg lies in the middle of the Nyen [Neva], and Narfwen [Narva] and Iwanogrod [Ivangorod] are on opposite sides of the Narfwiske [Narova] River, so that they can very well prevent the enemy from such an undertaking. . . .

Besides, these countries will be of great financial benefit to the nation, as they are very fertile. There is very little barren land, with no mountains or sandy plains. God has bestowed upon it arable land, meadows, and pastures in abundance, and there are rivers and lakes with a wealth of fish. Wherever there are forests, they have become large and dense during these many years of unrest, and are filled with all kinds of game, the pelts of which are very valuable. If God grants us an extension of the peace, this country with all its strange resources will greatly increase Sweden's revenue. I shall refrain from mentioning at this point the large sums of money a modest and uniform duty may bring, because the trade of all Russia has to go through these countries. Besides, these countries may not only increase the size of their cities and greatly improve the revenue of the crown; they will also improve the conditions and enhance the opportunities of every alert subject. And you nobles, and others who are anxious to obtain free estates, why do you crowd each other here, and fight and quarrel over your few farms? Go yonder to these countries and take for yourselves as large estates as you care to have and are able to manage. I shall grant you privileges and liberties, help you, and show you all the favors I can. Is this not a great benefit to come out of these countries to enhance our kingdom and fatherland?

It is hardly necessary to comment on the significance of this testimony by Gustavus Adolphus as proof of the validity of the fundamentals laid down in this study.

As Russia recovered from the Time of Troubles, it was only natural that the Russians should plan to recover these strategic points, as well as the other territory which they had lost. It looked as if they might achieve this in 1656–1658, when they seized Iamburg and Nienshants and held them for a while.[31] But the goal was not to be reached until Peter the Great, after forming the Northern Coalition, seriously embarked upon the task of regaining territorial access to the Baltic for Russia. After the Russian defeat at Narva in 1700 at the hands of Charles XII, who soon thereafter left for Poland, the reorganized Russian army under Sheremet'ev moved into Livonia from Pskov in 1702. In the meanwhile Peter the Great, having gone to Arkhangelsk, planned and executed a remarkable movement which ultimately placed Russian ships on Lake Ladoga, the river Neva, and the Baltic. He decided to build a fleet of warships and transports in the lake region between Arkhangelsk

---

[31] *Entsik. slovar'*, XXVII:1, 344.

and Lake Ladoga and bring them down by the rivers and lakes and by new roads over portages through Lake Onego and the river Svir'.[32] (See map 8.)

Spurred on by the Polish king's sarcastic remark that he, Peter I, "only sat quietly at home while Poland was being devastated by the Swedes," early in 1702 the Tsar[33] sailed from Arkhangelsk to Solovetskii Monastery, then to Niukhcha on the Gulf of Onega. From Niukhcha to Povenets on Lake Onego, roads and bridges were built and ships were portaged. At Povenets more ships were built and loaded with guns and ammunition and then the naval expedition left Lake Onego and sailed by way of the river Svir' to Lake Ladoga. The weather was so bad on Lake Ladoga that the contingent of men which he had assembled left overland for the ostrog of (Old) Ladoga at the mouth of the Volkhov. After recalling Sheremet'ev from Livonia, Peter I decided, on September 27, 1702, to attack, from this place, Nöteborg (Oreshek), which fell to the combined Russian land and naval forces on October 12.

Thereupon, after building more ships on the Neva, Peter I decided to begin, in April, 1703, an attack on Nienshants near the mouth of the Neva where it empties into the Gulf of Finland. This Swedish fortress fell on May 1. In the following year, Narva and Dorpat were taken. In 1710, Viborg and Kexholm were seized. The frontier set up at Nystadt in 1721 was very much the same as the new boundary arranged in 1940 between Soviet Russia and Finland. (See map 8.) It included Viborg and Kexholm and all of Lake Ladoga in Russia. Such a boundary appears rational only when the rivers and portages are taken into account. It also proves that Peter the Great understood the problem of northern Russia as well as did Gustavus Adolphus. In this way the Baltic–Caspian axis of Muscovite Russia was created.

---

[32] N. Ustrialov, *Istoriia tsarstvovaniia Petra Velikago* (St. Petersburg, 1863), IV:1 and IV:2.

[33] *Ibid.*, IV:1, 185–206, IV:2, 512–518.

It was on the basis of this Baltic–Caspian axis that Muscovite Russia was able to build an empire in three continents.

The expansion of Muscovite Russia to world empire: (1) *to the Black Sea.*—The absorption of Novgorod and its empire and the acquisition of the lower Volga basin opened the gates to the middle and upper Volga populations, which now spilled over to the south in the direction of the Black Sea and to the east and northeast toward Siberia.

At first the bulk of the migratory population went south; here we shall see again that the portages between the Dnieper and the Volga on the one side, and the Don and its tributaries on the other, played the decisive role.

To visualize accurately this southward Russian advance to the Black Sea, we must bear in mind that the Russians were at first represented here by infantry, which utilized, wherever possible, movement on river boats through portages, whereas the steppe-pony-riding Crimean and Nogai Tatars used *chaussées* or land trails (called *shliakhi, sakmy, dorogi*), which began at or near the Black Sea and ran northward through bottleneck portages along the watershed between the main rivers and their tributaries.[34] (See maps 9, 10.)

In the fourteenth, fifteenth, and sixteenth centuries the scene of stress was along the series of portages from the Oka (a main tributary of the Volga which flowed generally from the west to the east) to the Don and the Dnieper. In the earlier part of this period, this black soil region furnished grain first for Novgorod, as already indicated, through Volokolamsk and Torzhok,

---

[34] For important sources see *P.S.R.L.*, III–XIII; *S.G.G. i D.*; N. A. Popov (ed.), *Akty moskovskago gosudarstva* (3 vols., St. Petersburg, 1890–1901); A. A. Lishin (ed.), *Akty otnosiashchiesia k istorii voiska Donskogo* (3 vols. in 4, Novocherkassk, 1891–1894); and D. N. Bagalei, *Materialy dlia istorii kolonizatsii i byta stepnoi okrainy Moskovskago gosudarstva* (Kharkov, 1886). For the most useful historical atlas see K. V. Kudriashov, *Russkii istoricheskii atlas* (Moscow-Leningrad, 1928). For the best analysis see S. F. Platonov, "K istorii gorodov i putei na iuzhnoi okraine moskovskago gosudarstva v XVI veke," *Zhurnal M.N.P.*, XXXVI (March, 1898), 81–105. Additional information may be found in Paul Miliukov, *Ocherki po istorii russkoi kultury* (6th ed., St. Petersburg, 1909), Vol. I; V. Kliuchevskii, *Kurs*, II, 260 ff. (Hogarth tr., II, 112).

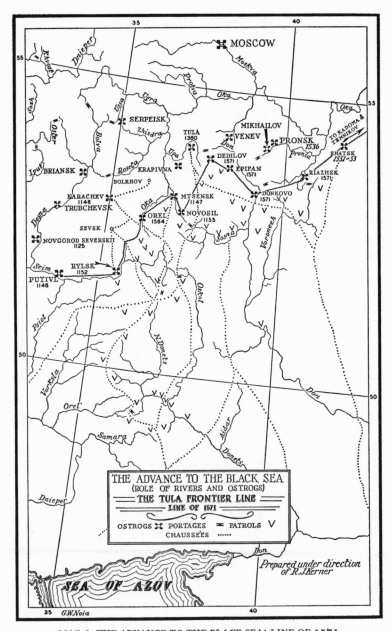

MAP 9. THE ADVANCE TO THE BLACK SEA: LINE OF 1571

and later for Moscow. It was also the region of defense against raids from the Tatars in the south. These raiders carried off valuable loot and numberless victims whom they sold into slavery. It was the area through which the population of the upper and middle Volga was always trying to penetrate in its search for fertile lands. It was therefore an area of vital strategic and economic importance to the Russian people.[35]

One concrete illustration may be found in the portage on the plain of Kulikovo between the Don and its tributaries, where the first great victory of Muscovite Russia over the Tatars was won in 1380. Here Dmitri Ivanovich, Grand Prince of Moscow, earned the title of Donskoi. The immediate region of Kulikovo includes the sources of the Upa and Zusha (tributaries of the Oka) and the sources of the Don and its tributaries, the Nepriadva and Krasivaia Mecha. This famous portage from the Oka to the Don has since become the crossroads of land highways at Bogoroditsk and the junction of railroads at Uzlovaia and at the village of Znamenskoe (Volovo?).[36] (See map 9; App. 1, A. Volga, iii, iv.)

While on the one hand the Tatars were to use trails, presently to be described, which penetrated into this first line of portages running roughly west to east between the Oka and the Don, on the other hand the Russians were to develop a military defense, the base of which was to be a line of ostrogs built to dominate the portages into the Don River system, as well as the river beds of that system itself, as a foothold was obtained on it.

For the sake of clarity, the chief land trails will first be described, and then the successive lines of ostrogs showing the Russian advance to the south will be indicated.

There were three main trails or roads that ran from the south: the Muravskii Shliakh, the Kalmiusskaia Sakma, and the Nogaiskaia Doroga (with its three branches).[37] Of these the Mu-

---

[35] Some observations may be found in Presniakov, *op. cit.*, pp. 227–228.

[36] See Kudriashov, *op. cit.*, table VI, map 19.

[37] The best description is to be found in Platonov, "K istorii gorodov...," pp. 86–89. For a map showing their directions see Kudriashov, *op. cit.*, table VIII, map 23.

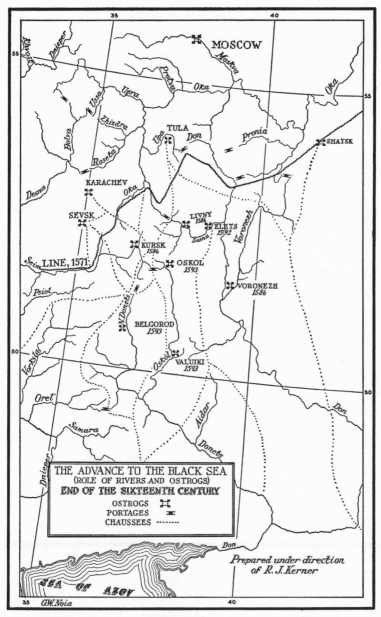

MAP 10. THE ADVANCE TO THE BLACK SEA: END OF THE 16TH CENTURY

ravskii Shliakh can be most accurately traced. (See map 9.) On the others the information is at times vague and conflicting.

The Muravskii Shliakh may be traced from Perekop on the Black Sea (on the isthmus leading into the Crimean peninsula) to Tula. (See maps 9–11.) It ran between the Don and the Dnieper river systems as follows:

1. Perekop

2. Along the watershed or portage between Konskie Voɑy (tributary of the Dnieper) and Molochnye Vody (which flows into the Sea of Azov).

3. Along the watershed or portage between the Volch'i Vody (tributary of the Samara-Dnieper) and the Kalmius (Sea of Azov). (Here a branch called the Kalmiusskaia Sakma took a northeasterly direction, crossing the Donets between the Borovaia and the Aidar.)

4. Along the watershed or portage between the Byk (tributary of the Samara-Dnieper) and the Velikii Tor (tributary of the Donets-Don). (Here the Muravskii Shliakh continued northwest, while a branch of it [known as the Iziumskaia Sakma] crossed the Donets at Izium directly north and thereafter ran due north between the Donets and the Oskol to join the Muravskii Shliakh once more along the watershed or portage between the Seim [tributary of the Desna-Dnieper] and the Oskol [tributary of the Donets-Don].)

5. Along the watershed or portage between the Orel'ka (tributary of the Orel'-Dnieper) and the Bol'shaia Bereka (tributary of the Donets-Don).

6. Along the watershed or portage between the Orchik (tributary of the Orel'-Dnieper) and the Kolomak (tributary of the Vorskla-

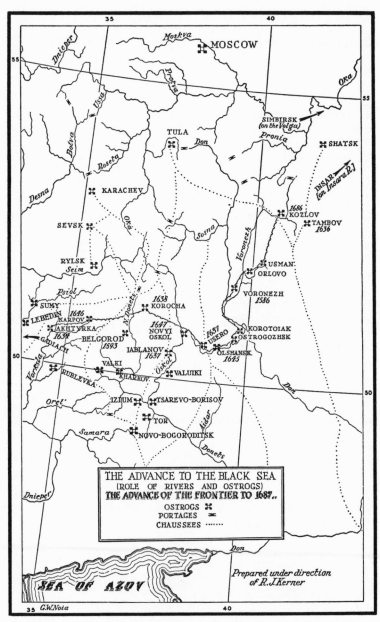

MAP 11. THE ADVANCE TO THE BLACK SEA: THE ADVANCE OF THE
FRONTIER TO 1687

Dnieper) on the west, and the Vodolaga (tributary of the Mozh-
Donets-Don) and the Mozh (tributary of the Donets-Don) on the
east.

7. Along the watershed or portage between the Merchik (tributary
of the Vorskla-Dnieper) and the Merl' (tributary of the Merchik-
Vorskla-Dnieper) on the west, and the Uda (or Udy) (tributary of
the Donets-Don).

8. Along the watershed or portage between the sources of the Vorskla (tributary of the Dnieper) and Donets (tributary of the Don).

9. Along the watershed or portage between the sources of the following rivers: Psel (tributary of the Dnieper), Seim (tributary of
the Desna-Dnieper), and Donets (tributary of the Don). (Here the
Bakaev Shliakh is reported to have joined it, and from here two
subsidiary roads started, the one called Svinaia Doroga, for Sevsk,
and the other called Pakhnuttsova Doroga, for Mtsensk.)

10. Along the watershed or portage between the sources of the Seim
(tributary of the Desna-Dnieper) and the Oskol (tributary of the
Donets-Don), where it was joined by the Iziumskaia Sakma (see
4 above).

11. Due north between the Tim and the Olym (tributaries of the
Bystraia Sosna-Don) and then across the Bystraia Sosna at Livny.

12. Along the watershed or portage between the Zusha (tributary
of the Oka) and the Mecha (tributary of the Don), where it was
joined by the Nogaiskaia Doroga.

13. Down the valley of the Upa past Dedilov to Tula.

The Kalmiusskaia Sakma, as indicated under 3, began as an offshoot of the Muravskii Shliakh between the sources of the Volch'i Vody (tributary of the Samara-Dnieper) and the Kalmius (which flows into the Sea of Azov). After crossing the Donets between its two branches, the Borovaia and the Aidar, this trail joined another originating in the southeast at the junction of the Donets and Belaia Kalitva. The junction of these two trails was along the watershed or portage between the sources of the Aidar and the Chernaia Kalitva (a tributary of the Don). It thereupon continued due north, crossing the Tikhaia Sosna, until it reached the Olym (a tributary of the Bystraia-Don). Running north along the Olym, it ended at a place which after 1636 was known as Chernavsk, on the Bystraia Sosna.

The Nogaiskaia Doroga was the trail used chiefly by the Nogai Tatars, whereas the trails previously described were the highways of the Crimean Tatars. Its origin was the Don below the mouth of the Tsymla, and its direction was north and northeast between the sources of the Bystraia (tributary of the Donets-Don) and the Tsymla (tributary of the Don) until it crossed the Chir and then the Don below the mouth of the Elan' (tributary of the Don). Thereafter it ran between the sources of the Peskovataia Tulucheeva (or Podgornaia), the Seret (or Osered) on the west, and the Khoper on the east. These are all tributaries of the Don. Thereafter the road ran between the Chigla (tributary of the Bitiug-Don), Bitiug (tributary of the Don), and Kurlak (tributary of the Bitiug-Don) on the west, and the Elan' (tributary of the Suvela-Khoper-Don) and the Takai (or Taka) (tributary of the Elan'-Suvela-Khoper-Don) on the east. At this portage the Nogaiskaia Doroga divided into two branches. The one toward the west joined the Muravskii Shliakh south of Dedilov (on the road to Tula), after crossing first the Voronezh (tributary of the Don) at Tarbeev Brod, then the Stanovaia Riasa (tributary of the Voronezh-Don), then the Don itself below Donkov (or Dankov), and finally emerged through the portage between the Mecha (tributary of the Don) and the Upa (tributary of the Oka). The other branch, which ran directly north to Shatsk, proceeded between the Chelnava (tributary of the Isna-Moksha-Oka) and the Tsna (tributary of the Moksha-Oka), then either crossed the Chelnava or ran west of it, and got to Shatsk between the Tsna and the Para (tributary of the Oka).

Undoubtedly the oldest fortified line which protected the middle and upper Volga region was that of the Oka, dating back to the middle of the sixteenth century. It began at Nizhnii Novgorod and extended westward, with its army centered at Serpukhov, the right wing being at Kaluga and the left wing at Kashira. The line then turned south toward Tula, and thence southwest to Kozelsk. (See map 9.) Generally to the south of this, but still on the Oka side of the portages from the Oka to the Don, was an advance line stretching from Riazan and running through Tula and Odoev to Likhvin.[38]

In 1480 Achmet, Khan of the Golden Horde, undertook a punitive expedition, in alliance with King Casimir of Poland-Lithuania, against Ivan III, who had rebelled against the Tatar yoke. Ivan III sent his family to Lake Beloe (Beloozero) for safety, but he himself, in great fear and doubt, finally had to face Achmet, who, having eluded such Russian defenses as there were, arrived on the Ugra. After facing each other here for several months, until the coming of the winter frost, both armies retreated hastily from the projected field of battle. This episode marked the liberation of Muscovite Russia from the Tatar yoke; but not from the peril of Tatar raids, as this was demonstrated for a century thereafter, and at no time more poignantly or more disastrously, even after the fall of Kazan, than in 1571, when Devlet-Girei, Khan of the Crimean Tatars, who dreamed of restoring the Tatars to their previous glory, suddenly made a raid through the portages and crossed the

[38] On this see Kliuchevskii, *Kurs*, II, 116–117; Miliukov, *op. cit.*, I, 56–57; for documentary evidence on the strategic importance of Tula, Kaluga, Briansk, and Kalachev see *S.G.G. i D.*, III, 125–130, 131–136, 156–163.

Oka, having been guided by Russian refugees through such lines of defense as existed. Moscow was sacked. The Tatars got away with much booty and caused an enormous loss of life.[39]

Means of defense against such occurrences were investigated by a special commission in 1571, whose deliberations resulted in the creation thereafter of a new line of defense, known as the *Line of 1571*.[40] (See map 9, App. 1, A. Volga, i–iv; B. Don, i–iii; and App. 3.)

This second main line of defense ran from Alatyr on the Sura through Shatsk, Riazhsk, Epifan, Donkov, Rylsk, and Putivl. It commanded the portages from the tributaries of the Oka and Dnieper to the tributaries of the Don, and in only one triangle (Epifan, Donkov, Riazhsk) did it actually get a foothold on the Don. Here it was to assure control of the most important portage from the Oka tributary of the Upa to the Don.[41] This feature of the line was intended primarily as a defense for the Oka country rather than as an aggressive foothold on the Don.

However, it was not long before the line advanced by several stages to the domination of the middle Don and Donets, once this foothold on the Don was obtained. In 1586 Kursk was rebuilt and Livny and Voronezh were founded or fortified. Kursk on the Seim, Livny on the Bystraia Sosna, and Voronezh at the junction of the Voronezh and the Don served as an advance net to catch the Tatar raids along the Pakhnuttsova Doroga or the Muravskii Shliakh.[42]

In 1593 the establishment of Belgorod on the Donets, (Old) Oskol on the Oskol, and Valuiki farther down on the Oskol,

[39] Karl Stählin, *Geschichte Russlands von den Anfängen bis zur Gegenwart* (4 vols. in 5, Berlin, 1923–1939), I, 219–220. For the Battle on the Ugra (1480) see also A. E. Presniakov, "Ivan III na Ugre," *Sbornik statei posviashchennykh S. F. Platonovu* (St. Petersburg, 1911).

[40] For the events leading to the sack of Moscow see Stählin, *op. cit.*, I, 282–283. For documentary material on the results of the work of the commission which created the defense line of 1571 see Popov, *op. cit.*, I, 1–17.

[41] Popov, *op. cit.*, I, 3–15; Kudriashov, *op. cit.*, table VIII, map 23.

[42] Platonov, "K istorii gorodov . . . ," pp. 88–89.

and in 1600 Tsarevo-Borisov near the junction of the Oskol
and Donets, indicated that a determined effort was being made
to block the Tatar trails on either side of the Donets and Oskol.[43]
(See map 10.) That fords also played an important part in
Muscovite and Tatar strategy is to be perceived from these instructions of 1594 and 1633, respectively, of the Tsar:

> If the men of the Crimea or Azov wage war on our frontier, you
> [cossacks] must fight them on the Don, the Donets, and other rivers,
> wherever there are fords to cross.[44]
> The cossacks are to fight the men from Azov, the Crimea, and the
> Nogai country in the steppe, along the rivers, and at the fords. The
> cossacks are to supply boats and rowers for the Russian embassy
> returning from Turkey along the Don and the Voronezh.[45]

However, it seems evident that these advances between 1586
and 1600 were not sufficient to dominate the Tatar trails. Between 1637 and 1680—during the period of the annexation of
the Ukraine (1654)—it became necessary to consolidate Moscow's grip on the middle Donets and Don in order to hold the
Tatars at bay by a complex and intricate system of ostrogs and
fortified lines, some of which are to be found in the Russian
Academy Atlas of 1745. This system—it was much more than
a single line—brought the entire region from the Vorskla to
the Don, with all its trails and rivers, under Russian control.
Its chief line ran from Akhtyrka on the Vorskla to Karpov, Belgorod, Korocha, Iablonov, (New) Oskol, Usero, Olshansk, Ostrogozhsk, Voronezh, Kozlov, Tambov, Insar.[46] There remained
no portage and no ford through which the Tatars might pour
into the region from the Vorskla to the Don that was not fortified by an ostrog.[47] Izium (founded in 1680) guarded, with

[43] *P.S.R.L.*, XIV, 45; Bagalei, *op. cit.*, p. 8.
[44] Lishin, *op. cit.*, I, 4.
[45] *Ibid.*, I, 11–13, 31.
[46] For the line see Kudriashov, *op. cit.*, table VIII, map 23; for sources, see *Akty
arkheograficheskoi ekspeditsii*, III, 397, 410–411, IV, 30; Bagalei, *op. cit.*, 54–73,
118–127; Miliukov, *op. cit.*, I, 58–60; Lishin, *op. cit.*, pp. 92, 150, 175, 179.
[47] A partial list of the ostrogs built in this region, apart from those on the line
just indicated, consisted of the following. On the Kolomak: Kolomak, Vysoko-

Tsarevo-Borisov, the ford or passage over the Donets of the Iziumskaia Sakma, a branch of the Muravskii Shliakh. The ostrog Tor on the Velikii Tor built in 1668 and the ostrog Novo-Bogoroditsk on the Byk constructed in 1687 controlled the portage through which the Muravskii Shliakh passed south of the Donets. Here it was possible to check the Tatars in the very beginnings of a raid.[48] (See map 11.)

Along this system between Kozlov and Tambov, the Nogai-skaia Doroga made its way and divided into two branches, the one aiming at Tula in the west and the other at Shatsk in the north. These two points controlled both trails. (See map 11.)

The portage (or portages) from the Volga to the Don continued, at this period, as in the most ancient times, to play a role of some importance. The protection for the direct portage from the Volga to the Don at Sarkel (Belaia Vezha) was indicated by the following ostrogs in the eighteenth century: Tsaritsyn (now Stalingrad), Meshochnaia, Grachi, Osokor, and Donskaia. Another portage much used was up the Kamyshinka (tributary of the Volga), and then over the portage to the Ilovlia (tributary of the Don). It is also likely that either of the following tributaries of the Don may have been used for direct portage to the Volga: the Chervlennaia, the Donskaia, the Tsaritsa, or the Esaulovskaia-Aksai. (See App. 1, A. Volga, i–iv.)

Just before the raid of 1480 by Achmet, that ruler planned to dig a canal joining the two rivers. Such a canal was later projected several times under Sultan Selim, and again by Peter the Great, and it is now one of the projects being undertaken by the Soviet government. In 1569 the military commander (*voevoda*) Saburov was appointed to serve at the portage. In 1691 the Tsar sent a message saying: ". . . it has become known

pol'e, Perekop; on the Merlia: Rublevka, Krasnyi Kut, Murafa, Merchik, Volnyi Kurgan; from the Donets westward: Bishkin, Zmiev, Sokolov, Merefa, Valki, Chuguev, Kharkov, Olshansk, Zolochev, Udy, Saltov; east from the Donets: Balakleia, Volch'e, Nizhgolsk; on the Oskol: Tsarevo-Borisov, Solenaia, Goro-khovatka, Borovaia, Senkovo, Kupenka, Dvurechnaia, Kamenka.

[48] See Kudriashov, *op. cit.*, table VIII, map 23, and Lishin, *op. cit.*, p. 150.

to us that the . . . cossacks, Ataman Philip Sula and his comrades, who had previously been on the Volga, . . . intend to take boats and supplies from the Don to the Volga."[49]

The elaborate system of lines connecting ostrogs and fortified towns and advance ostrogs consisted of abatis in the forest, and bulwarks and ditches on the plains. These made up a continuous line (called *cherta*), defended by stationary guards (called *storozhi*) and by mobile patrols (called *stanitsy*).[50] In this way, every trail, every ford, and every river was obstructed and under surveillance.

Thus in little more than one hundred years from the erection of the defense line of 1571 Moscow gained control of the middle courses of the Donets and the Don. The subsequent history of this region indicates that the Russians descended the Donets and the Don and that Russian expansion, blocked at first by Lithuanians and Poles, and then by Tatars and Turks, made its way from river bank to river bank on the northern shores of the Black Sea, both east and west from the Don, until in the reign of Catherine II the entire northern and eastern shores fell into the hands of the Russians.

The expansion of Muscovite Russia to world empire: (2) to the Pacific.—When we turn to this phase of the Russian urge to the sea, we find that basic materials for research are more copious and as a consequence reveal more clearly the dynamics of the advance and the policy pursued by the government and by individuals. We see again the same basic elements that emerged from our examination of the centuries of Russian experience in Europe: rivers, portages, ostrogs, monasteries, and furs. Only the data most necessary to illustrate the theme of this study will be included here.[51]

---

[49] *S.G.G. i D.*, II, 52; Lishin, *op. cit.*, pp. 164–165; *Bol'shaia sov. entsik.*, XII, 685 ff., XL, 404–406; *Atlas rossiiskoi* (St. Petersburg, 1745), map 10.

[50] S. F. Platonov, *Ivan Groznyi* (Berlin, 1924), pp. 124–125.

[51] The present author has in preparation a series of volumes on Russian eastward expansion, in part monographic, in part documentary, which will cover all phases of this development. At present the best general accounts of the history

For the application of centuries of experience a magnificent opportunity was offered by Siberia, with its series of river basins and easy portages from the tributaries of the Pechora and the Kama in Europe, through the Ob', Enisei, Lena, and Amur to the Pacific. Siberia still remains the world's greatest source of supply of furs. Here, more clearly than in European Russia,[52] we sense that the advance came as a result of the relative exhaustion of fur-bearing animals in easily accessible areas. The rate of exhaustion determined the speed of the expansion. The Siberian fur trade in the sixteenth and seventeenth centuries, we know, was one of the best sources of revenue of the Russian state and was the largest single item in its foreign trade.[53]

The Urals, rising from 1000 to 5500 feet above sea level, have never been a barrier. The portages from the Kama and the Pechora in Europe to the Ob' in Siberia are not much higher than 2000 feet above sea level at any point and generally the approach to them is gradual. When fur-bearing animals began to diminish in the Russian northeast, Siberia beckoned.

East across the Urals is the great River Ob' with its important tributaries, the Tavda, Tura, Tobol, and Irtysh. Hardy traders and trappers of Novgorod often penetrated the Pechora–Ural–Ob' portages. (See maps 4, 12, 13, 18.) The lower reaches of the Ob' were exploited definitely from about the fourteenth century, if not earlier. The advance into this region from the basin of the Pechora and its tributaries by portage over the

---

of Siberia are V. I. Ogorodnikov, *Ocherk istorii Sibiri do nachala XIX veka* (3 vols. in 2 parts, Irkutsk-Vladivostok, 1920–1924), and other studies by the same author; S. V. Bakhrushin, *Ocherki po istorii kolonizatsii Sibirii v XVI i XVII vv.* (Moscow, 1927–1928); Gerhard F. Mueller, *Istoriia Sibiri* (St. Petersburg, 1750, also 1787; Moscow-Leningrad, 1937 [this edition is used hereafter]); P. N. Butsinskii, *Zaselenie Sibiri i byt pervykh ee nasel'nikov* (Kharkov, 1889); V. K. Andrievich, *Istoriia Sibiri* (in 2 parts, St. Petersburg, 1889), and four other volumes of Siberian history by this author. For further bibliographical items see Robert J. Kerner, *Northeastern Asia: A Selected Bibliography* (2 vols., Berkeley, 1939).

[52] See Miliukov, *op. cit.*, I, 71–73.

[53] The best monograph is that of Raymond H. Fisher, *The Russian Fur Trade* (*1550–1700*) (doctoral dissertation, University of California, 1937; now in press).

Urals was in the manner of the raid: by levying tribute (*iasak*) of furs and of such silver as could be obtained from the natives, by exacting homage and further promises of tribute, followed by withdrawal, this formula to be repeated from time to time if promises were not fulfilled. Similar in nature were the expeditions carried out by Moscow in the years 1465, 1483, and 1499, and executed by portage over the Urals from the Pechora basin; they, too, were raids.[54] So, in fact, was the so-called conquest of Siberia by Yermak in the years from 1579 to 1584.[55] Yermak, however, definitely undermined and almost succeeded in shattering the power of the Tatar khan, Kuchum, in the basin of the Ob'.

The enterprising family of Stroganovs, however, planned to occupy the territory into which the former Volga pirate advanced. It was only when Yermak's initial success in taking the Siberian capital, Sibir, became known that Moscow realized what an opportunity was presented, not only for using the region to defend the back yard of European Russia against the raids of Siberian peoples, but also to establish there a profitable base for an advance into Asia. For these reasons, apparently, Moscow sent reinforcements to Yermak, at his request as well as at the request of the Stroganovs, and finally completed the conquest after his death. But, in so doing, Moscow abandoned the policy of the raid for one of planned domination of rivers

---

[54] Arkhangelsk Chronicle (ed. 1781), p. 141, quoted by Bakhrushin, *op. cit.*, pp. 67, 89; Shcheglov, *op. cit.*, p. 10, who refers to the Arkhangelsk Chronicle without indication of page; F. G. Mueller, *op. cit.*, pp. 202–204, has quotations from unpublished archival material (pp. 203–204); S. Herberstein, *Zapiski o moskovitskikh delakh* (trans. A. I. Malein; St. Petersburg, 1908), pp. 125, 133; Voskresensk Chronicle, *P.S.R.I.*, VIII, 237; Sofia Chronicle, *P.S.R.L.*, VI, 43–44; Ogorodnikov, *op. cit.*, II:1, 12–16; A. Oksenov, "Slukhi i vesti o Sibiri do Yermaka," *Sibirskii sbornik* (St. Petersburg, 1887), IV, 108–116; for the background of the advance to the Urals see A. A. Kizevetter, *Russkii sever* (Vologda, 1919), and S. F. Platonov, *Proshloe russkoga severa* (Leningrad, 1923).

[55] Stroganov Chronicle, Arkheograficheskaia Kommissiia, *Sibirskiia letopisi* (St. Petersburg, 1907), pp. 11, 16, 21, 28, 37, 45, 59, 85; Esipov Chronicle, *ibid.*, p. 308; Remezov Chronicle, *ibid.*, pp. 313, 314, 316, 317, 322; Mueller, *op. cit.*, pp. 215–216, 219–221, 223–228; I. G. Akulinin, *Yermak i Stroganovy* (Paris, 1933), pp. 53–62.

and portages through the building of ostrogs. Three expeditions were sent into Siberia in the years 1583, 1585, and 1586, the second and third after the death of Yermak. Two of them abandoned Siberia; the third was ordered to build two ostrogs, which became known as Tiumen (1586) and Tobolsk (1587).[56] Tiumen guarded the Tura route into the Ob' basin. Tobolsk, at the junction of the Ob' and the Irtysh, became a center of power in all directions. In 1594 the building of Tara, farther to the east on the Irtysh, gave the Russians three points almost in an east and west line. Attention was given at once to gaining or maintaining complete domination of the highways into this area from Russia, when the first state road was charted along the Kama–Vishera–Lozva portage route. The Lozva was a tributary of the Tavda. In the upper reaches of the Lozva a temporary ostrog, Lozvinsk, was constructed in 1590. However, a better road was from Perm through Pelym. Lozvinsk was used to conquer Pelym in 1594. But the best and most direct route from the Volga-Kama basin along the Tura was finally controlled by building the ostrog and town of Verkhoturie in 1598 on the upper reaches of the Tura, and the ostrog Turinsk in its middle course in 1600. Tiumen defended the lower course of the Tura. Thus by 1600 Moscow had a fortified route from the Kama to the Tobol and Irtysh over which Verkhoturie, Turinsk, and Tiumen stood guard.[57] There remained only the building of ostrogs at other strategic points in the basin. In 1593 the ostrog

---

[56] Remezov Chronicle, *Sibirskiia letopisi*, pp. 339, 344, 348–349; Stroganov Chronicle, *ibid.*, pp. 76, 85, 87; Mueller, *op. cit.*, pp. 253, 266, 274–275; "Zapiski, k sibirskoi istorii sluzhashchiia . . . ," *Drevniaia rossiiskaia vivliofika*, III, 107–108; Ogorodnikov, *op. cit.*, II:1, 32–35; Butsinskii, *op. cit.*, pp. 84, 104.

[57] See instructions to A. Eletskoi about building a town on the river Tara (1593–1594) in Mueller, *op. cit.*, pp. 354–361; for Lozvinsk see *ibid.*, p. 277, referring to material in the archives, and Butsinskii, *op. cit.*, p. 16; for Pelym see the instructions to Gorchakov, about 1594, Arkheograf1cheskaia Kommissiia, *Russkaia istoricheskaia biblioteka* (39 vols., St. Petersburg, 1875–1927; hereafter cited as *R.I.B.*), II, 103–120; also Mueller, *op. cit.*, pp. 346–354; for Verkhoturie see instructions to Golovin, 1597, about the construction of a town on the Tura, *R.I.B.*, II, 56–61; for Turinsk see instructions to Ianov about the construction of an ostrog in Epanchin (Turinsk), 1600, *R.I.B.*, II, 66–74; also Mueller, *op. cit.*, pp. 383–385.

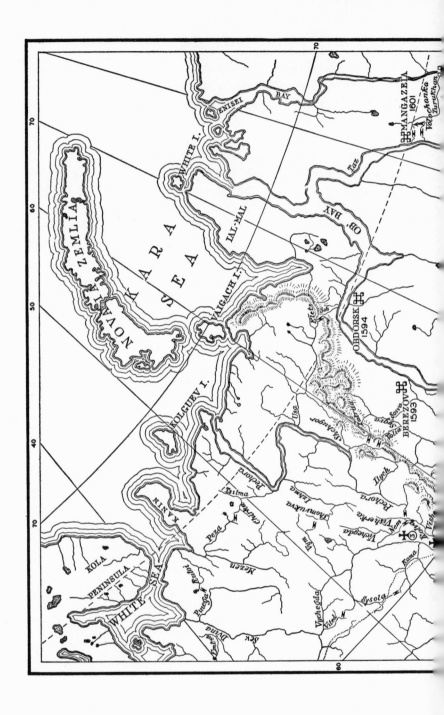

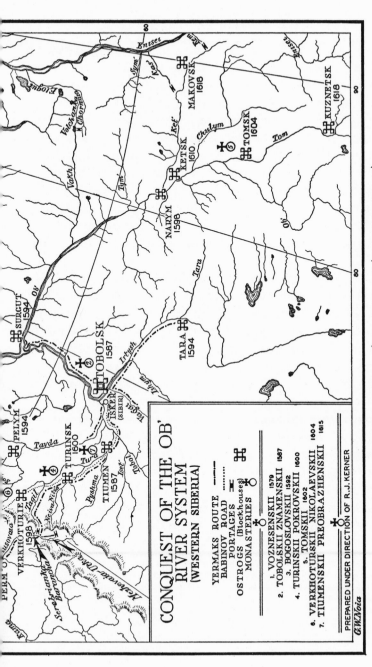

MAP 13. CONQUEST OF THE OB' RIVER SYSTEM (WESTERN SIBERIA)

CONQUEST OF THE OB'
RIVER SYSTEM
(WESTERN SIBERIA)

YERMAKS ROUTE ———
BABINOV ROAD ·········
PORTAGES ⚓
OSTROGS (Blockhouses) ✠
MONASTERIES ☦

1. VOZNESENSKII 1579
2. TOBOLSKII ZNAMENSKII 1587
3. BOGOSLOVSKII 1592
4. TURINSKII POKROVSKII 1600
5. TOMSKII 1602
6. VERKHOTURSKII NIKOLAEVSKII 1604
7. TIUMENSKII PREOBRAZHENSKII 1615

PREPARED UNDER DIRECTION OF R.J.KERNER

G.W.Voia

KUZNETSK 1618
MAKOVSK 1618
TOMSK 1604
KETSK 1610
NARYM 1598
TARA 1594
SURGUT 1594
TOBOLSK 1587
ISKER (SIBIR)
PELYM 1594
TURINSK 1600
TIUMEN 1587
VERKHOTURIE 1598

Berezov was built along the lower Ob', and in 1595 that of Obdorsk at the mouth. Five years later the Taz River to the east was reached and Tazovsk (later called Mangazeia) was built. Surgut was founded in 1594 on the middle course of the Ob', and farther up the river to the east, Narym in 1596 and Ketsk in 1597 (1602?), on the Ket' tributary of that river. Narym and Ketsk opened up and commanded the middle and upper reaches of the Ob' inhabited by Tatar and Kirghiz tribes. In 1604 at the junction of the Ob' and the Tom was built the ostrog of Tomsk, which guarded the gateway from the steppes into the Ob' basin. Later, in 1618, as an advanced outpost, Kuznetsk was built farther up (to the south) on the Tom.[58] (See App. 4.)

In this way, and chiefly during the first decade and a half after the death of Yermak, nearly all the strategic points in the basin were occupied and the region thoroughly subjugated. In the course of this process the native Ostiak, Vogul, Samoied, Tatar, and Kirghiz tribes were forced to pay tribute in fur. The process of subjugation itself was control of river and portage by ostrogs from the Volga-Kama basin to the Ob' and the establishment of ostrogs as outposts against nomad populations to the south and southeast.

Starting out as the private, chartered enterprise of the Stroganov family, the venture was taken over by the state, which ended the period of raids and began the occupation of the territory, creating thereby a defense for European Russia against raids from Asia, and at the same time a profitable and solid base for Russian expansion into Asia. It was the result of a planned movement based on previous Russian national experience.

---

[58] On Berezov see instructions to Gorchakov, 1592, Mueller, *op. cit.*, pp. 283, 346; on Obdorsk see *ibid.*, p. 498; on Tazovsk and Mangazeia see instructions to Mosalskii and Pushkin, 1601, *R.I.B.*, pp. 814–833; P. N. Butsinskii, *Mangazeia* (Kharkov, 1893), pp. 1–66, *passim;* on Surgut, Narym, and Ketsk, see Butsinskii, *K istorii Sibiri: Surgut, Narym i Ketsk do 1645 g.* (Kharkov, 1893), pp. 2, 16, 19, 24; on Tomsk see instructions to Bezobrazov, 1604, *R.I.B.*, II, 78–79; on Kuznetsk see the correspondence of the Siberian military commanders (*voevodas*) concerning the building of Kuznetsk, 1617–1621, Mueller, *op. cit.*, pp. 451–455.

Thousands of sables and other furs now enriched the treasury of the state and the pockets of many private traders.[59]

The same process led ever eastward. State enterprise had brought western Siberia into the Russian empire; individual initiative, in which the few and scattered officials participated, was chiefly the cause for Russia's reaching the Pacific a generation later. Individuals and groups of entrepreneurs (*opytovshchiks*) sought "unused lands and natives not paying tribute." The state followed after them, constructing ostrogs to command rivers and portages and supervising the collection of tribute from the natives.

We turn now from the basin of the Ob' to the basin of the Enisei. The latter was penetrated chiefly from two points. (See maps 14, 18.)

At the north, up the Taz from Mangazeia to its source and by portage to the Turukhan was a relatively short distance. In 1607, at the junction of the Turukhan and the Enisei and opposite the Lower (Nizhniaia) Tunguska there was built the little ostrog (*ostrozhek*) of Turukhansk. From this point, clearly commanding the lower half of the Enisei, Russian traders and trappers went up the river after 1607 and down the river to the sea after 1610.[60]

In the south, the Russians advanced up the Ket' River (a tributary of the Ob') from Ketsk to its upper reaches, where the ostrog of Makovsk was built in 1618. Makovsk guarded a portage of some seventy versts (forty-six miles) to the Enisei. Crossing the portage, an ostrog was built under the name of Eniseisk

[59] Akulinin, *op. cit., passim,* esp., p. 56; Ogorodnikov, *op. cit.,* II, 26–27; Bakhrushin, *op. cit.,* p. 99; Stroganov Chronicle, *Sibirskiia letopisi,* pp. 10–11; *ibid.,* Esipov Chronicle, p. 317.

[60] Fisher, *op. cit.,* p. 67; Bakhrushin, *op. cit.,* pp. 146, 151, 155–157; "Istoricheskie akty o podvigakh Erofeiia Khabarova na Amure v. 1649–1651 gg.," *Zhurnal dlia chteniia vospitannikam voenno-uchebnykh zavedenii* (St. Petersburg, 1840), No. 105, p. 62; report of Voevoda Frantsbekov concerning the expedition of Khabarov to the Amur River, 1650, Arkheograficheskaia Kommissiia, *Dopolneniia k aktam istoricheskim* (12 vols., St. Petersburg, 1846–1872; hereafter cited as *D.A.I.*), III, 258–261; Ogorodnikov, *op. cit.,* II, 32, 35, 40–44; J. E. Fischer, *Sibirskaia istoriia* (St. Petersburg, 1774), p. 237.

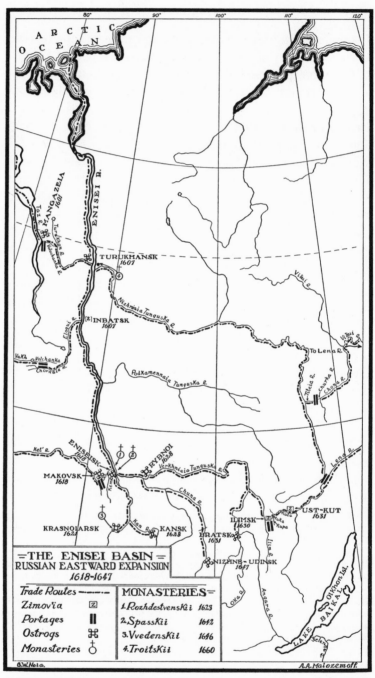

MAP 14. RUSSIAN EASTWARD EXPANSION: THE ENISEI BASIN (1618–1647)

in 1619. It was destined, after Tobolsk, to be a most important source of activity in Siberia. It stood at the junction of the Enisei and the Upper (Verkhniaia) Tunguska. To dominate the basin of the Enisei from the south, the ostrog of Krasnoiarsk was constructed high up on the Enisei in 1628, and that year also the ostrog of Kansk was built on the Kan tributary of the Enisei. Thus in two decades (1607–1626) this river system was brought into Russian hands and the native Tungus and other tribes were forced to pay tribute.[61] (See App. 4.)

Two elements in the situation always led the Russians on: the rivers, and the hope of greater riches in furs farther ahead. The numbers of easily accessible fur-bearing animals soon showed signs of diminishing. This was an added incentive to move on.

And so the next river system, that of the Lena to the east, was penetrated. (See maps 15, 19.) In the late 'twenties, fur-bearing animals in the Enisei basin began to diminish rapidly, and traders and trappers, penetrating into the Lena basin, found themselves in difficulties before hostile natives.[62] As a result, the military commanders of Tobolsk and Eniseisk took a hand, impelled by visions of increased tribute returns and illegal personal profits. They competed with each other. The Lena region was entered from the north, especially from Mangazeia and Turukhansk, by advancing up the Lower Tunguska to its source and then across the Chichuisk portage near the mouth of the Kirenga River to the Lena. From south of the Enisei private individuals and officials entered that region over the Ilim portage from the Upper Tunguska and its tributary, the Angara. The Ilim portage became, in 1630, the site for the Ilimsk winter quarters. In that same year, Kirensk on the

---

[61] G. F. Mueller, "Sibirskaia istoriia," *Ezhemesiachnyia sochineniia ... akademii nauk* (St. Petersburg, October, 1763), pp. 363–365; A. A. Titov (ed.), *Sibir v XVII veke* (Moscow, 1890), pp. 47, 82; Ogorodnikov, *op. cit.*, II:1, 44–47; Bakhrushin, *op. cit.*, pp. 110–112, 124–125, 127; Fischer, *op. cit.*, pp. 276–277, 282.

[62] Instructions to Golovin, 1638, *R.I.B.*, II, 961–972; on Iakutsk, see Titov, *Sibir v XVII veke*, p. 22; report of Lena (Iakutsk) military commanders (*voevodas*) concerning furs gathered on the Viliui and about depredations by the natives, 1639, *D.A.I.*, II, 230–231; Ogorodnikov, *op. cit.*, II, 48–50.

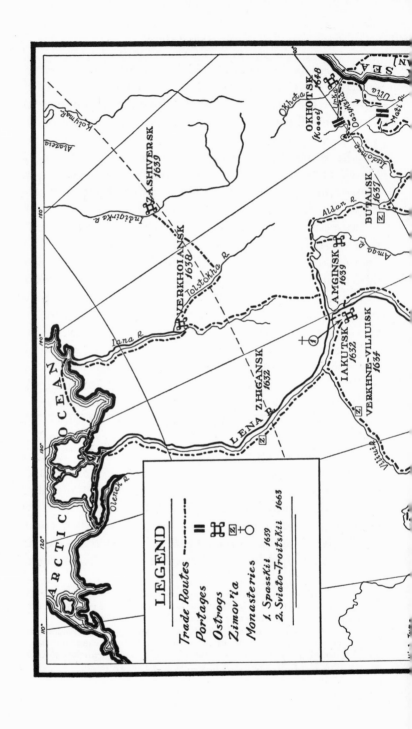

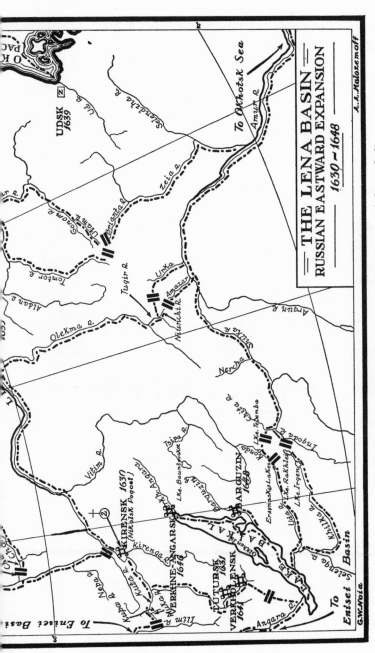

MAP 15. RUSSIAN EASTWARD EXPANSION: THE LENA BASIN (1630–1648)

Lena was constructed, and two years later, much farther down
that river, the ostrog of Iakutsk, which, after Tobolsk and
Eniseisk, became the next center of importance. Quickly other
ostrogs were built: Zhigansk in 1632, between Iakutsk and
the mouth of the Lena, to dominate its lower course; Amginsk
in 1633, on the Aldan River, a tributary of the Lena, which

OUTER WALLS OF THE OSTROG OF IAKUTSK

indicated the road to the Pacific on the east and the Amur
on the south; Viliuisk, in 1634, controlling the connection between the Lower Tunguska and the Chona with the Viliui
River, which flowed east into the Lena; and Olekminsk in 1635,
at the junction of the Olekma and the Lena. In 1636 Kopylov
went up the Aldan beyond Amginsk to the mouth of the Maia,
where he constructed the Butalsk winter quarters. It was from
here three years later, in 1639, that a detachment of twenty
men, sent up the Maia and the Iudoma, crossed the divide,
descended the Ulia to the Sea of Okhotsk, and explored that
body of water from the Tauia on the north, where winter quarters were set up, to the River Uda on the south, where the Udsk

ostrozhek was founded. In this way the shores of the Pacific were reached.[63] (See maps 15, 16, 20.)

For the next decade and a half the wild and remote country of the Iukagirs—the basins of the Iana, Indigirka, Alazeia, Kolyma, and Anadyr rivers—was overrun by men sailing down the Lena to the sea and up the Iana, where the Verkhoiansk ostrog was built in 1638; or crossing the Verkhoiansk range and

A VIEW OF IAKUTSK IN THE EIGHTEENTH CENTURY

descending the Indigirka, where the Zashiversk ostrog was constructed in 1639, or going across country from the Indigirka to the Alazeia. The Kolyma was discovered from the sea, and Nizhne-Kolymsk, near its mouth, was founded in 1644. In 1649 the Anadyrsk ostrog went up on the middle course of the Anadyr.[64] In the meanwhile, led on by the prospect of getting a haul of tusks, Dezhnev and others in 1648 sailed down the Kolyma to the sea, rounded the eastern end of Siberia, and

[63] On Iakutsk see instructions to Golovin, 1638, *R.I.B.*, II, 961–972; description of rivers, 1640–1641, *D.A.I.*, II, 243–248; on Ilimsk see Fischer, *op. cit.*, pp. 351, 354; on Okhotsk see the Petition of Serving Men, 1651, and the description of the route of Okhotsk, 1651, *D.A.I.*, III, 320–325; report of the serving man Epishev, 1652, *D.A.I.*, III, 332–343; Ogorodnikov, *op. cit.*, II, 50–53. (*Sluzhilye liudi,* literally "serving men," indicates men in military service.)

[64] V. I. Ogorodnikov, *Iz istorii pokoreniia Sibiri. Pokorenie Iukagirskoi zemli* (Chita, 1922), *passim; idem, Ocherki po istorii ...* , II, 54–57; Bakhrushin, *op. cit.,* pp. 128–132.

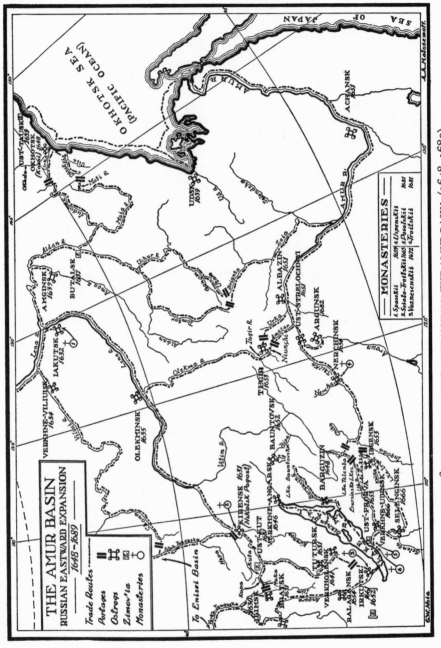

MAP 16. RUSSIAN EASTWARD EXPANSION: THE AMUR BASIN (1648–1689)

returned safely up the Anadyr. Thus they proved, nearly a hundred years before Bering, that Asia and North America were separated by a body of water.[65]

The Buriat country in and around Lake Baikal was penetrated in about three decades. This region was most difficult to master, the Buriats, who were Mongols, being warlike, and topographic conditions hard. Raids were made into this region from Eniseisk, Krasnoiarsk, and Iakutsk, not only because it lay near and, in fact, across the route to the sea, but also because, besides furs, there was a rumor that silver could be found there. This rumor was to lead hunters later into the basin of the Amur. The forces stationed at the three ostrogs competed strenuously for the prize.

The region west of Lake Baikal was dominated through the Ilim portage from the Enisei into the Lena basin. Here the powerful ostrog (1630), and later town, of Ilimsk (in 1649) had been founded. Eniseisk military commanders, basing their headquarters on this strategic point, advanced their detachments along the Upper Tunguska and then along the Angara, establishing the Bratsk ostrog (1631) and, twenty-one years later, on the same river nearer Lake Baikal, winter quarters at the Irkut, which became the ostrog of Irkutsk (1661). In 1654, midway between Bratsk and Irkutsk on the Angara, the ostrog of Balagansk went up. Thus the road to Lake Baikal was opened from the west, with Irkutsk and its rising town as the center of power in this region.[66] (See map 16.)

[65] L. S. Berg, *Otkrytie Kamchatki i ekspeditsii Beringa, 1725–1742* (Leningrad, 1935), pp. 28 ff.—note esp. his destructive criticism of F. A. Golder, *Russian Expansion on the Pacific, 1641–1850* (Cleveland, 1914), pp. 67–95, 268–288; N. N. Ogloblin, "Semen Dezhnev (1638–1671 gg.)," *Zhurnal M.N.P.,* CCLXXII (November-December, 1890), 249–306; Ogorodnikov, *op. cit.,* II, 57–61.

[66] Reports of Iakutsk military commanders (*voevodas*) Golovin and Glebov, 1641, *D.A.I.,* II, 258–261; reports of serving men, 1641, *ibid.,* II, 261; report of the Eniseisk military commander (*voevoda*) Uvarov, 1646, *ibid.,* III, 68–70; report of the Krasnoiarsk military commander (*voevoda*) Skriabin, 1653, *ibid.,* III, 387–390; Fischer, *op. cit.,* pp. 350, 354, 540–541, 557; N. N. Ogloblin, *Obozrenie stolbtsov i knig Sibirskago Prikaza* (4 vols., Moscow, 1895), IV, 37; Ogorodnikov, *Ocherki po istorii* . . . , II, 62–65.

In the meanwhile the Buriats along the Ud River to the west were subjugated from Krasnoiarsk by the construction in 1648 of the Udinsk ostrozhek, later known as Nizhne-Udinsk.[67] The Iakutsk military commanders undertook the conquest of the Buriats living in the upper Lena and northern Baikal region, where in the far upper reaches of the Lena they built the ostrozhek of Verkholensk in 1641, from which they could penetrate the northern half of Lake Baikal. Further expeditions advanced from the Lena up the Vitim on the northeastern side of the lake, where in 1646 the ostrozhek Verkhne-Angarsk went up; farther down on the east shore of the lake, at the mouth of the Barguzin River, the ostrog of Barguzinsk was built in 1648. From here the way into the Amur River system was explored. In 1653 two ostrogs, Ust'-Prorva, at the mouth of the Selenga, and Irgensk on Lake Irgen, and in the next year Nerchinsk, at the mouth of the Nercha where it flows into the Shilka (a tributary of the Amur), were built. Although the ostrog of Nerchinsk was destroyed by the Tunguses, it was rebuilt in 1658. Thus began the process of protecting the route leading from the Baikal region into the Amur basin. To this system of protected points were added three other ostrogs, Telembinsk on the Khilka (1658) and Verkhne-Udinsk and Selenginsk (1665) on the Selenga. In this way the domination of the Buriat region was completed and a direct route into the Amur basin opened up and controlled.[68]

But the Eniseisk people were not alone in forging a road into the inviting region of the Amur, which rumor filled not only with furs and food, but with silver as well. The Iakutsk military commanders sent out Vasilii Poiarkov, and his famous explorations resulted. In 1643 he went up the Aldan, the Uchur, and the Gonam, crossed the Iablonnoi range and

[67] Fischer, op. cit., p. 541; Ogorodnikov, op. cit., II, 66.

[68] Letter of the Eniseisk military commander (voevoda) Pashkov, to the Tomsk military commander (voevoda) Volynskii concerning ostrogs on the River Shilka and Lake Irgen, 1652, D.A.I., III, 343–345; Fischer, op. cit., pp. 532, 561, 567; Ogorodnikov, op. cit., II, 66–73.

portage, and then went down the Brianta, the Zeia, and the Amur to its mouth. He returned to Iakutsk in 1646 from the Sea of Okhotsk, after crossing the Stanovoi ridge and sailing down the Maia and the Aldan to the Lena. Poiarkov dispelled the beautiful dream of a Promised Land of silver, but he discovered a fertile agricultural region, the possession of which by Russia would mean not only strategic security for eastern Siberia and easy access to the Pacific, but also a center of grain cultivation for that area. The lack of an adequate grain-producing region in eastern Siberia was to make Russia's hold on the Pacific precarious for two centuries.[69]

It was soon found by private traders and trappers that the best route from the Lena to the Amur was up the Olekma and its tributary the Tugir over the Iablonnoi range, called here the Tugir portage, and down to the Shilka and the Amur. To make this route secure the ostrozhek of Ust'-Strelochnyi was constructed in 1651 at the junction of the Shilka and the Argun'.

Tugirsk, built at the portage in 1653, was abandoned when Nerchinsk was founded the next year. The most used route from the west, however, became the Baikal–Selenga–Ud–Telemba–Chita–Ingoda–Shilka road, of which we have already spoken.[70] (See maps 15, 16.)

For the purposes of this study it is not necessary to narrate the activities of the Russians under E. P. Khabarov and others in the Amur valley or to explain why they failed, in their conflict with the Manchus, to establish themselves there, as is indicated by the Treaty of Nerchinsk in 1689. To have done so

[69] Documents concerning the journey of Vasilii Poiarkov . . . , 1646, *D.A.I.*, III, 50–60; report from Iakutsk, 1651, Arkheograficheskaia Kommissia, *Akty istoricheskie* (5 vols., St. Petersburg, 1841–1842, index, 1843), IV, 76; V. I. Ogorodnikov, "Tuzemnoe i russkoe zemledelie na Amure v XVIII v.," *Trudy gosudarstvennogo dal'nevostochnogo universiteta* (Vladivostok, 1927), Ser. III, No. 4, p. 9; Robert J. Kerner, "Russian Expansion to America," *Papers of the Bibliographical Society of America*, XXV (1931), 111–129; Ogorodnikov, *Ocherki po istorii . . . ,* II, 74–82.

[70] Report of the lesser noble, Beketov, to the military commander (*voevoda*) of Eniseisk, Pashkov, 1653, *D.A.I.*, III, 390–396; Bakhrushin, *op. cit.*, pp. 138–139; N. Spafarii, "Puteshestvie chrez Sibir . . . Nikolaia Spafariia v 1675 . . . ," *Zapiski imperatorskago russkago geograficheskago obshchestva po otdeleniiu etnografii*, Vol. X, No. 1 (1882), pp. 136–140; Ogorodnikov, *Ocherki po istorii . . . ,* II, 83–84.

would have required much more than raids, which was all they had in their bag of tricks. It would have required, besides ostrogs, an armed colonizing population capable of developing agriculture as a defense against the Manchus, who, to make Russian tenure impossible, destroyed the fields and brought hunger upon the invading Russians in a relatively fertile region.[71] The task here has been to show how the process of expansion worked. The policy of raids failed in the Amur River valley, just as did the policy of raids both by Novgorod and Moscow throughout the first century of their contacts with the region beyond the Urals. Siberia was only conquered with the adoption of the policy of planned occupation by river and portage and ostrog, carried out with a sufficiently numerous group of colonizers. Such would have been the fate of the Amur valley had Moscow been able to back up the raiders with a sufficiently strong army and numerous colonists. Caught by war in Europe and suffering disastrous defeats at the hands of the Crimean Tatars, Russia was unable, at the end of the seventeenth century, to repeat what she had done in western Siberia. This was not accomplished until almost two centuries later. Other operative factors in the process were, mainly, the fur trade, which was the predominant incentive, and the activities of government officials, missionaries, and churchmen.

It has already been stated that the fur trade was synonymous with the conquest of Siberia. The Moscow government was the chief fur trader.[72] It collected the tribute or tax in furs from the natives. It collected a 10-per cent tax in the best furs from the private traders and trappers. In addition, it insisted on the

---

[71] Reports of serving men concerning Khabarov's activities on the Amur, 1652, *D.A.I.*, III, 346–348; instruction of the Iakutsk military commander (*voevoda*) to the serving man Prokofiev (1652), reports of the serving men Uvarov and Ermolin (1652), report of Erofei Khabarov (1652), *D.A.I.*, III, 352–371; E. Robinson, "The First Conquest of the Amur" (seminar report, History 249B, University of California, 1938), *passim;* Chen (Tsiutao Ho, *So Fang Pei Sheng*) (68 vols., Peking, 1868), introduction to VI, 17, App. A; Ogorodnikov, *Ocherki po istorii* . . . , II, 85–102.

[72] Kerner, "Russian Expansion to America," *op. cit.*, pp. 111–112, 114–115; Bakhrushin, *op. cit.*, pp. 140, 168–169; Ogorodnikov, *Ocherki po istorii* . . . , II, 100–101.

right of buying from merchants and trappers the best furs they obtained. Furthermore, the government exercised a monopoly on the sables and black foxes sold to China. This made possible a lucrative foreign trade, with Russian furs playing a

FUR TRIBUTE (IASAK) PAID AT A SIBERIAN OSTROG

leading role in the fur markets of Europe (Leipzig) and China. We know that furs were the most important single item in the foreign and domestic commerce of Russia in the sixteenth and seventeenth centuries. There is a statement to the effect that as early as 1586 the state treasury received 200,000 sables,

10,000 black foxes, 500,000 squirrels, besides beavers and ermines, from Siberia. Estimates of the income of the state from Siberian furs in the middle of the seventeenth century range from about 7 to about 30 per cent (or approximately from 125,000 to 600,000 rubles) of the total revenue of the state. The weight of the evidence, however, is on the side of the lower percentage. What value was represented by the ruble of that day is to be noted from the fact that two black fox pelts in 1623 brought 110 rubles. With these 110 rubles the owner could buy fifty-five acres of land, erect a good cabin, buy five horses, twenty head of cattle, twenty sheep, several dozen fowl, and still have half his capital left. The government paid the administrative expenses in Siberia out of the fur trade, retained a large surplus, and added an immense region to the state.[73]

Hand in hand with the military commander, accompanied by his assistants and soldiers, went the priest and the monk. Yermak had a "religious assistant" with him. The first church was founded in the ostrog of Tiumen in 1586, the first monastery at Tobolsk in 1601, and in 1620 the first diocese of Siberia was established with its seat at Tobolsk. (See App. 5.) What the private trader and trapper or the military commander with his "serving men" and cossacks could not do in bringing about pacification, the priest and monk or nun did.[74] The govern-

---

[73] P. Miliukov, "Gosudarstvennoe khoziaistvo Rossii v sviazi s reformoi Petra Velikago," *Zhurnal M.N.P.*, CCLXXI:301–357; G. Kotoshikin, *O Rossii v tsarstvovanie Alekseia Mikhailovicha* (3d ed., St. Petersburg, 1884), pp. 104–138; N. M. Karamzin, *Istoriia gosudarstva Rossiiskago* (2d ed., 12 vols., St. Petersburg, 1818–1829), X, 26; I. M. Kulisher, *Istoriia russkogo narodnogo khoziaistva* (2 vols., Moscow, 1925), II, 238; Fisher, *op. cit.*, pp. 183–185, 192–196, 291–369; Butsinskii, *Mangazeia*, pp. 1–2.

[74] The role of the Russian Orthodox Church and its monasteries in the history of Russian expansion, especially its economic and military significance, still awaits thorough research. Some hints of the importance of monasteries may be found in such brief accounts as Kizevetter's *Russkii sever*, 27 ff., and Platonov's *Proshloe . . .* , 33 ff. For Siberia, see esp. N. Abramov, "Materialy dlia istorii khristianskago prosveshcheniia Sibiri," *Zhurnal M.N.P.*, LXXXI:2, 15–56, and *Sibirskaia sovetskaia entsiklopediia* (3 vols., Novosibirsk, 1929–1931), III, 506–507; G. V. Lantzeff, *Siberia in the Seventeenth Century: A Study of Colonial Administration* (doctoral dissertation, University of California, 1938; now in press), MS pp. 296–339. There is an excellent opportunity to do for Russian his-

A SIBERIAN VILLAGE IN THE SEVENTEENTH CENTURY

ment did not want the native population oppressed, because that would mean a decline in the tribute,—that is to say, the revenue,—but official graft and private brigandage on the part of the merchants and trappers brought about a fearful decline in the native population and woeful oppression of the survivors. A bootleg fur trade flourished, resulting from the monopolistic tendencies of the government. Siberia became, with the Russian conquest, the scene of a disastrous exploitation both of its most readily accessible article of wealth—furs—and of its native population.

When the Russians reached the Pacific, the Kurile and Aleutian islands with their fur-bearing animals beckoned them on. With slight modifications, fundamentally the same principle, historically evolved in Europe and consciously planned and applied in Siberia, was now applied to Russian expansion to North America. The sea was like a river; the key island, guarding passages between islands and dominating chains of islands, was an ostrog. Thus on the Aleutian chain of islands Unalaska and Kodiak [Kadiak] were, so to speak, ostrogs. The present strategic key of American defense in the Aleutians is Dutch Harbor (Captain's Bay). It is situated on Unalaska Island, which guards Umnak Pass to the west and the Akutan and Unimak passes to the east. The Diomede Islands in the narrowest channel between Alaska and Siberia seemed destined to play similar roles. What is now Alaska was, under Russian rule, controlled from an island on which Novo-Arkhangelsk or Sitka, an ostrog, was founded.[75]

tory what Professor Herbert Eugene Bolton has so brilliantly done for American history in his essay: "The Mission as a Frontier Institution in the Spanish American Colonies," *Wider Horizons of American History* (New York, 1939), pp. 107–148.

[75] Komitet ob ustroistve russkikh amerikanskikh kolonii, *Doklad Komiteta ob ustroistve russkikh-amerikanskikh kolonii* (2 vols., St. Petersburg, 1863–1864), I, 9–11; P. Tikhmenev, *Istoricheskoe obozrenie obrazovaniia rossiisko-amerikanskoi kompanii i deistvii eia do nastoiashchago vremeni* (2 vols., St. Petersburg, 1861–1863), esp. I, 15; Lantzeff, *op. cit.*, pp. 154–155, 188–190; S. B. Okun', *Rossiisko-amerikanskaia kompaniia* (Leningrad, 1939).

Chapter V ⚓ Waterways, Railroads, and Land Highways

~~~~~~~~~~~~~~~~~~~~~~~~~~~~~~~~

CANALS, railroads, and land highways emphasize the importance of the several factors which have been analyzed in previous chapters of this study. It may be stated that, as a rule, railroads followed along rivers and over portages; that canals were usually dug through portages; and that many important arterial highways, both ancient and modern, were built along the watersheds on the portages. A few illustrations will serve the purpose here intended.

The building of canals naturally came before the construction of railroads and modern highways. There are several systems of canals in Russia that ought to be better known than they have been,[1] since, in 1913, Russian river transportation amounted to 46,300,000 tons.[2]

[1] See Ministerstvo Putei Soobshcheniia, *Karta vnutrennikh vodnykh i shosseinykh soobshchenii Evropeiskoi Rossii* (St. Petersburg, 1894); I. Stuckenberg, *Beschreibung aller im russischen Reiches gegrabenen oder projectierten Schiff und flussbaren Kanäle* (St. Petersburg, 1841); Gershelman, *Istoricheskii ocherk vnutrennikh vodnykh soobshchenii* (St. Petersburg, 1892); A. A. Neopikhanov, *Russkii transport i ego planirovanie* (Moscow-Leningrad, 1924), I; *Gosudarstvennyi rechnoi transport v 1925* (Moscow, 1925); S. V. Bernstein-Kogan, *Vnutrennii vodnyi transport* (Moscow, 1927), I; *Materialy po statistike putei soobshchenniia*, issue 1 (Moscow, 1926); *Sotsialisticheskii transport* (Moscow, 1926–). For maps see the collection (by A. V. Strel'bitskii and V. A. Bashlavin, ed. 1934?) under title of *Karty evropeiskoi chasti S.S.S.R.* (1:1,500,000), and the collection of separate maps, *Karta vostochnoi chasti S.S.S.R.* (1884 publication of the Military Topographic Section), corrected to 1932 by the cartographic Section U.V.T. (1:4,200,000), and *Bol'shoi sovetskii atlas mira* (Moscow, 1937), plates 162–163.

[2] *Bol'shaia sov. entsik.*, XI, 756.

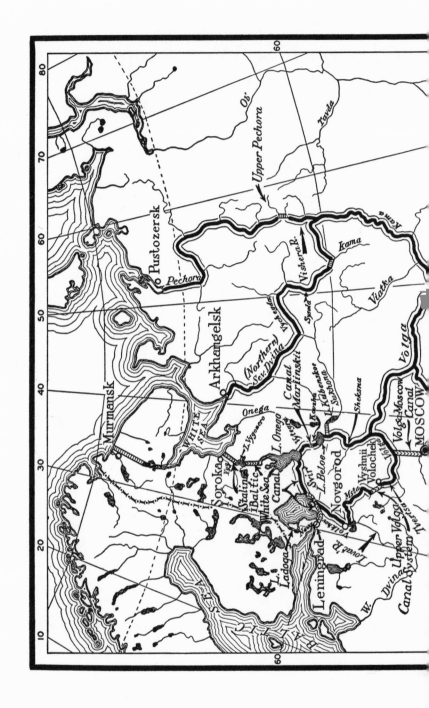

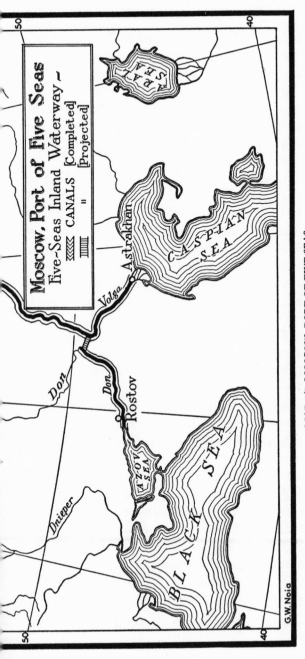

Moscow, Port of Five Seas
Five-Seas Inland Waterway ~
CANALS [Completed]
≡ [Projected]

Dnieper

Don

Don

Rostov

AZOV SEA

B L A C K   S E A

Volga Astrakhan

C A S P I A N
S E A

ARAL SEA

G.W. Noia

MAP 17. MOSCOW, PORT OF FIVE SEAS

The first and oldest of these canals is the Upper Volga Waterway, created by the Tvertsa and Tsna canals (through the key portage of Vyshnii Volochek), which join the upper Volga with the Baltic. The construction of this waterway was begun in 1703 and completed in 1709 under Peter the Great. (See maps 2, 17; App. 1, A. Volga, xxvii.) It was in practical use well into the nineteenth century and was the first, and for a long time (until the St. Petersburg–Moscow railway superseded it) the only connection between the Volga and the Baltic Sea. The waterway originated in the upper Volga, where it was supplied by reservoirs. The river Tvertsa (which empties into the Volga opposite Tver) was used to its source, where the Tvertsa or Upper Volga Canal, the river Tsna, and the Tsna Canal took up the waterway, which then led through Lake Mstino, then the river Msta, then through canals running parallel to and along the shores of Lake Ilmen, down the river Volkhov, through the canals along the shores of Lake Ladoga, to and through the river Neva to the Gulf of Finland and the Baltic.[3] It need not be emphasized that this waterway led directly past Torzhok through Vyshnii Volochek—probably the best known of all the portages of Russia—and that it connected Moscow and St. Petersburg by water. Its importance can hardly be overestimated. At one time early in the nineteenth century thousands of canal boats—as many as 5000 in one year—made their way from the Volga to the Baltic.

Next in time and importance was the Tikhvin Waterway, the construction of which was debated by Peter the Great in 1710, but which was not completed until 1811. It connects the upper Volga through its tributary, the Mologa, with the Siaz, which flows into Lake Ladoga. From ancient times a trade route passed through this water system over the Tikhvin portage. The exact route was as follows: the Volga, the Mologa (as far as the mouth of the Chagodoshcha), the Chagodoshcha,

---

[3] See esp. *Bol'shaia sov. entsik.*, XIV, 82, and *Entsik. slovar'*, XXXII:2, 708, and XXXIII:1, 278–279.

the Goriun, Lake Vozhanskoe, the Sominka, Lake Somino, the Valchina, the Tikhvin Canal (over the ancient portage made in part by Lakes Krupino and Lebedino), the river Tikhvinka, the river Siaz, Lake Ladoga, and the river Neva. This system carried a heavy traffic in foodstuffs in the last half of the nineteenth century, when hundreds of canalboats moved over it annually. (See map 17; App. 1, A. Volga, xxx.) The St. Petersburg (or Leningrad–Vologda) railway in part parallels this waterway and actually runs through the portage at Tikhvin.[4]

The third and last waterway from the upper Volga to the Baltic was known as the Mariinsk System. It became the most important of the three waterways. Like the Tikhvin Canal, its building was seriously considered by Peter the Great, but actually it was not constructed until 1808, while the parallel canal between Lake Beloe (Beloozero) and Lake Onego was completed only in 1852. It leaves the Volga at Rybinsk by way of the Sheksna, passes through the canal of Lake Beloe (Beloozero) into the Kovzha, through the New Mariinsk Canal (the place of the portage) to the Vytegra, and down that river to Lake Onego or the canal along its shores; from there it follows the river Svir' to Lake Ladoga, and, through that lake or the canal along its shores, passes to the river Neva, and thence to the Gulf of Finland.[5] (See App. 1, A. Volga, xxxii.) Just above where the Sheksna enters Lake Beloe (Beloozero) this system was united with the Northern Dvina System by means of the Württemberg Canals constructed between 1824 and 1828. The Württemberg Canal System leaves the Northern Dvina at the mouth of the Sukhona and then proceeds westward through the Sukhona, Lake Kubenskoe, the Porozovitsa, Lake Blagoveshchenskoe, the river Itkla, the canal (through the portage),

[4] *Entsik. slovar'*, XXXIII:1, 278.

[5] Sviagintsev, *Kratkoe opisanie Mariinskago vodnago puti* (St. Petersburg, 1882); Eidragevich, "Obzor sudokhodnago sostoianiia vodnago puti gertsoga Viurtembergskago," *Zhurnal ministerstva putei soobshcheniia* (St. Petersburg, 1886); *Entsik. slovar'*, XVIII:2, 621–626; I. F. Tiumenev, "Po Mariinskoi sisteme," *Istoricheskii vestnik*, XCI (1903), 226–265, 655–693, 1057–1108.

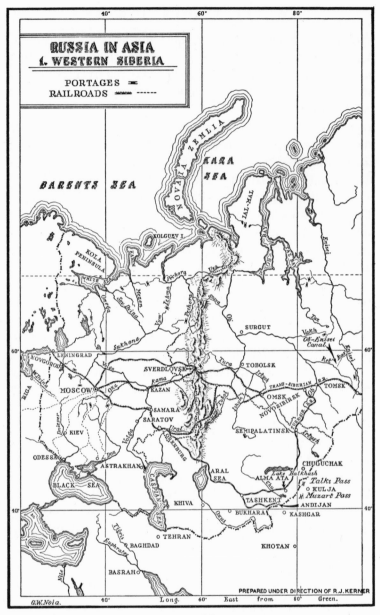

MAP 18. RUSSIA IN ASIA: (1) WESTERN SIBERIA

Lake Keshemskoe, Lake Vazerinskoe, the river Pozdyshka, Lake
Bab'e, the canal paralleling the former river Karbatka, Lake
Siverskoe, and the canal (through the portage) joining the
Sheksna near the village of Topornia.⁶ (See map 17; App. 1, A.
Volga, xxxiv.)

The important portages between the Northern Dvina, Pechora, Kama, and Ob' naturally raise questions relating to
canal-building projects. A project to connect the rivers Chusovaia (tributary of the Kama-Volga) and Iset (tributary of the
Tobol-Ob') near Ekaterinburg (now called Sverdlovsk) was developed in the eighteenth century. (See maps 12, 13, 14, 18;
App. 1, A. Volga, lvi.) The meridional folds of the Urals make
connections possible between the tributaries of the Ob' and
those of the Kama, Pechora, and Northern Dvina. The Northern Catherina (Severo-Ekaterininskii) Canal was constructed
between 1785 and 1822 to join the Kama and Northern Dvina
river systems, as follows: the Northern Dvina, the Vychegda,
the Northern Kel'tma, the canal (portage), the Dzurich, the
Southern Kel'tma, and the Kama. (See map 12; App. 1, A.
Volga, 1.) This canal was closed in 1838 from lack of traffic.
More recent developments in this region point toward its re-
construction. Another connection, with a portage called the
Bukhinskii Volok, joins these two basins as follows: the Northern Dvina, the Vychegda, the Nem, the Bukhinskii Volok, the
Berezovka, Lake Chusovskoe, the Visherka, the Kolva, the Vi-
shera, and the Kama. (See App. 1, A. Volga, lii.)

The Kama–Pechora route begins with the Kama and contin-
ues with the Vishera, the Kolva, the Visherka, Lake Chusovskoe,
the Berezovka, the Elovka (landing place, Ust'-Elovka), the
Vogulka (landing places at Pupovo and Ostozh'e), the Pechorskii Volok, the Volosnitsa, and ends in the Pechora. (See App. 1,
A. Volga, liii.) Along this route it is now proposed to create
a deep-waterway system that will connect the White or Arctic

---

⁶ *Entsik. slovar'*, VII:2, 704–705; V. G. German, "Proekt Volga-Belomorskogo
kanala v XVII v.," *Istoricheskii sbornik*, Ak. Nauk S.S.S.R., I (1934), 254.

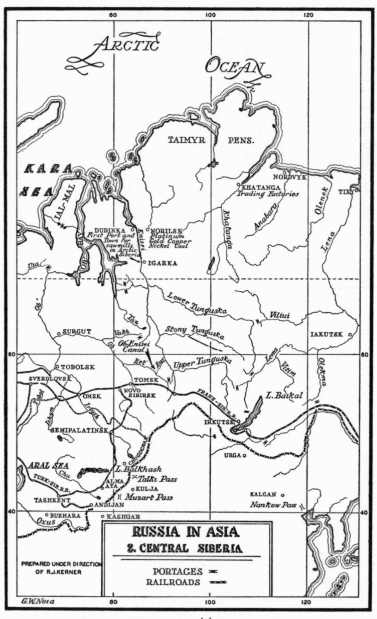

MAP 19. RUSSIA IN ASIA: (2) CENTRAL SIBERIA

Sea with the Caspian by the construction of two reservoirs, one in the basin of the Kolva and the other at the sources of the Pechora. A short navigable canal is to be built to join them. The Northern Dvina–Vychegda basin is to be connected with this system by a canal from the Nem to the Vychegda.[7] (See App. 1, A. Volga, lii.)

In 1882 construction of the Ob'–Enisei Canal in Siberia was begun, and it was completed within the decade. This canal joined the Ket', a tributary of the Ob', with the Kas', a tributary of the Enisei. (See App. 1, L. Ob', viii.) Thus a Siberian waterway of some five thousand versts, extending from Tiumen to Irkutsk, was made possible.[8]

Any study of the rivers and artificial waterways of Russia leads to the conclusion that the central water system is that of the Volga, which has a basin including 1080 rivers, rivulets, streams, and lakes, and comes nearest to linking the European with the Siberian river systems.[9] It is no wonder that the next step in the development of the artificial waterways of Russia, after the removal of the capital from Leningrad to Moscow, was the construction of additional canals that would make Moscow a port accessible to all the seas into which the rivers of the present Soviet Union flow.

It was in this connection that three great canals were projected: the Moscow–Volga Canal, the White Sea–Baltic Canal, and the Volga–Don Canal. The completion of these waterways would make Moscow a port of five seas: the White, the Baltic, the Caspian, the Azov, and the Black. Two of these projects,

---

[7] V. Semenov Tian'-Shanskii, "Kama," *Bol'shaia sov. entsik.*, XXX, 792; "Severo-Ekaterininskii Kanal," *Entsik. slovar'*, XXXII:1, 310; P. Beliavskii, "Kama," *ibid.*, XIV:1, 123–124; and "Kamo-Pechorskii vodnyi put'," *Bol'shaia sov. entsik.*, XXXI, 135; "Vishera," *ibid.*, XI, 357.

[8] A. I. Dmitriev-Mamonov and A. F. Zdiarskii, *Guide de grand chemin de fer trans-sibérien* (St. Petersburg, 1900), p. 249.

[9] See articles: V. K., "Volga kak vodnyi put'," *Bol'shaia sov. entsik.*, XII, 685–691; A. Rybnikov, "Istoriko-khoziaistvennyi ocherk Volzhskogo puti," *ibid.*, pp. 691–693; and G. Sitnikov, "Volga v ekonomicheskom otnoshenii," *ibid.*, pp. 693–701.

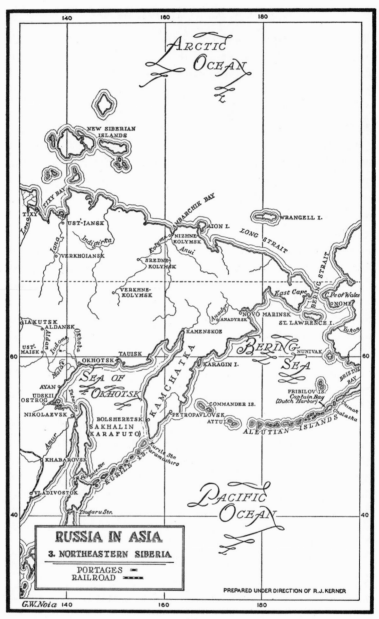

MAP 20. RUSSIA IN ASIA: (3) NORTHEASTERN SIBERIA

the Moscow–Volga and the White Sea–Baltic canals, have been completed.

The purpose of the Moscow–Volga Canal[10] is to connect the capital by a deep waterway as directly as possible with the Volga River, even though Moscow is at present situated on a tributary of the Oka, which in turn is a tributary of the Volga. (See App. 1, A. Volga, xii, xix.) This canal shortens the distance to Rybinsk (toward the White and Baltic seas) by 1100 kilometers and the distance to Gor'kii (toward the Caspian and Black seas) by 110 kilometers; it also creates a suitable water supply for Moscow and for the Moskva River. The Moscow–Volga Canal begins at the village of Ivan'kovo, eight kilometers above the mouth of the river Dubna, and turns south to the town of Dmitrov, where the stream is raised by five locks. Five reservoirs are made by damming up the rivers Iksha, Ucha, Kliazma, and Khimka. Near the village Shchukino the canal, after having proceeded a distance of 128 kilometers, joins the river Moskva. At Rybinsk, now Russia's waterway center, a vast reservoir or lake has been created.

The White Sea–Baltic Canal,[11] now called the Stalin Canal, begins at Soroka on the Gulf of Onega and extends to the river Vyg, then runs through the river Vyg, Lake Vyg, the river Telekina, Lake Telekinskoe, Lake Matko, Lake Dolgoe, and Vol Lake, reaching Povenets on Lake Onego through an unnamed stream. Thereupon the already familiar routes to the Volga or to the Baltic may be followed by the boats. It will be noted, as indicated above, that Peter the Great started on his expedition to the Baltic in 1702 from Niukhcha (on the Gulf of Onega) and reached Povenets chiefly over the same route.

The portage route of the Volga–Don Canal (described on pages 65, 107) is scheduled for completion in 1945. The five seas will therefore be linked together through the territory of the Soviet Union when these canals are all functioning. It would not be fantastic to complete the scheme by a canal between

---

[10] *Bol'shaia sov. entsik.*, XL, 404–408.   [11] *Ibid.*, XXXI, 232–233.

the Volga and the Ob' systems, as has been suggested at various times since the eighteenth century. In this way access by inland waterway could be realized from the heart of Russia to Lake Baikal.

When one comes to the relationship of railroads[12] to the set of factors under observation here, one may point to a number of illustrations among the many at hand. The railroad from Moscow to Smolensk follows the old Smolensk road, which passes through the leading portages between these two cities. These have already been described above in connection with Napoleon's invasion. Here the main road and the railroad virtually parallel each other. The railroad from Moscow to Rzhev runs through Volokolamsk—the most important portage in this area—and so does the highway. The railroad from Moscow to St. Petersburg (Leningrad), in spite of the famous instructions of Nicholas I to his engineers to follow a straight line, runs from Tver through Vyshnii Volochek, a portage the importance of which has been touched upon many times in this study. Here it meets the Tvertsa Canal. The railroad from Soroka to Medvezhia Gora is parallel to the White Sea–Baltic Canal along a considerable part of its course. The Transsiberian Railway was built with a view to a relationship with the river systems of Siberia as well as with the Ob'–Enisei Canal. Here the rail and water systems were meant to supplement each other.[13] The Transsiberian was built in such a way as to run through certain portages in territory not competing directly with the Ob'–Enisei Canal. At Ekaterinburg, the key station in the Urals, we are

[12] See note 1 to this chapter.

[13] A. N. de Koulomzine, *Sibirskaia zheleznaia doroga* (St. Petersburg, 1903), pp. 24–39; in French, *Le Trans-sibérien* (Paris, 1904), pp. 27–36; N. A. Voloshinov, "Sibirskaia zheleznaia doroga," *Izvestiia imperatorskago russkago geograficheskago obshchestva*, XXVII (1891), 11–39, points out that there were also proposals to build the railway only through the portages to link up with the river traffic; see also D. M. M(erkhalev), *Zheleznye dorogi Sibiri. Sbornik sibstatupravleniia* (2d ed., Novo-Nikolaevsk, 1921); A. IU. Rudzit, "Magistral' Sibir'-Sredniaia Aziia," *Sev. Aziia* (1928) ; *Generalnyi plan rekonstruktsii narodnogo khoziaistva Iakutskoi A.S.S.R.* (Iakutsk, 1928) has plans for 1927–1941.

at the portage between the Chusovaia (of the Kama–Volga system) and the Pyshma and the Iset (of the Tobol–Ob' system).
From Kurgan on the Tobol to Petropavlovsk on the Ishim;
from Petropavlovsk to Omsk on the Irtysh; from Barabinsk
close to the Om, tributary of the Irtysh, to Novosibirsk (formerly Novonikolaevsk) on the Ob'; from Achinsk on the Chulym to Krasnoiarsk on the Enisei: from Krasnoiarsk on the
Enisei to Kansk on the Kan; from the Zima on the Oka, tributary of the Angara, to Irkutsk on the Angara, the Transsiberian
Railway runs through watersheds which have served or are
serving as portages.

The references here made to land highways, and those previously made, as for example the Tatar trails and the later Russian highways which developed out of them (see pages 56–61),
indicate clearly that the most important of them ran through
portages.

Chapter VI ✑ General Obser-
vations and Conclusions

~~~~~~

THE CONCLUSION to be drawn from this analysis extending over a thousand years of recorded history is, I believe, obvious. Here is a process—the elements of which are the people, rivers, and portages, the ostrogs, monasteries, and furs—which may be traced in its action and development from tribal community to world empire. The railroad, canal, and motor highway have followed through the portages chiefly along the lines laid down by this process.

Over these rivers and portages went representative members and groups of several types of society: the hunting-pastoral, the patriarchal, the feudal-serf, and the modern. Each, whatever its ideology, utilized them. These changing types could come and go, but the elements of the process always remained. The urge to the sea always dominated.

To break up the Russian empire, as has been considered and attempted in the past, would be to work in opposition to basic forces which are creating a geographical, economic, and functional unity and which centuries of history have revealed as constantly operating. Here on these vast limitless plains nature and man have achieved most when man has understood these basic truths and, by adjusting himself to them, has mastered a new continent, Eurasia.

To say that this process explains all there is to Russian history is to claim far too much. No such claim is made for it. But that it explains much cannot be denied. That it fundamentally affected and indeed vitally helped to shape the course of Russian history seems clear. Like a newly discovered tool or invention it awaits use by the historian or statesman with its revealing explanations of the past and its prophecy of the future.

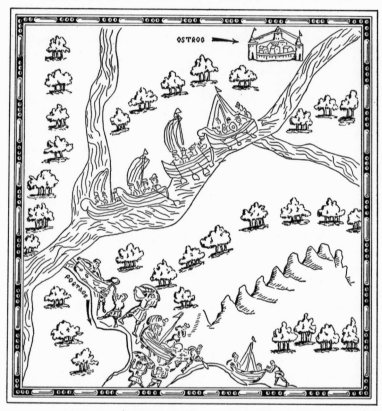

AN OSTROG (BLOCKHOUSE) AND PORTAGE IN SIBERIA

APPENDIXES

Appendix 1 ⚓ Portages and the Important Russian River Systems

HERE are included the important Russian river systems and most of the portages. No attempt has been made to make this list absolutely exhaustive; nevertheless, no other list of like character or degree of completeness exists, and since it may prove useful to historians and geographers it is here included. It represents a small part of the intensive work necessary before fundamental conclusions in the text could be reached.

A. THE VOLGA AND ITS TRIBUTARIES

i. *The Volga-Kamyshinka-Ilovlia-Don Portage*[1]
> R. Volga
> R. Kamyshinka
> > Portage (*Volok*)
> R. Ilovlia
> R. Don

ii. *The Volga-Khupta-Riasa-Don Portage*[2]
> R. Volga
> R. Oka
> R. Pronia
> R. Ranovaia
> R. Khupta
> > Portage (*Volok*)
> R. Riasa
> R. Voronezh
> R. Don

---

[1] V. Semenov-Tian'-Shanskii, "Volga v fiziko-geograficheskom otnoshenii," *Bol'-shaia sov. entsik.*, XII, 672–682, esp. 677:
"Near Kamyshin the Volga is in the near vicinity (17 km.) of the upper part of the river Ilovlia, the tributary of the Don. The distance between the sources of the rivulet Kamyshinka, the tributary of the Volga, and the Ilovlia is only a little more than 4 km. In this place ... in ancient times there existed a portage many times used by the troops invading the land of the Khazars and moving from the Don basin to the Volga. In the sixteenth century the Turkish Sultan Selim attempted to build a canal here. A similar attempt was later made by Peter I. Both enterprises remained unfinished, but the remains of the work are still to be seen."
[2] V. Rudakov, "Vodnye puti v drevnei Rossii," *Entsik. slovar'*, VI:2, 757–758, esp. 758; W. Coxe, *Travels into Poland, Russia, Sweden, and Denmark* (4th ed., 5 vols., London, 1792), III, 451–452.

iii. *The Volga-Shat'-Don Portage*[3]

    R. Volga
    R. Oka
    R. Upa
    R. Shat'
        Portage (*Volok*)
    R. Don

iv. *The Volga-Pshevka-Perevolochnia-Don Portage*[4]

    R. Volga
    R. Oka
    R. Zusha
    R. Pshevka
        Portage (*Volok*)
    R. Perevolochnia
    R. Liubovsha
    R. Trudy
    R. Sosna
    R. Don

v. *The Volga-Reseta-Snezhat'-Dnieper Portage*[5]

    R. Volga
    R. Oka
    R. Zhizdra
    R. Reseta (Resseta, Roseta)
        Portage (*Volok*)
    R. Snezhat'
    R. Desna
    R. Dnieper

---

[3] V. Rudakov, *loc. cit.;* Z. Khodakovskii, "Puti soobshcheniia v drevnei Rossii," *Russkii istoricheskii sbornik* (Moscow, 1838), I, 5, states:
"After being informed that the tributaries of the Upa-Shat' and Shivorona closely approach the Don, Sviatoslav dragged his boats across the narrow space here and went down the Don."

[4] Khodakovskii, *op. cit.*, p. 39; Rudakov, *loc. cit.*, who mentions only the Oka-Zusha-Sosna-Don links.

[5] N. P. Barsov, *Ocherki russkoi istoricheskoi geografii* (Warsaw, 1885), p. 23, mentions a village called Staika, on the Reseta, and another Staika on the Ugra River as evidence that they were landing places. Barsov deduces from the events of the twelfth century that the route from Novgorod Severskii into the land of the Viatichi went by way of Karachev, a town on the Snezhat' River. Khodakovskii, *op. cit.*, p. 33, points out the evidences of navigation along the river Zhizdra.

vi. *The Volga-Ressa-Volok-Dnieper Portage*[6]

R. Volga
R. Oka
R. Ugra
R. Ressa (Resa)
    Portage (*Volok*)
R. Volok
R. Neruch
R. Bolva
R. Desna
R. Dnieper

vii. *The Volga—either Ugra-Osma-Dnieper, or Ugra tributaries-Viazma-Dnieper, or Voria-Gzhat'-Volga Portage*[7]

Variant 1:	Variant 2:
R. Volga	R. Volga
R. Oka	R. Oka
R. Ugra	R. Ugra
	Ugra tributaries
Portage (*Volok*)	Portage (*Volok*)
R. Osma	R. Viazma
R. Dnieper	R. Dnieper

Variant 3:
R. Volga
R. Oka
R. Ugra
R. Voria
    Portage (*Volok*)
R. Gzhat'
R. Vazuza
R. Volga

---

[6] Barsov, *op. cit.*, p. 23, indicates a number of places whose names suggest the once existing routes: Stoiki and Stoi on the Bolva. Khodakovskii, *op. cit.*, pp. 32–33, does not think that the route indicated in the text was very much in use on account of the shallowness of the rivers.

[7] For variant 1 see Barsov, *op. cit.*, pp. 20–21; for variants 2 and 3—possible portages—see the U.S.S.R. map.

viii. *The Volga-Protva-Moskva-Volga Portage*[8]

>R. Volga
>R. Oka
>R. Protva
>>Portage (*Volok*)
>R. Moskva
>R. Oka
>R. Volga

ix. *The Volga-Lopasnia-Pakhra-Volga Portage*[9]

>R. Volga
>R. Oka
>R. Lopasnia
>>Portage (*Volok*)
>R. Pakhra
>R. Moskva
>R. Oka
>R. Volga

x. *The Volga-Ruza-Derzha-Volga Portage*[10]

>R. Volga
>R. Oka
>R. Moskva
>R. Ruza
>>Portage (*Volok*)
>R. Derzha
>R. Volga

---

[8] Barsov, *op. cit.*, p. 30.

[9] *Loc. cit.*, esp. reference to the Ipat Chronicle under 1176.

[10] Khodakovskii, *op. cit.*, p. 33, mentions this route as one used by an official of Novgorod on the way to Vladimir.

xi. *The Volga—either Voloshna, or Istra-Lama-Volga Portage*[11]

Variant 1:	Variant 2:
R. Volga	R. Volga
R. Oka	R. Oka
R. Moskva	R. Moskva
R. Ruza	R. Istra
R. Voloshna	
Portage (Volok Lamskii)	Portage (Volok Lamskii)
R. Lama	R. Lama
R. Shosha	R. Shosha
R. Volga	R. Volga

xii. *The Volga-Skhodnia-Kliazma-Volga Portage*[12]

R. Volga
R. Oka
R. Moskva
R. Skhodnia
    Portage (*Volok*)
R. Kliazma
R. Oka
R. Volga

xiii. *The Volga-Iauza-Kliazma-Volga Portage*[13]

R. Volga
R. Oka
R. Moskva
R. Iauza
    Portage (*Volok*)
R. Kliazma
R. Oka
R. Volga

---

[11] S. M. Seredonin, *Istoricheskaia geografiia* (Petrograd, 1916), pp. 236–237, discusses the significance of Volok Lamskii; Rudakov, *loc. cit.;* Barsov, *op. cit.,* p. 30, refers to the Laurentian Chronicle under the year 1135, see Arkheograficheskaia Kommissiia, *Polnoe sobranie russkikh letopisei* (24 vols., St. Petersburg, 1846–1914; hereafter cited as *P.S.R.L.*), I, 132; Khodakovskii, *op. cit.,* pp. 31–32, discusses the significance of Volok Lamskii; "Volokolamsk," *Bol'shaia sov. entsik.,* XII, 785–786; K. V. Kudriashov, *Russkii istoricheskii atlas* (Moscow-Leningrad, 1928), table III; Kliuchevskii, *Kurs,* II, 6.

[12] Barsov, *loc. cit.*

[13] *Loc. cit.;* Kliuchevskii, *loc. cit.*

xiv. *The Volga-Buzha-Kliazma-Volga Portage*[14]

R. Volga
R. Oka
R. Pra
Series of lakes
R. Polia
R. Buzha
    Portage (*Volok*)
R. Kliazma
R. Oka
R. Volga

xv. *The Volga-Solma-Sarra-Rostovskoe Portage*[15]

R. Volga
R. Nerl' (Bol'shaia)
R. Solma
    Portage (*Volok*)
R. Sarra (Sara)
L. Rostovskoe

xvi. *The Volga-Solma-Malaia Nerl'-Volga Portage*[16]

R. Volga
R. Nerl' (Bol'shaia)
R. Solma
    Portage (*Volok*)
R. Malaia Nerl'
R. Kliazma
R. Oka
R. Volga

xvii. *The Volga-Pleshcheevo-Koloksha-Volga Portage*[17]

R. Volga
R. Nerl' (Bol'shaia)
L. Somino
R. Veska (Vioksa)
L. Pleshcheevo
    Portage (*Volok*)
R. Koloksha
R. Kliazma
R. Oka
R. Volga

---

[14] Khodakovskii, *op. cit.*, p. 35.
[15] Rudakov, *loc. cit.*; Barsov, *op. cit.*, p. 31; *P.S.R.L.*, XX, 148–149, XXIII, 65.
[16] Rudakov, *loc. cit.*; Barsov, *loc. cit.*
[17] Rudakov, *loc. cit.*; Barsov, *op. cit.*, pp. 30–31.

xviii. *The Volga-Vlena-Kliazma-Volga Portage*[18]

> R. Volga
> R. Sestra
> R. Dubna
> R. Vlena (Viela)
> > Portage (*Volok*)
> R. Kliazma
> R. Oka
> R. Volga

xix. *The Volga-Iakhroma-Kliazma-Volga Portage*[19]

> R. Volga
> R. Sestra
> R. Iakhroma
> > Portage (*Volok*)
> R. Kliazma
> R. Oka
> R. Volga

xx. *The Volga-Gzhat'—either Obsha-Dnieper, or Voria-Gzhat'-Volga Portage*[20]

> Variant 1:   Variant 2:
> > R. Volga   (See Volga vii, variant 3)
> > R. Vazuza
> > R. Gzhat'
> > > Portage (*Volok*)
> > R. Obsha (?)
> > R. Dnieper

xxi. *The Volga-Vazuza-Dnieper Portage*[21]

> R. Volga
> R. Vazuza
> > Portage (*Volok*)
> R. Dnieper

---

[18] *Ibid.,* p. 30.

[19] *Loc. cit.*

[20] V. A. Brim, "Put' iz Variag v Greki", *Izvestiia akademii nauk S.S.S.R.*, Ser. VII, Otdelenie obshchestvennykh nauk, No. 2 (1931) (pp. 201–249), p. 231; Seredonin, *op. cit.*, p. 229.

[21] Barsov, *op. cit.*, pp. 20, 28; Khodakovskii, *op. cit.*, pp. 24–26.

xxii: *The Volga-Vazuza-Viazma-Dnieper Portage*[22]

    R. Volga
    R. Vazuza
        Portage (*Volok*)
    R. Viazma
    R. Dnieper

xxiii. *The Volga-Peno-Zhadenie-Western Dvina Portage*[23]

    R. Volga
    R. Selizharovka
    L. Seliger (western side)
    L. Iamanets (Emenets)
    L. Sterzh
    L. Vselug
    L. Peno
        Portage (*Volok*)
    L. Zhadenie
    R. Western Dvina

xxiv. *The Volga-Runa-Pola-Lovat' Portage*[24]

    R. Volga
    R. Selizharovka
    L. Seliger
    L. Sterzh
    R. Runa
        Portage (*Volok*, 10 versts long)
    R. Pola
    R. Lovat'

[22] Rudakov, *loc. cit.*
[23] Brim, *op. cit.*, p. 232; Barsov, *op. cit.*, pp. 26, 28–29.
[24] *Ibid.*, p. 28; Khodakovskii, *op. cit.*, pp. 33–34.

xxv. *The Volga-Seliger-Volotskoe-Lovat' Portage*[25]

R. Volga
R. Selizharovka
L. Seliger
    Portage (*Volok* across the hills, 5 versts long)
L. Volotskoe
L. Dolgoe
L. Samintsovo
L. Stromilovo
L. Istochino
R. Chernoruchenka
R. Iavon'
R. Pola
R. Lovat'

xxvi. *The Volga-Kosha-Volochnia-Volga Portage*[26]

R. Volga
R. Kosha
    Portage (*Volok*)
R. Volochnia
R. Osuga
R. Tvertsa
R. Volga

xxvii. *The Volga-Tsna-Mstino-Msta Portage*[27]

R. Volga
R. Tvertsa
R. Tsna
    Portage (*Volok*—Vyshnii Volochek)
L. Mstino
R. Msta

---

[25] T. J. Arne, "La Suède et l'Orient. Etudes archéologiques sur les relations de la Suède et de l'Orient pendant l'âge des Vikings," *Archives d'Etudes Orientales*, VIII (Uppsala, 1914), p. 16; Rudakov, *loc. cit.*; Barsov, *op. cit.*, p. 27; Khodakovskii, *op. cit.*, p. 33.

[26] *Ibid.*, p. 32. This route was of importance in communications from Torzhok to the region of Lake Seliger.

[27] Arne, *loc. cit.*, is the only one who mentions the Tsna as one of the links. Rudakov, *loc. cit.*; Barsov, *op. cit.*, p. 29, emphasizes the significance of this route for Novgorod. The Tvertsa was a key to Novgorod. Occupation of the upper Tvertsa by the princes of the lower Volga always interrupted the trade of Novgorod with the Volga region; it also led to the rise of prices in Novgorod and sometimes to famine. Khodakovskii, *op. cit.*, p. 26; Seredonin, *op. cit.*, pp. 234–238, has a discussion of the importance of this route. Coxe, *op. cit.*, III, map, pp. 444–445.

xxviii. *The Volga-Keza-S'ezzha-Msta Portage*[28]

    R. Volga
    R. Mologa
    R. Keza (Kesadra)
        Portage (*Volok* near L. Navolok)
    R. S'ezzha
    R. Msta

xxix. *The Volga-Pechenovo-Msta Portage*[29]

    R. Volga
    R. Mologa
    R. Chagodoshcha
    R. Pes'
    L. Mezhvoloch'e
    L. Iasino (Iamnoe, according to Barsov)
    L. Sitno
    R. Sitinets
    L. Sheregodra
    R. Sheregodra
    L. Liuto
    R. Liuta
    L. Pechenovo (Pelenovo, according to Khodakovskii)
        Portage (Volok Derzhkovskii, below Borovichi)
    R. Msta

xxx. *The Volga-Chagoda-Volozhba-Ladoga Portage*[30]

Variant 1:	Variant 2:
R. Volga	R. Volga
R. Mologa	R. Mologa
R. Chagodoshcha	R. Chagodoshcha
R. Chagoda	R. Somina
	R. Valchina
Portage (Volok Volokoslavskii or Khot'slavskii)	
R. Volozhba (Volosha)	R. Tikhvinka
R. Siaz' (Sias')	R. Siaz'
L. Ladoga	L. Ladoga

---

[28] Khodakovskii, *op. cit.*, p. 32, is of the opinion that "this route enabled the Varangians to go to the sources of the Mologa, the banks of which are covered with ancient burying grounds. Through this route Novgorod communicated with its *volost* (province) of Bezhitsy." See also the map inclosed in *Entsik. slovar'*, XXI:1, pp. 236–237.

[29] Arne, *loc. cit.*, leaves out lakes and rivers between Volok Derzhkovskii and the River Pes'; Rudakov, *loc. cit.*; Barsov, *op. cit.*, p. 31.

[30] For variant 1 see Arne, *loc. cit.*; Rudakov, *loc. cit.*; Khodakovskii, *op. cit.*, p. 21; Barsov, *op. cit.*, p. 31. Variant 2—possible portage—present Tikhvin canal system.

xxxi. *The Volga-Kolp'-Lid'-Volga Portage*[31]

    R. Volga
    R. Sheksna
    R. Suda
    R. Kolp'
        Portage (*Volok*)
    R. Lid'
    R. Chagodoshcha
    R. Mologa
    R. Volga

xxxii. *The Volga-Kovzha-Vytegra-Ladoga Portage*[32]

    R. Volga
    R. Sheksna
    L. Beloe (Beloozero)
    R. Kovzha
        Portage (*Volok*, 7 versts long)
    R. Vytegra
    L. Onego (Onezhskoe)
    R. Svir'
    L. Ladoga

[31] Arne, *loc. cit.*; Khodakovskii, *loc. cit.*; Barsov, *op. cit.*, pp. 31–32.

[32] Arne, *loc. cit.*, thinks that this was the most convenient route between the Volga and the Baltic Sea. Rudakov, *loc. cit.*, describes it also as a Volga–Baltic Sea route.

xxxiii. *The Volga-L. Volotskoe-L. Dolgoe-Onega Portage*[33]

R. Volga
R. Sheksna
L. Beloe (Beloozero)
R. Ukhtoma
L. Volotskoe (Volodskoe)
    Portage (Volok Ukhtomskii)
L. Dolgoe
R. Ukhtoma (another river of the same name as above)
R. Modlona
L. Vozhe
R. Svid
L. Lache
R. Onega

xxxiv. *The Volga-Slavianka-Porozovitsa-Northern Dvina Portage*[34]

R. Volga
R. Sheksna
R. Slavianka
    Portage (Volok Korotkii near L. Korotkoe, con-
    nected with L. Beloe (Beloozero) through the R.
    Borodava)
R. Porozovitsa
L. Kubenskoe
R. Sukhona
R. Northern Dvina

---

[33] V. G. Geiman, "Proekt Volgo-Belomorskogo kanala v XVII v.," *Istoricheskii sbornik*. Akademiia nauk S.S.S.R.(Leningrad, 1934), I, 254. Khodakovskii, *op. cit.*, p. 28, indicates that the portages Ukhtomskii and Korotkii are among the most ancient ones. The country beyond them was called Zavolochie (Country-beyond-the-Portage). These portages were the gates into the land of furs. Originally they were under the control of the Kievan princes (N. N. Karamzin, *Istoriia gosudarstva rossiiskago* [2d ed., 12 vols., St. Petersburg, 1818–1829], II, nn. 138, 141). Later these portages were controlled by the princes of Beloozero, always faithful servants of the Vladimir and Moscow princes. Control over these portages by hostile princes seriously handicapped the Novgorodian trade (Karamzin, *op. cit.*, III, nn. 3, 100, 182, etc.).

[34] Arne, *loc. cit.*; Rudakov, *op. cit.*, p. 757, describes this route as a part of the "Zavoloch'skii vodnyi put'," branching through the Mologa to the Msta and going by way of the Vychegda to the Kama and to the Pechora. Barsov, *op. cit.*, p. 32, speaks of the Sheksna as the "gate to the Zavolochie," and of the route given here as the "Zavoloch'skii put'"; Khodakovskii, *op. cit.*, pp. 27–28.

xxxv. *The Volga-Pidma-Bolshma-Onega Portage*[35]

  R. Volga
  R. Sheksna
  R. Pidma
      Portage (*Volok,* 10 versts long)
  R. Bolshma
  L. Vozhe or Charandskoe
  R. Svid
  L. Lache
  R. Onega

xxxvi. *The Volga-Sheksna-Perechnaia-Onega Portage*[36]

  R. Volga
  R. Sheksna
      Portage (Volok Korotkii)
  R. Perechnaia
  R. Punema
  L. Vozhe
  R. Svid
  L. Lache
  R. Onega

xxxvii. *The Volga-Sogozha-Toshna-Northern Dvina Portage*[37]

  R. Volga
  R. Sheksna
  R. Sogozha
      Portage (*Volok*)
  R. Toshna
  R. Vologda
  R. Sukhona
  R. Northern Dvina

xxxviii. *The Volga-Obnora-Lezha-Northern Dvina Portage*[38]

  R. Volga
  R. Kostroma
  R. Obnora
      Portage (*Volok*)
  R. Lezha
  R. Sukhona
  R. Northern Dvina

[35] Barsov, *loc. cit.*
[36] Khodakovskii, *op. cit.*, p. 27.
[37] A possible portage, see the U.S.S.R. map.
[38] *Idem.*

xxxix. *The Volga-Monza—either Lezha, or Shuia-Northern Dvina Portage*[39]

Variant 1:	Variant 2:
R. Volga	R. Volga
R. Kostroma	R. Kostroma
R. Monza	R. Monza
Portage (*Volok*)	Portage (*Volok*)
R. Lezha	R. Shuia
R. Sukhona	R. Sukhona
R. Northern Dvina	R. Northern Dvina

xl. *The Volga-Tutka-Khmelnitsa-Northern Dvina Portage*[40]

R. Volga
R. Kostroma
R. Tutka
   Portage (*Volok*)
R. Khmelnitsa
R. Sukhona
R. Northern Dvina

xli. *The Volga-Kostroma-Tolshma-Northern Dvina Portage*[41]

R. Volga
R. Kostroma
   Portage (*Volok*)
R. Tolshma
R. Sukhona
R. Northern Dvina

xlii. *The Volga-Iuza-Sharzhenga-Northern Dvina Portage*[42]

R. Volga
R. Unzha
R. Iuza
   Portage (*Volok*)
R. Sharzhenga
R. Iug
R. Northern Dvina

---

[39] For variant 1 see Khodakovskii, *op. cit.*, p. 30. Variant 2 a possible portage, see the U.S.S.R. map.

[40] A possible portage, see the U.S.S.R. map.

[41] *Idem.*

[42] Khodakovskii, *loc. cit.*, indicates a possibility of the Volga-Unzha-Iuza-Iug route. In this case the river Sharzhenga is the logical link, see the U.S.S.R. map.

xliii. *The Volga-Pyshchug-Kudanga-Northern Dvina Portage*[43]

> R. Volga
> R. Vetluga
> R. Pyshchug
> > Portage (*Volok*)
> R. Kudanga
> R. Iug
> R. Northern Dvina

xliv. *The Volga-Vokhma-Entala-Northern Dvina Portage*[44]

> R. Volga
> R. Vetluga
> R. Vokhma
> > Portage (*Volok*)
> R. Entala
> R. Iug
> R. Northern Dvina

xlv. *The Volga-Maramitsa-Kichug-Northern Dvina Portage*[45]

> R. Volga
> R. Kama
> R. Viatka
> R. Moloma
> R. Maramitsa
> > Portage (*Volok*)
> R. Kichug
> R. Pushma
> R. Iug
> R. Northern Dvina

[43] A possible portage, see the U.S.S.R. map.

[44] Khodakovskii, *op. cit.*, p. 30. The river Entala is a possible link, according to the U.S.S.R. map.

[45] A possible portage, see the U.S.S.R. map.

xlvi. *The Volga—either Suran-Setka, or Kobra-Lunia-Northern Dvina Portage*[46]

Variant 1:
- R. Volga
- R. Kama
- R. Viatka
- R. Kobra
- R. Suran
     Portage (*Volok*)
- R. Setka
- R. Luza
- R. Iug
- R. Northern Dvina

Variant 2:
- R. Volga
- R. Kama
- R. Viatka
- R. Kobra

     Portage (*Volok*)
- R. Lunia
- R. Luza
- R. Iug
- R. Northern Dvina

xlvii. *The Volga-Volosnitsa—either Nydyb, or Sysola-Northern Dvina Portage*[47]

Variant 1:
- R. Volga
- R. Kama
- R. Volosnitsa
     Portage (*Volok*)
- R. Nydyb
- R. Sysola
- R. Vychegda
- R. Northern Dvina

Variant 2:
- R. Volga
- R. Kama
- R. Volosnitsa
     Portage (*Volok*)

- R. Sysola
- R. Vychegda
- R. Northern Dvina

xlviii. *The Volga-Kama-Uzhga-Northern Dvina Portage*[48]

- R. Volga
- R. Kama
     Portage (*Volok*)
- R. Uzhga
- R. Sysola
- R. Vychegda
- R. Northern Dvina

---

[46] *Idem.*

[47] *Idem.*

[48] S. V. Bakhrushin, *Ocherki po istorii kolonizatsii Sibiri v XVI i XVII vv.* (Moscow, 1927–1928), p. 89.

xlix. *The Volga-Vesliana-Syz-Northern Dvina Portage*[49]

 R. Volga
 R. Kama
 R. Vesliana
 R. ? (tributary of the Vesliana)
   Portage (*Volok*)
 R. Syz
 R. Sysola
 R. Vychegda
 R. Northern Dvina

l. *The Volga-Dzhurich-Severnaia Keltma-Northern Dvina Portage*[50]

 R. Volga
 R. Kama
 R. Iuzhnaia Keltma
 R. Dzhurich
   Portage (*Volok*)
 R. Severnaia Keltma
 R. Vychegda
 R. Northern Dvina

li. *The Volga-Pil'va-Yk-Northern Dvina Portage*[51]

 R. Volga
 R. Kama
 R. Pil'va
   Portage (*Volok*)
 R. Yk
 R. Nem (Nem', Nema)
 R. Vychegda
 R. Northern Dvina

---

[49] A possible portage, see the U.S.S.R. map.

[50] Rudakov, *op. cit.*, p. 757; "Severo-Ekaterininskii kanal," *Entsik. slovar'*, XXXII:I, 310; V. Semenov-Tian'-Shanskii, "Kama," *Bol'shaia sov. entsik.*, XXX, 792.

[51] A possible portage, see the U.S.S.R. map.

lii. *The Volga-Berezovka-Nem-Northern Dvina Portage*[52]

    R. Volga
    R. Kama
    R. Vishera (Vishera on the pre-Soviet maps, Kolva on the
        U.S.S.R. map)
    R. Kolva
    R. Visherka
    L. Chusovskoe
    R. Berezovka
        Portage (Volok Bukhinskii)
    R. Nem (Nem', Nema)
    R. Vychegda
    R. Northern Dvina

liii. *The Volga-Vogulka-Volosnitsa-Pechora Portage*[53]

    R. Volga
    R. Kama
    R. Vishera (see Volga lii)
    R. Kolva
    R. Visherka
    L. Chusovskoe
    R. Berezovka
    R. Elovka
    R. Vogulka
        Portage (Volok Pechorskii)
    R. Volosnitsa
    R. Pechora

liv. *The Volga-Vishera-Lozva-Ob' Portage*[54]

    R. Volga
    R. Kama
    R. Vishera
        Portage (*Volok*)
    R. Lozva
    R. Tavda
    R. Tobol
    R. Irtysh
    R. Ob'

[52] "Vishera," *Bol'shaia sov. entsik.*, XI, 357, says: "... In ancient times the Vishera was a part of the important waterway from the Kama to the Northern Dvina and Pechora rivers." See also "Kamsko-Pecherskii vodnyi put'," *Bol'shaia sov. entsik.*, XXXI, 135; Bakhrushin, *loc. cit.*

[53] See references in the preceding footnote. Also P. Beliavskii, "Kama," *Entsik. slovar'*, XIV:1, 123–124.

[54] Bakhrushin, *op. cit.*, pp. 88–89; V. I. Ogorodnikov, *Ocherk istorii Sibiri do nachala XIX veka* (3 vols. in 2 parts, Irkutsk-Vladivostok, 1920–1924), II, 35.

lv. *The Volga-Mezhevaia Utka-Neiva (or Rezh?)-Ob' Portage*[55]

> R. Volga
> R. Kama
> R. Chusovaia
> R. Mezhevaia Utka
> > Portage (*Volok*)
> R. Rezh ?
> R. Neiva
> R. Nitsa
> R. Tura
> R. Tobol
> R. Irtysh
> R. Ob'

lvi. *The Volga-Chusovaia—either Pyshma, or Iset-Ob' Portage*[56]

Variant 1:	Variant 2:
R. Volga	R. Volga
R. Kama	R. Kama
R. Chusovaia	R. Chusovaia
Portage (*Volok*)	Portage (*Volok*)
R. Pyshma	R. Iset
R. Tobol	R. Tobol
R. Irtysh	R. Irtysh
R. Ob'	R. Ob'

lvii. *The Volga—either Serebrianka, or Chusovaia Sylva-Zheravlia-Ob' Portage*[57]

Variant 1:	Variant 2:
R. Volga	R. Volga
R. Kama	R. Kama
R. Chusovaia	R. Chusovaia
R. Serebrianka	R. Chusovaia Sylva
Portage (Volok Tagilskii)	Portage (Volok Tagilskii)
R. Zheravlia	R. Zheravlia
R. Barancha	R. Barancha
R. Tagil	R. Tagil
R. Tura	R. Tura
R. Tobol	R. Tobol
R. Irtysh	R. Irtysh
R. Ob'	R. Ob'

[55] Bakhrushin, *op. cit.*, p. 102.
[56] A possible portage, see the U.S.S.R. map.
[57] Bakhrushin, *op. cit.*, p. 90.

B. THE DON AND ITS TRIBUTARIES

i. *The Don-Severnyi Donets-Berestovaia-Dnieper Portage*[58]

    R. Don
    R. Severnyi Donets
        Portage (*Volok*)
    R. Berestovaia
    R. Orel'
    R. Dnieper

ii. *The Don-Severnyi Donets-Seim-Dnieper Portage*[59]

    R. Don
    R. Severnyi Donets
        Portage (*Volok*)
    R. Seim
    R. Dnieper

iii. *The Don-Oskolets-Seim-Dnieper Portage*[60]

    R. Don
    R. Severnyi Donets
    R. Oskol
    R. Oskolets
        Portage (*Volok*)
    R. Seim
    R. Dnieper

iv. *The Don-Perevolochnia-Pshevka-Volga Portage*

    (See Volga iv)

v. *The Don-Shat'-Volga Portage*

    (See Volga iii)

vi. *The Don-Riasa-Khupta-Volga Portage*

    (See Volga ii)

vii. *The Don-Ilovlia-Kamyshinka-Volga Portage*

    (See Volga i)

---

[58] Rudakov, *op. cit.*, p. 758.
[59] Khodakovskii, *op. cit.*, p. 38.
[60] *Loc. cit.*

C. THE DNIEPER AND ITS TRIBUTARIES

i. *The Dnieper-Pripet'-Seret-Dniester Portage*[61]

R. Dnieper
R. Pripet'
R. Styr
    Portage (*Volok*)
R. Seret
R. Dniester

ii. *The Dnieper-Pina-Mukhovets-Vistula Portage*[62]

R. Dnieper
R. Pripet'
R. Iasolda (Iazolda)
R. Pina
    Portage (*Volok* where the Dnieper-Bug canal is
    now)
R. Mukhovets
R. Zapadnyi Bug
R. Vistula

iii. *The Dnieper-Iasolda-Shara-Niemen Portage*[63]

R. Dnieper
R. Pripet'
R. Iasolda
    Portage (*Volok* where the Oginskii canal is now)
R. Shara
R. Niemen

[61] Barsov, *op. cit.*, p. 22. The river Styr is a likely link, according to the U.S.S.R. map.

[62] Barsov, *loc. cit.*, mentions the Dnieper, Pripet', Zapadnyi Bug, and the Vistula. Other links are suggested by the present Dnieper–Zapadnyi Bug canal system described in "Bug Zapadnyi," *Bol'shaia sov. entsik.*, VII, 767; and also in "Dnepr," *Entsik. slovar'*, X:II, 792–793.

[63] A possible and probable portage in the place of the present-day Oginskii canal system that is described in "Oginskii kanal," *Entsik. slovar'*, XXI:II, 690, and in "Neman," *Bol'shaia sov. entsik.*, XL, 520.

iv. *The Dnieper-Svisloch-Usha-Western Dvina Portage*[64]

 R. Dnieper
 R. Berezina
 R. Svisloch
  Portage (*Volok*)
 R. Usha
 R. Viliia (Wilia)
 R. Naroch
 L. Naroch
 L. Miadel
 R. Miadelka
 R. Disna
 R. Western Dvina

v. *The Dnieper-Svisloch-Usha-Niemen Portage*[65]

 R. Dnieper
 R. Berezina
 R. Svisloch
  Portage (*Volok*)
 R. Usha
 R. Viliia (Wilia)
 R. Niemen

vi. *The Dnieper-Svisloch-Ptich-Niemen Portage*[66]

 R. Dnieper
 R. Berezina
 R. Svisloch
  Portage (*Volok*)
 R. Ptich
 R. Usa
 R. Uzda
 R. Niemen

vii. *The Dnieper-Berezina-Ushacha-Western Dvina Portage*[67]

 R. Dnieper
 R. Berezina
  Portage (*Volok*)
 R. Ushacha
 R. Western Dvina

---

[64] Khodakovskii, *op. cit.*, p. 37. [65] *Loc. cit.* [66] *Loc. cit.*
[67] *Loc. cit.*: this was "the shortest route between Kiev and Polotsk."

viii. *The Dnieper-Drut'-Usvitsa-Western Dvina Portage*[68]

    R. Dnieper
    R. Drut'
        Portage (Volok Perevolochna)
    R. Usvitsa (Usveia)
    R. Ulla (Ula)
    R. Western Dvina

ix. *The Dnieper-Drut'-Obol-Western Dvina Portage*[69]

    R. Dnieper
    R. Drut'
        Portage (Volok Perevolochna)
    R. Obol
    R. Luchesa
    R. Western Dvina

x. *The Dnieper-Luchesa-Western Dvina Portage*[70]

    R. Dnieper
        Portage (*Volok*)
    R. Veritsa (?)
    L. Luchesa (?)
    R. Luchesa
    R. Western Dvina

---

[68] Brim, *op. cit.*, p. 232, refers to P. G. Liubomirov's "Torgovye sviazi Rusi s Vostokom v VIII–IX vv." *Uchenye zapiski saratovskogo universiteta,* Vol. I, issue 3 (1923). Liubomirov suggests on the basis of numismatic findings a route through the town of Lukoml', which is on the river Lukomlia, a tributary of the Usvitsa. Khodakovskii, *op. cit.*, pp. 36–37, thinks that Perevolochna was on the Kiev-Polotsk route. He also says that "once in 1158 there were more than 300 *lodii* (boats) belonging to the men of Polotsk and Drutsk near the town of Drutsk [on the upper Drut']," and refers to Karamzin, *op. cit.*, II, nn. 134, 386. See also Kudriashev, *op. cit.*, map III.

[69] Brim, *loc. cit.*; Khodakovskii, *loc. cit.*

[70] See the map of the Mogilev gubernia, *Entsik. slovar'*, XIX:II, 572–573.

xi. *The Dnieper-Katynka-Krapivka-Western Dvina Portage*[71]

R. Dnieper
R. Katynka
  Portage (*Volok*)
R. Krapivka (Lelevka or Lelekva)
L. Kuprino
R. Vydra
L. Kasplia
R. Kasplia
R. Western Dvina

xii. *The Dnieper-Khvost-Vydra-Western Dvina Portage*[72]

R. Dnieper
R. Khvost
  Portage (*Volok*)
R. Vydra
L. Kasplia
R. Kasplia
R. Western Dvina

xiii. *The Dnieper-Votria-Elsha-Western Dvina Portage*[73]

R. Dnieper
R. Vop'
R. Votria
  Portage (*Volok*)
R. Elsha
R. Mezha
R. Western Dvina

xiv. *The Dnieper-Obsha-Gzhat'-Volga Portage*

  (See Volga xx)

xv. *The Dnieper-Vazuza-Volga Portage*

  (See Volga xxi)

---

[71] Brim, *loc. cit.*; Arne, *op. cit.*, p. 15, locates the portage near the village of Lodyzhnitsa or Lodeinitsa, west of Smolensk, close to Gnezdovo; Seredonin, *op. cit.*, p. 229; Barsov, *op. cit.*, p. 24; S. M. Solov'ev, *Istoriia Rossii s drevneishikh vremen* (29 vols. in 7, St. Petersburg, 1894–), I, 16; Khodakovskii, *op. cit.*, pp. 13–14, who refers to the treaty of Mstislav of Smolensk with Riga and Gotland in 1229 (*S.G.G. i D.*, II, 3–4), where this portage is mentioned; Kudriashov, *loc. cit.*

[72] Kudriashov, *loc. cit.*

[73] *Loc. cit.*; Brim, *op. cit.*, p. 232; Seredonin, *op. cit.*, p. 229.

xvi. *The Dnieper-Viazma-Vazuza-Volga Portage*
    (See Volga xxii)

xvii. *The Dnieper-Viazma-Ugra tributaries-Volga Portage*
    (See Volga vii, variant 2)

xviii. *The Dnieper-Osma-Ugra-Volga Portage*
    (See Volga vii, variant 1)

xix. *The Dnieper-Volok-Ressa-Volga Portage*
    (See Volga vi)

xx. *The Dnieper-Snezhat'-Reseta-Volga Portage*
    (See Volga v)

xxi. *The Dnieper—either Iput', or Oster-Desna-Dnieper Portage*[74]

Variant 1:	Variant 2:
R. Dnieper	R. Dnieper
R. Sozh	R. Sozh
R. Iput'	R. Oster
Portage (*Volok*)	Portage (*Volok*)
R. Desna	R. Desna
R. Dnieper	R. Dnieper

xxii. *The Dnieper-Seim-Oskolets-Don Portage*
    (See Don iii)

xxiii. *The Dnieper-Seim-Severnyi Donets-Don Portage*
    (See Don ii)

xxiv. *The Dnieper-Berestovaia-Severnyi Donets-Don Portage*
    (See Don i)

xxv. *The Dnieper-Volch'ia-Kalmius-Sea of Azov Portage*[75]
    R. Dnieper
    R. Samara
    R. Volch'ia
        Portage (*Volok*)
    R. Kalmius
    Sea of Azov

---

[74] Barsov, *op. cit.*, pp. 22–23, points out that in the twelfth century a route went by way of the Sozh-Desna to the Volga; this route was called "na Radimiche" and is mentioned in the Ipat Chronicle under 1169, *P.S.R.L.*, II, 97.

[75] Rudakov, *op. cit.*, p. 758; Barsov, *op. cit.*, p. 21.

xxvi. *The Dnieper-Volch'ia-Krynka-Sea of Azov Portage*[76]

    R. Dnieper
    R. Samara
    R. Volch'ia
        Portage (*Volok*)
    R. Krynka
    R. Mius
    Sea of Azov

xxvii. *The Dnieper-Konskaia-Berda-Sea of Azov Portage*[77]

    R. Dnieper
    R. Konskaia
        Portage (*Volok*)
    R. Berda
    Sea of Azov

D. THE WESTERN DVINA AND ITS TRIBUTARIES

i. *The Western Dvina-Disna-Miadel-Niemen Portage*[78]

    R. Western Dvina
    R. Disna
        Portage (*Volok*)
    L. Miadel
    L. Naroch
    R. Naroch
    R. Viliia (Wilia)
    R. Niemen

ii. *The Western Dvina-Usha-Svisloch-Dnieper Portage*
    (See Dnieper iv)

iii. *The Western Dvina-Ushacha-Berezina-Dnieper Portage*
    (See Dnieper vii)

iv. *The Western Dvina-Usvitsa-Drut'-Dnieper Portage*
    (See Dnieper viii)

---

[76] Rudakov, *loc. cit.*; Barsov, *loc. cit.*

[77] D. F. Shcheglov, "Pervyia stranitsy russkoi istorii," *Zhurnal M.N.P.* (St. Petersburg), CLXXXIV (1874) (221–269), 254.

[78] Khodakovskii, *op. cit.*, p. 37.

v. *The Western Dvina-Obol-Drut'-Dnieper Portage*
    (See Dnieper ix)

vi. *The Western Dvina-Luchesa-Dnieper Portage*
    (See Dnieper x)

vii. *The Western Dvina-Krapivka-Katynka-Dnieper Portage*
    (See Dnieper xi)

viii. *The Western Dvina-Vydra-Khvost-Dnieper Portage*
    (See Dnieper xii)

ix. *The Western Dvina-Elsha-Votria-Dnieper Portage*
    (See Dnieper xiii)

x. *The Western Dvina-Zhadenie-Peno-Volga Portage*
    (See Volga xxiii)

xi. *The Western Dvina-Zhadenie-Luchanskoe-Lovat' Portage*[79]
    R. Western Dvina
    L. Zhadenie (Zhadore)
    R. Vologda ?
    L. Otolovo ?
        Portage (*Volok*)
    L. Luchanskoe
    R. Pola
    R. Lovat'

xii. *The Western Dvina-Vydbino-Pola-Lovat' Portage*[80]
    R. Western Dvina
    R. Toropa
    L. Boino
    L. Brosno
    L. Luchanskoe
    L. Vydbino
        Portage (*Volok*)
    R. Pola
    R. Lovat'

---

[79] Khodakovskii, *op. cit.*, p. 15; Barsov, *op. cit.*, p. 25.
[80] Brim, *op. cit.*, p. 232; Seredonin, *op. cit.*, pp. 228–229.

xiii. *The Western Dvina-Zhelno-Serezha-Lovat' Portage*[81]

    R. Western Dvina
    R. Toropa
    L. Zhelno
        Portage (*Volok*)
    R. Serezha
    R. Kunia
    R. Lovat'

xiv. *The Western Dvina-Dvin'e-Kunia-Lovat' Portage*[82]

    R. Western Dvina
    R. Dvinka
    L. Dvin'e
        Portage (*Volok*)
    R. Kunia
    R. Lovat'

xv. *The Western Dvina-Usviat-Kunia-Lovat' Portage*[83]

    R. Western Dvina
    R. Zhizhitsa
    L. Zhizhitskoe
    R. Usviat (Usviacha)
        Portage (*Volok*)
    R. Kunia
    R. Lovat'

[81] Barsov, *op. cit.*, pp. 25–26, thinks that this route was used in 1168–69 by Prince Rostislav Mstislavovich in his expedition from Novgorod against Smolensk. He disagrees with Khodakovskii, the latter maintaining that this route was also used in the events of 1234. Barsov refers to the 1st Novgorodian Chronicle, *P.S.R.L.*, III, 49. Khodakovskii, *op. cit.*, pp. 13–14, refers to Karamzin, *op. cit.*, III, n. 343. See also Kudriashov, *loc. cit.*; Solov'ev, *op. cit.*, I, 16.

[82] Barsov, *op. cit.*, p. 26, calls this route a branch of the "Variazhskii put'." He refers to the 1st Novgorodian Chronicle, *P.S.R.L.*, III, 49, proving that this was the road used by the Lithuanians in the invasion of 1234. The chronicler points out Klin as the place where the Lithuanians retreated. Klin served as a center of communication between the Lovat' and the region of the Dvina. The town Zhizhichi, situated on this route, was already in the twelfth century one of the richest in this region. It paid very considerable taxes (of which 130 *grivny* went to the prince) and feudal fees, as is shown by the charter of the bishopric of Smolensk, 1150.

[83] Brim, *op. cit.*, p. 232; Seredonin, *op. cit.*, p. 228.

xvi. *The Western Dvina-Usmen-Lovat' Portage*[84]

    R. Western Dvina
    R. Usviat (Usviacha)
    L. Usviat
    L. Usmen
        Portage (*Volok*)
    R. Lovat'

xvii. *The Western Dvina-Ozerishche-Emenets-Lovat' Portage*[85]

    R. Western Dvina
    R. Obol
    L. Ozerishche (Ezerishche)
        Portage (*Volok*)
    L. Odrovo ?
    L. Emenets
    R. Emenka
    L. Nevel
    R. Emenka [*sic*]
    L. Molosno
    L. Kamshino
    R. Lovat'

xviii. *The Western Dvina-Usha—either Nasva, or Udraika-Lovat' Portage*[86]

Variant 1:	Variant 2:
R. Western Dvina	R. Western Dvina
R. Drisa	R. Drisa
R. Usha (Ushcha)	R. Usha (Ushcha)
Portage (*Volok*)	Portage (*Volok*)
R. Nasva (Nosva)	R. Udraika
R. Lovat'	R. Lovat'

xix. *The Western Dvina-Usha-Velikaia Portage*[87]

    R. Western Dvina
    R. Drisa
    R. Usha (Ushcha)
        Portage (*Volok*)
    R. Velikaia

---

[84] Brim, *loc. cit.;* Seredonin, *loc. cit.*
[85] Barsov, *op. cit.*, pp. 24–25, refers to the 1st Novgorodian Chronicle, under 1185, *P.S.R.L.*, III, 19, and to the Ipat Chronicle, under 1178, *P.S.R.L.*, II, 120. See also Brim, *op. cit.*, p. 231; Seredonin, *loc. cit.*
[86] Brim, *op. cit.*, p. 226; Khodakovskii, *op. cit.*, pp. 30–31.
[87] Brim, *loc. cit.;* Khodakovskii, *loc. cit.*

E. THE VELIKAIA AND ITS TRIBUTARIES

i. *The Velikaia-Virts-Pernava Portage*[88]

    R. Velikaia
    L. Pskovskoe (Velikoe)
    L. Chudskoe (Peipus)
    R. Embakh (Omovzha)
    L. Virts
    R. Paala ? (See the U.S.S.R. map)
        Portage (*Volok*)
    R. Kavast ? (See the U.S.S.R. map)
    R. Pernava

ii. *The Velikaia-Cherekha—either Uza, or Sudoma-Shelon' Portage*[89]

Variant 1:	Variant 2:
R. Velikaia	R. Velikaia
R. Cherekha	R. Cherekha
Portages (Bol'shoi Volochek and Malyi Volochek)	
R. Uza	R. Sudoma
R. Shelon'	R. Shelon'

iii. *The Velikaia—either Nasva, or Udraika-Lovat' Portage*[90]

Variant 1:	Variant 2:
R. Velikaia	R. Velikaia
Series of lakes	Series of lakes
Portage (*Volok*)	Portage (*Volok*)
R. Nasva	R. Udraika
R. Lovat'	R. Lovat'

iv. *The Velikaia-Usha-Western Dvina Portage*

    (See Western Dvina xix)

---

[88] Rudakov, *op. cit.*, p. 758; Brim, *loc. cit.*; Khodakovskii, *op. cit.*, p. 21.

[89] Laurentian Chronicle, *P.S.R.L.*, I, 63; 1st Novgorodian Chronicle, *P.S.R.L.*, III, 85; Rudakov, *op. cit.*, p. 758; Barsov, *op. cit.*, p. 27; Kudriashov, *loc. cit.*

[90] Brim, *op. cit.*, p. 226; Khodakovskii, *op. cit.*, pp. 30–31.

F. THE SHELON' AND ITS TRIBUTARIES

i. *The Shelon'—either Hotynka, or Soba-Luga Portage*[91]

Variant 1:	Variant 2:
R. Shelon'	R. Shelon'
R. Mshaga	R. Mshaga
R. Hotynka	R. Soba
Portage (*Volok*)	Portage (*Volok*)
R. Luga	R. Luga

ii. *The Shelon'—either Uza, or Sudoma-Cherekha-Velikaia Portage*
(See Velikaia ii)

G. THE LOVAT' AND ITS TRIBUTARIES

i. *The Lovat'-Volotskoe-Seliger-Volga Portage*
(See Volga xxv)

ii. *The Lovat'-Pola-Runa-Volga Portage*
(See Volga xxiv)

iii. *The Lovat'-Luchanskoe-Zhadenie-Western Dvina Portage*
(See Western Dvina xi)

iv. *The Lovat'-Pola-Vydbino-Western Dvina Portage*
(See Western Dvina xii)

v. *The Lovat'-Serezha-Zhelno-Western Dvina Portage*
(See Western Dvina xiii)

vi. *The Lovat'-Kunia-Usviat-Western Dvina Portage*
(See Western Dvina xv)

vii. *The Lovat'-Kunia-Dvin'e-Western Dvina Portage*
(See Western Dvina xiv)

viii. *The Lovat'-Usmen-Western Dvina Portage*
(See Western Dvina xvi)

---

[91] Arne, *op. cit.*, p. 15; Brim, *loc. cit.*; Barsov, *loc. cit.*; Khodakovskii, *op. cit.*, pp. 18–19, mentions the fact that "the right tributary of the Luga, Oredezh, was navigable as far as Lake Tesovo." Khodakovskii hints at the possibility of a Luga-Oredezh-Tesovo-Neva portage.

ix. *The Lovat'-Emenets-Ozerishche-Western Dvina Portage*
    (See Western Dvina xvii)

x. *The Lovat'—either Nasva, or Udraika-Usha-Western Dvina
    Portage*
    (See Western Dvina xviii)

H. THE MSTA AND ITS TRIBUTARIES

i. *The Msta-Pechenovo-Volga Portage*
    (See Volga xxix)

ii. *The Msta-S'ezzha-Keza-Volga Portage*
    (See Volga xxviii)

iii. *The Msta-Mstino-Tsna-Volga Portage*
    (See Volga xxvii)

I. THE ONEGA AND ITS TRIBUTARIES

i. *The Onega-Voloshozero-Chereva-Ladoga Portage*[92]
    R. Onega
    R. Kena
    L. Kenozero
    R. Pocha
    L. Pochozero
    R. Voloshka (Volosha)
    L. Voloshozero (Voloshevo, Volotskoe)
        Portage (*Volok*, 6 versts long)
    R. Chereva
    R. Vodla
    L. Onego
    R. Svir'
    L. Ladoga

[92] S. F. Platonov, *Proshloe russkago severa* (St. Petersburg, 1923), p. 15; Ruda-kov, *loc. cit.*, states that "the Novgorodians knew this route in 1137. It preserved its importance to the beginning of the nineteenth century for transit of goods from Arkhangelsk by way of the Onega."

ii. *The Onega-Lache-Vytegra-Ladoga Portage*[93]
>   R. Onega
>   L. Lache
>   Portage (*Volok*)
>   R. Vytegra
>   L. Onego
>   R. Svir'
>   L. Ladoga

iii. *The Onega-Dolgoe-Volotskoe-Volga Portage*
>   (See Volga xxxiii)

iv. *The Onega-Bolshma-Pidma-Volga Portage*
>   (See Volga xxxv)

v. *The Onega-Perechnaia-Sheksna-Volga Portage*
>   (See Volga xxxvi)

vi. *The Onega-Voloshka-Vel'-Northern Dvina Portage*[94]

Variant 1:	Variant 2:
R. Onega	R. Onega
R. Voloshka	R. Voloshka
Portage (*Volok*)	Portage (*Volok*)
R. Vel'	R. Vel'
R. Vaga	R. Vaga
	R. Kokshenga
R. Northern Dvina	R. Northern Dvina

Variant 3:
>   R. Onega
>   R. Voloshka
>   Portage (*Volok*)
>   R. Vel'
>   R. Vaga
>   R. Ust'ia
>   R. Northern Dvina

---

[93] Platonov, *loc. cit.*

[94] M. Edemskii, "O starykh torgovykh putiakh na severe," *Zapiski russkago arkheograficheskago obshchestva* (St. Petersburg), IX (1913) (39–62), 61–62.

vii. *The Onega-Emtsa-Northern Dvina Portage*[95]
>R. Onega
>>Portage (*Volok*)
>R. Emtsa
>R. Northern Dvina

J. THE NORTHERN DVINA AND ITS TRIBUTARIES

i. *The Northern Dvina-Emtsa-Onega Portage*
>(See Onega vii)

ii. *The Northern Dvina-Vel'-Voloshka Portage*
>(See Onega vi)

iii. *The Northern Dvina-Kokshenga-Sukhona-Northern Dvina Portage*[96]
>>R. Northern Dvina
>>R. Vaga
>>R. Kokshenga
>>>Portage (*Volok*)
>>R. Sukhona
>>R. Northern Dvina

iv. *The Northern Dvina-Porozovitsa-Slavianka-Volga Portage*
>(See Volga xxxiv)

v. *The Northern Dvina-Toshna-Sogozha-Volga Portage*
>(See Volga xxxvii)

vi. *The Northern Dvina-Lezha—either Obnora, or Monza-Volga Portage*
>(See Volga xxxviii and xxxix, variant 1)

vii. *The Northern Dvina-Shuia-Monza-Volga Portage*
>(See Volga xxxix, variant 2)

viii. *The Northern Dvina-Khmelnitsa-Tutka-Volga Portage*
>(See Volga xl)

ix. *The Northern Dvina-Tolshma-Kostroma-Volga Portage*
>(See Volga xli)

---

[95] Platonov, *loc. cit.*; Khodakovskii, *op. cit.*, p. 29.   [96] Edemskii, *op. cit.*, p. 55.

x. *The Northern Dvina-Sharzhenga-Iuza-Volga Portage*
(See Volga xlii)

xi. *The Northern Dvina-Kudanga-Pyshchug-Volga Portage*
(See Volga xliii)

xii. *The Northern Dvina-Entala-Vokhma-Volga Portage*
(See Volga xliv)

xiii. *The Northern Dvina-Kichug-Maramitsa-Volga Portage*
(See Volga xlv)

xiv. *The Northern Dvina-Viled'-Sysola-Northern Dvina Portage*[97]
R. Northern Dvina
R. Vychegda
R. Viled'
Portage (Volok Viledskii)
R. Sysola
R. Vychegda
R. Northern Dvina

xv. *The Northern Dvina—either Setka-Suran, or Lunia-Kobra-Volga Portage*
(See Volga xlvi)

xvi. *The Northern Dvina—either Sysola, or Nydyb-Volosnitsa-Volga Portage*
(See Volga xlvii)

xvii. *The Northern Dvina-Uzhga-Kama-Volga Portage*
(See Volga xlviii)

xviii. *The Northern Dvina-Syz-Vesliana-Volga Portage*
(See Volga xlix)

xix. *The Northern Dvina-Severnaia Keltma-Dzhurich-Volga Portage*
(See Volga l)

[97] Bakhrushin, *op. cit.*, p. 89, describes this portage as a route to the Kama.

xx. *The Northern Dvina-Yk-Pil'va-Volga Portage*
(See Volga li)

xxi. *The Northern Dvina-Nem-Berezovka-Volga Portage*
(See Volga lii)

xxii. *The Northern Dvina-Iuzhnaia Mylva-Severnaia
Mylva-Pechora Portage*[98]

R. Northern Dvina
R. Vychegda
R. Iuzhnaia Mylva (Myl'ia)
Portage (*Volok*)
R. Severnaia Mylva (Myl'ia)
R. Pechora

xxiii. *The Northern Dvina-Govniukha-Ukhta-Pechora Portage*[99]

R. Northern Dvina
R. Vychegda
R. Vym
R. Shomvukva (ancient Tetera)
R. Govniukha
Portage (Volok Vymskii; there is a village
Perevolok)
R. Ukhta
R. Izhma
R. Pechora

xxiv. *The Northern Dvina-Pinega-Kuloi-White Sea*[100]

R. Northern Dvina
R. Pinega
Portage (Volok Pinezhskii)
R. Kuloi
White Sea

---

[98] Rudakov, *op. cit.*, p. 757.
[99] Bakhrushin, *op. cit.*, p. 61; A. A. Titov (ed.) , *Sibir' v XVII veke* (Moscow, 1890), p. 51; Ogorodnikov, *Ocherki istorii Sibiri*, II, 8.
[100] Bakhrushin, *op. cit.*, p. 62.

K. THE PECHORA AND ITS TRIBUTARIES

i. *The Pechora-Lake (name unknown)-Peza-Mezen Portage*[101]

Variant 1:	Variant 2:
R. Pechora	R. Pechora
R. Tsilma	R. Tsilma
R. Chirka	
R. Rubikha	
Lake (unknown)	Lake (unknown)
Portage (Volok Pezskii)	Portage (Volok Pezskii)
R. Peza	R. Peza
R. Mezen	R. Mezen

ii. *The Pechora-Ukhta-Govniukha-Northern Dvina Portage*
  (See Northern Dvina xxiii)

iii. *The Pechora-Severnaia Mylva-Iuzhnaia Mylva-Northern Dvina Portage*
  (See Northern Dvina xxii)

iv. *The Pechora-Volosnitsa-Vogulka-Volga Portage*
  (See Volga liii)

v. *The Pechora-Ilych-Sosva-Ob' Portage*[102]
  R. Pechora
  R. Ilych
    Portage (*Volok*)
  R. Sosva
  R. Ob'

vi. *The Pechora-Shchugor—either Iatriia, or Vol'ia-Sosva-Ob' Portage*[103]

Variant 1:	Variant 2:
R. Pechora	R. Pechora
R. Shchugor	R. Shchugor
Portage (*Volok*)	Portage (*Volok*)
R. Iatriia	R. Vol'ia
R. Sygva	
R. Kirtas	
R. Sosva	R. Sosva
R. Ob'	R. Ob'

---

[101] *Loc. cit.*   [102] *Ibid.*, p. 63; Rudakov, *loc. cit.*

[103] For variant 1 see Bakhrushin, *op. cit.*, pp. 63, 77; also the U.S.S.R. map; P. N. Butsinskii, *Zaselenie Sibiri i byt eia pervykh nasel'nikov* (Kharkov, 1889), pp. 178–179. For variant 2, see Rudakov, *loc. cit.*

vii. *The Pechora-Elets-Sob'-Ob' Portage*[104]
    R. Pechora
    R. Usa (ancient Sob'-Musa)
    R. Elets
        Portage (Volok Kamennyi)
    R. Sob'
    R. Ob'

L. THE OB' AND ITS TRIBUTARIES

i. *The Ob'-Sob'-Elets-Pechora Portage*
    (See Pechora vii)

ii. *The Ob'-Sosva-Ilych-Pechora Portage*
    (See Pechora v)

iii. *The Ob'—either Vol'ia, or Iatriia-Shchugor-Pechora Portage*
    (See Pechora vi)

iv. *The Ob'-Lozva-Vishera-Volga Portage*
    (See Volga liv)

v. *The Ob'-Zheravlia—either Serebrianka, or Chusovaia*
Sylva-Volga Portage
    (See Volga lvii)

vi. *The Ob'-Neiva (or Rezh?)-Mezhevaia Utka-Volga Portage*
    (See Volga lv)

vii. *The Ob'—either Pyshma, or Iset-Chusovaia-Volga Portage*
    (See Volga lvi)

---

[104] Bakhrushin, *op. cit.*, pp. 62, 75; Rudakov, *loc. cit.*; Titov, *op. cit.*, pp. 50–51; Butsinskii, *op. cit.*, p. 176.

viii. *The Ob'—either Ket', or Kem, or Kas'-Enisei Portage*[105]

Variant 1:   Variant 2:
  R. Ob'   R. Ob'
  R. Ket'   R. Ket'
  Portage (Volok   Portage (Volok
    Makovskii)   Makovskii)
  R. Toma
  R. Kem   R. Kas'
  R. Enisei   R. Enisei

Variant 3:
  R. Ob'
  R. Ket'
  Portage (Volok Makovskii)
  R. Enisei

ix. *The Ob'-Tym-Sym-Enisei Portage*[106]

R. Ob'
R. Tym
  Portage (*Volok*)
R. Sym
R. Enisei

x. *The Ob'-Volochanka-Volochanka-Enisei Portage*[107]

R. Ob'
R. Vakh
R. Volochanka
  Portage (Volok Eloguiskii, 15 versts long)
R. Volochanka (same name as above, otherwise known as
  Chernaia)
R. Elogui
R. Enisei

---

[105] For variant 1, see Bakhrushin, *op. cit.*, p. 112; G. F. Mueller, "Sibirskaîa istoriia," *Ezhemesiachnyia sochineniia ... akademii nauk* (St. Petersburg, March, 1764), pp. 207–208.
    For variant 2, see the the map of the U.S.S.R. for a possible portage.
    For variant 3, see Bakhrushin, *op. cit.*, pp. 110–111; Titov, *op. cit.*, pp. 30, 46–47, 81–82; Spafarii, "Puteshestvie chrez Sibir ... Nikolaia Spafariia v 1675 ... ," *Zapiski imperatorskago russkago geograficheskago obshchestva po otdeleniiu etnografii* (St. Petersburg), X, no. 1 (1882), pp. 67–83.
  [106] Bakhrushin, *op. cit.*, p. 114; Mueller, "Sibirskaia istoriia," *Ezhemesiachnyia sochineniia ... (June, 1764), pp. 512–513.
  [107] Bakhrushin, *op. cit.*, p. 112; Titov, *op. cit.*, p. 36.

xi. *The Ob'-Krugloe-Volochanka-Enisei Portage*[108]

    R. Ob'
    Gulf of Ob' (Obskaia Guba)
    Gulf of Taz (Tazovskaia Guba)
    R. Taz
    R. Volochanka (Volochaika)
    L. Krugloe
    Small streams
       Portage (Volok Eniseiskii)
    R. Volochanka (same name as above)
    R. Turukhan
    R. Enisei

M. THE ENISEI AND ITS TRIBUTARIES

i. *The Enisei-Volochanka-Krugloe-Ob' Portage*

    (See Ob' xi)

ii. *The Enisei-Volochanka-Volochanka-Ob' Portage*

    (See Ob' x)

iii. *The Enisei-Sym-Tym-Ob' Portage*

    (See Ob' ix)

iv. *The Enisei—either Kas', or Kem, or Ket'-Ob' Portage*

    (See Ob' viii)

---

[108] Bakhrushin, *op. cit.*, pp. 114, 120; Ogorodnikov, *op. cit.*, II, 47; Titov, *op. cit.*, pp. 21–22, 37, uses the name Volochaika instead of Volochanka both times.

v. *The Enisei-Erakleia-Ingoda-Amur Portage*[109]

R. Enisei
R. Verkhniaia Tunguska (Upper Tunguska) (called Angara near the source)
L. Baikal
R. Selenga
R. Khilka
L. Irgen
L. Erakleia
   Portage (Volok Irgenskii)
R. Ingoda
R. Shilka (formed by the junction of the Ingoda and Nercha)
R. Amur

vi. *The Enisei-Ilim-Muka-Lena Portage*[110]

R. Enisei
R. Verkhniaia Tunguska
R. Ilim
   Portage (Volok Lenskii)
R. Muka
R. Kupa
R. Kuta
R. Lena

vii. *The Enisei-Nizhniaia Tunguska-Kulenga-Lena Portage*[111]

R. Enisei
R. Nizhniaia Tunguska (Lower Tunguska)
   Portage (Volok Chichuiskii or Tungusskii)
R. Kulenga (Kulinga)
R. Lena

---

[109] "Report of the military commander (*voevoda*) Pashkov, 1652," *D.A.I.*, III, 343–345; "Report of the lesser noble Beketov, 1653," *D.A.I.*, III, 390–396; "Instructions to the lesser noble Kolesnikov, 1656," *D.A.I.*, IV, 53; Spafarii, *op. cit.*, pp. 126–127; Bakhrushin, *op. cit.*, pp. 136–137; Titov, *op. cit.*, pp. 31, 47, 106; J. E. Fischer, *Sibirskaia istoriia . . .* (St. Petersburg, 1774), p. 566; V. K. Andrievich, *Istoriia Sibiri* (in 2 parts, St. Petersburg, 1889), I, 81–82; Ogorodnikov, *op. cit.*, II, 71–72.

[110] "Petition of serving men, 1640," *D.A.I.*, II, 172–174; "Report of the military commander (*voevoda*) Golovin, 1640," *D.A.I.*, II, 238–239: "Description of rivers, 1640–1641," *D.A.I.*, II, 243–248; "Report of the military commanders (*voevodas*) Pushkin and Suponev, 1645," *D.A.I.*, III, 37–40; "Instructions to Golovin, 1638," *R.I.B.*, II, 961–972; Fischer, *op. cit.*, p. 354; Bakhrushin, *op. cit.*, pp. 123–126.

[111] "Report of the military commander (*voevoda*) Golovin, 1640," *D.A.I.*, II, 248–249; "Report of the military commanders (*voevodas*) Golovin and Glebov, 1641," *D.A.I.*, II, 252–254; Bakhrushin, *op. cit.*, p. 128; Fischer, *op. cit.*, pp. 360–361; Ogorodnikov, *op. cit.*, II, 48.

viii. *The Enisei-Titeia-Churka-Lena Portage*[112]

    R. Enisei
    R. Nizhniaia Tunguska
    R. Titeia
        Portage (Volok Viliuiskii)
    R. Churka
    R. Chona
    R. Viliui
    R. Lena

ix. *The Enisei-Piasina-Khatanga Portage*[113]

    R. Enisei
        Portage (*Volok*)
    R. Piasina
        Portage (*Volok*)
    R. Khatanga

N. THE LENA AND ITS TRIBUTARIES

i. *The Lena-Churka-Titeia-Enisei Portage*
    (See Enisei viii)

ii. *The Lena-Kulenga-Nizhniaia Tunguska-Enisei Portage*
    (See Enisei vii)

iii. *The Lena-Muka-Ilim-Enisei Portage*
    (See Enisei vi)

iv. *The Lena-Niugzi-Urka-Amur Portage*[114]

    R. Lena
    R. Olekma
    R. Tugir
    R. Niugzi (Nuigchi, Niunzi, Niunchi, Niuga, Niuzia)
        Portage (Volok Tugirskii)
    R. Urka (Ura, Ui)
    R. Amur

---

[112] Bakhrushin, *op. cit.*, pp. 123, 127; Fischer, *op. cit.*, p. 30; Ogorodnikov, *op. cit.*, II, 47.

[113] Ogorodnikov, *loc. cit.*

[114] "Questioning of . . . Vizhevtsov and . . . Poiarkov, 1647," *D.A.I.*, III, 102–104; "Instructions to . . . Prokof'ev, 1652," *D.A.I.*, III, 352–354; "Questioning of . . . Andreev, 1652," *D.A.I.*, III, 371–373; Spafarii, *op. cit.*, pp. 133, 164; Titov, *op. cit.*, p. 33; Bakhrushin, *op. cit.*, p. 134; Ogorodnikov, *op. cit.*, II, 87.

v. The Lena-Niugzi-Amazar-Amur Portage[115]

R. Lena
R. Olekma
R. Tugir
R. Niugzi (Niugchi, Niunzi, Niunchi, Niuga, Niuzia)
    Portage (Volok Tugirskii)
R. Amazar
R. Amur

vi. The Lena-Katym-Zeia-Amur Portage[116]

R. Lena
R. Aldan
R. Tontora
R. Katym
    Portage (Volok Aldanskii)
R. Zeia
R. Amur

vii. The Lena-Niuemka-Brianda-Amur Portage[117]

R. Lena
R. Aldan
R. Uchur
R. Gonom
R. Niuemka
    Portage (*Volok*)
R. Brianda (Brianta)
R. Zeia
R. Amur

viii. The Lena-Volochanka-Siksha-Ul'ia Portage[118]

R. Lena
R. Aldan
R. Maia
R. Volochanka (modern Mati?)
    Portage (*Volok*)
R. Siksha (modern Dasyksha?)
R. Ul'ia

[115] "Petition of Maksimov, 1657," *D.A.I.*, IV, 94–95; Bakhrushin, *op. cit.*, p. 134.
[116] Spafarii, *op. cit.*, p. 165; Bakhrushin, *op. cit.*, p. 135.
[117] "Acts about the voyage of . . . Poiarkov, 1646," *D.A.I.*, III, 50–60; "Questioning of . . . Vizhevtsov and . . . Poiarkov, 1647," *D.A.I.*, III, 102–104; "Instructions to . . . Poiarkov, 1643," *Chteniia v imperatorskom obshchestve istorii i drevnostei rossiiskikh* (Moscow, 1861), I, pt. 5, 1–14.
[118] "Acts about the voyage of . . . Poiarkov, 1646," *D.A.I.*, III, 50–60; "Reports of . . . Epishev, 1652," *D.A.I.*, III, 332–343; Bakhrushin, *op. cit.*, p. 139.

ix. *The Lena-Iudoma—either Bludnaia, or Urak-Okhota Portage*[119]

Variant 1:   Variant 2:

    R. Lena   R. Lena

    R. Aldan   R. Aldan

    R. Maia   R. Maia

    R. Iudoma   R. Iudoma

                   Portage (Iudomskii Krest or Volok Okhotskii)

    R. Bludnaia

    R. Urak   R. Urak

         Portage (*Volok*)   Portage (*Volok*)

    R. Okhota   R. Okhota

x. *The Lena-Iana Portage*[120]

    R. Lena

         Portage (*Volok* across the Verkhoiansk Mountains)

    R. Iana

O. THE IANA AND ITS TRIBUTARIES

i. *The Iana-Lena Portage*

    (See Lena x)

ii. *The Iana-Indigirka Portage*[121]

    R. Iana

         Portage (*Volok*)

    R. Indigirka

P. THE KOLYMA AND ITS TRIBUTARIES

i. *The Kolyma-Uiagan-Penzhina Portage*[122]

    R. Kolyma

    R. Oemokon (Omolon)

    R. Uiagan

         Portage (Volok Penzhinskii)

    R. Penzhina

---

[119] "Instructions to Skvortsov, 1660," *D.A.I.*, IV, 200–214; "Report of . . . Maksimov and . . . Antipin, 1715," Arkheograficheskaia Kommissiia, *Pamiatniki sibirskoi istorii XVIII veka* (2 vols., St. Petersburg, 1885), II, 62–64; "Distances between Siberian towns, 1724," *ibid.*, II, 461–468.

[120] Ogorodnikov, *op. cit.*, II, 56.

[121] *Loc. cit.*

[122] Bakhrushin, *op. cit.*, p. 129; *D.A.I.*, VIII, 175.

ii. *The Kolyma-Aniui-Anadyr Portage*[123]

    R. Kolyma
    R. Aniui
        Portage (*Volok*)
    R. Anadyr

Q. THE AMUR AND ITS TRIBUTARIES

i. *The Amur-Ingoda-Erakleia-Enisei Portage*
    (See Enisei v)

ii. *The Amur-Urka-Niugzi-Lena Portage*
    (See Lena iv)

iii. *The Amur-Amazar-Niugzi-Lena Portage*
    (See Lena v)

iv. *The Amur-Zeia-Katym-Lena Portage*
    (See Lena vi)

v. *The Amur-Brianda-Niuemka-Lena Portage*
    (See Lena vii)

R. ARCTIC OCEAN PENINSULAR PORTAGES

i. *The Mezen Gulf-Chizha-Chesha-Cheshskaia Gulf Portage*[124]

    Mezen Gulf
    R. Chizha
        Portage (Volok Cheshskii)
    R. Chesha
    Cheshskaia Gulf

ii. *The Kara Gulf-Mutnaia-Zelenaia-Gulf of Ob' Portage*[125]

    Kara Gulf
    R. Mutnaia
        Portage (*Volok*)
    R. Zelenaia
    Gulf of Ob'

---

[123] Bakhrushin, *loc. cit.;* "Report of Dezhnev and Semenov, 1655," *D.A.I.,* IV, 16–27.

[124] *R.I.B.,* II, 1091; Bakhrushin, *op. cit.,* p. 80.

[125] *R.I.B.,* II, 1051–1052 ff.; Bakhrushin, *op. cit.,* p. 82.

Appendix 2 ✍ Extracts from the Smolensk Trade Codes of 1229 and 1274, Illustrating the Regulations in Regard to the Portage from the Western Dvina to the Dnieper[1]

~~~~~~

Code of 1229
§ 15

If the Bailiff [of the Portage] should hear of the arrival of a Latin merchant, he is to send men with wagons (*kola*) to transport the goods [across the Portage], and not detain the merchant, [for] in this, damage might be caused.

Code of 1274
§ 15

If the Bailiff of the Portage (*Voloch'skyi Tiun*) should hear that a German merchant and men of Smolensk have arrived at the Portage, he is to send his man without delay to the Portagers (*Volochane*) so that they may transport the German merchant and the men of Smolensk with [their] goods [across the Portage]. No one should cause them any hindrance, because ... it may lead to a great deal of damage to the men of Smolensk and to the Germans at the hands of the pagans.

§ 16

a. If Latin and Smolensk merchants should arrive at the Portage [at the same time], lots should be drawn to determine who should be transported first [across the Portage] to Smolensk.

b. If men should arrive from other lands, they are to be transported [across the Portage] later.

§ 16

Lots are drawn to determine who is to cross the Portage first.

If a Russian merchant [from some other place than Smolensk] should arrive, he is to follow afterward.

---

[1] P. V. Golubovskii, *Istoriia smolenskoi zemli do nachala XV stoletiia* (Kiev, 1895), pp. 156–170; see also L. K. Goetz, *Deutsch-Russische Handelsgeschichte des Mittelalters* (Lübeck, 1922), pp. 439–543. In the Code of 1229, "Latin merchants" undoubtedly means "non-Orthodox," "non-Russian" and, most likely, "German."

c. The same regulations apply to the Russians in Riga and on the coast of Gothland.

§ 17

If a Latin merchant arrives in the town [Smolensk] from the Portage, he is to give to the Princess a roll of cloth and to the Bailiff of the Portage a pair of gloves, so that there will be no delay in transporting the goods.

§ 17

If a German merchant arrives in the town [Smolensk], he is to give to the Princess a roll of cloth and to the Bailiff of the Portage Gothic gloves with fingers.

§ 18

If any Portager should undertake to transport Latin goods across the Portage and should any part of these goods perish, then all the Portagers must pay [the damages].

§ 18

If any Portager should load German or Smolensk goods on his wagons in order to transport them across the Portage and should any part of the goods perish, then all the Portagers must pay [the damages].

§ 36

The Bishop of Riga, the Master of the Godly Nobles, and all landholders permit free passage along the Dvina from its source to its mouth on the sea, whether by water or land, to all [merchants] Latin or Russian.

§ 36

The Bishop of Riga, Folkoun, the Master of the Godly Nobles, and all Lords of the Riga country permit free passage along the Dvina from its source to its mouth, by water or land, to every Russian merchant going up or down the river.

§ 37

If, God forbid, anybody in these lands [along the Dvina] should lose a boat (*uchan*) or skiff (*cheln*), whether [he be] Russian or Latin, his goods should not be seized either in the water or on the shore.

§ 37

If, God forbid, anybody suffers a wreck or loses a boat, whether [he be] a Russian or a German, he is allowed to bring his goods without any harm to the shore.

Appendix 3 ⚕ Extracts from Documents and Other Sources Illustrating the Fortified Line of 1571 and Its Successors

YEAR 1571 (7079), January 1, the Sovereign Tsar and Grand Prince Ivan Vasilievich of all the Russias commanded his Boiar Prince Mikhailo Ivanovich Vorotynskii to assume charge of the patrols and outposts and of the entire Sovereign's service on the open frontier (*polskie sluzhby*).

January 7, in accordance with the command of the Sovereign Tsar and Grand Prince, the Boiar Prince Mikhailo Ivanovich Vorotynskii passed the word of the Sovereign to the Secretary (*Diak*) Ondrei Klobukov and his associates in the Military Office (*Rozriad*). The Sovereign ordered him [Vorotynskii] to take charge of and to reorganize the patrols and outposts and ordered him to find former lists of the patrols. Summonses should be sent to Putivl, Tula, Riazan, Meshchera, and other frontier towns, and to Severa [a region in the Ukraine], calling for the lesser nobility ("sons of boiars") [there follows an enumeration of other groups], patrol guards, and frontier guards who make rounds from Putivl [an enumeration of the towns named above follows] toward different places in the open frontier and who have served during the last ten to fifteen years. Men from the nearest towns are to appear in Moscow the day following Epiphany, men from Putivl two weeks later. [There follow instructions to the local officials asking them to send also veterans crippled in the frontier service and those (Russians) who had been in Tatar captivity. Then a statement follows that the instructions calling for men were sent out, and that the men arrived in Moscow, some in January, others in February.]

The Boiar Prince Mikhailo Ivanovich Vorotynskii reviewed the lists of the lesser nobility of all towns [an enumeration of other categories called to Moscow follows] and reported concerning them to the Sovereign Tsar and Grand Prince.

The Sovereign . . . Ivan Vasilievich ordered . . . Vorotynskii to attend to the business of the patrols, outposts, and various frontier

---

[1] N. A. Popov (ed.), *Akty moskovskago gosudarstva* (St. Petersburg, 1890), I, 1–2.

services, to question [the men who had been summoned and here enumerated], and, upon receiving information, to write in detail: from what town or place the patrols should come and where they should be sent; where the stationary guards should be posted; how far and in what direction patrols should be sent from the outposts; where the commanders (*golovy*) should be stationed to watch for the hostile invasion; how many men there should be under each commander and from what town they should come. . . . After the questioning was over and the lists of men were ready, the Sovereign appointed Prince Mikhailo Tiufiakin and the Secretary Rzhevskii to supervise the commanders (*dosmotriti golov*) on the Crimean frontier, and Iurii Bulgakov and Boris Khokhlov, those on the Nogai frontier. They were personally to determine where the headquarters of the commanders should be established and where patrols should be placed. . . .

LIST OF OUTPOSTS BASED ON INFORMATION OBTAINED BY THE
BOIAR PRINCE MIKHAILO IVANOVICH VOROTYNSKII IN 1571[2]

i. *Donets outposts*

> First outpost between the Mzha and the Kolomak [rivers] [on the portage through which went a trail called the Muravskii Shliakh]. . . .
>
> Second outpost of Obyshkinskaia . . . to guard along the Donets [River] . . . as far as the Shebalinov Ford.
>
> Third outpost of Bolykleia . . . to guard along the Donets as far as the Savinskii Ford. . . .
>
> Fourth outpost to Savinskaia and Iziumskaia . . . to guard along the Donets . . . as far as the Savinskii Ford. . . .
>
> Fifth outpost of Sviatogorskaia . . . to guard along the Donets. . . .
>
> Sixth outpost of Bakhmutovskaia . . . to guard along the Donets. . . .
>
> Seventh outpost of Aidarskaia . . . discontinued in 1571. . . .

ii. *Putivl outposts*

> First outpost between the Psiol and the Vorskla [rivers] on the pass (*v prokhodekh*) [portage between these two rivers on the route of a trail called the Bakaev Shliakh]. . . .
>
> Second outpost between the Psiol and the Seim [rivers] [portage between these rivers]. . . .
>
> Third outpost at Skala near Sarkel (Belaia Vezha).

---

[2] *Ibid.*, I, 7–12.

iii. *Additional Putivl outposts*

First, along the Seim, at Mokoshevichi. . . .
Second, along the Seim, at Rozsokhi. . . .
Third, on the Seim . . . five versts from Putivl. . . .
Fourth, at Belye Berega, ten versts from Putivl. . . .

iv. *Outposts from Rylsk*

First, on the Seim, at Pnevitsy . . . to guard the ford [on the route of a trail called the Svinaia Doroga]. . . .
Second, on the Koryzha [River] to guard the ford [on the route of the Svinaia Doroga]. . . .

v. *Outposts from the frontier towns . . . along the Sosna, Don, Mecha, and other rivers*

First outpost on the Sosna, at the mouth of the Livna [River] [route of the Muravskii Shliakh]. . . .
Second outpost on the Sosna, near the mouth of the Chernava [River] [route of a trail called the Kalmiusskaia Sakma]. . . .
Third outpost at the mouth of the Vorgla. . . .
Fourth outpost at the Talitskii Ford. . . .
Fifth outpost on the Don at the Galich Mountains. . . .
Sixth outpost at Krivoi Bor . . . to guard the Don . . . and to the left as far as the Voronezh [River] [portage between the Don and the Voronezh?]. . . .
Seventh outpost on the Don at the mouth of the Skverna. . . .
Eighth outpost on the upper Skverna [River] [near the portage between the Skverna and the Stanovaia Riasa]. . . .
Ninth outpost above Kobelsha and Iagodna [near the portage between the Skverna and the Riasa]. . . .
Tenth outpost at the sources of the Riasa [at the portage between the Skverna and the Riasa]. . . .
Eleventh outpost on the Mecha, at the Turmyshskii Ford. . . .
Twelfth outpost on the Mecha, between the Zelenkov and Sementsov Fords. . . .
Thirteenth outpost on the Viazovna [River] . . . on the Dryginskaia Doroga (Road). . . .
Fourteenth outpost on the Viazovna on the Turmyshevskaia Doroga. . . .

vi. [*Outposts*] *from Epifan*

> First outpost at the sources of the Nepriadva and Sukromna [rivers] [at the portage between the Nepriadva, Mecha (tributary of the Don) and the Upa (tributary of the Oka)]. . . .

vii. *Outposts from Dedilov*

> First outpost on the Uperta [River] at the Kamennyi Ford. . . .
> Second outpost at Lake Volovo [right on the portage between tributaries of the Oka and the Don]. . . .
> Third outpost at the sources of the Upa and Turdeeva Mecha [on the portage between tributaries of the Oka and the Don]. . . .
> Fourth outpost at Vladychnia Kria near the Muravskii Shliakh. . . .
> Fifth outpost at Kuzemkina Dubrova . . . to guard to the left as far as the Muravskii Shliakh, to the right as far as Plava. . . .

viii. *Outposts from Novosil*

> First outpost at the sources of the River Liubosha. . . .
> Second outpost at Kust. . . .
> Third outpost on the River Liubosha at the mouth of the Korytna. . . .
> Fourth outpost on the Sosna [River]. . . .
> Fifth outpost on the Sosna. . . .
> Sixth outpost between the Perestriazha and Iakovlevskii forests [near the portage between the tributaries of the Sosna and the Zusha rivers]. . . .
> Seventh outpost beyond the Zusha. . . .
> Eighth outpost at Pshevskii Hill. . . .
> Ninth outpost at Zarachunskii Hill. . . .
> Tenth outpost at Vezhki. . . .
> Eleventh outpost near the mouth of the river Kakolna. . . .

ix. *Outposts from Mtsensk*

> First outpost at the mouth of the Kolpna [River], on the Sosna. . . .
> Second outpost on the Sosna. . . .
> Third outpost on the Neruch [River]. . . .
> Fourth outpost on the Neruch. . . .

x. *Outposts from Orel and Karachev*

First outpost on the Seim, opposite Gorodenskoe Gorodishche....

Second outpost ... between the road to Karachev and the
Mestilov Gates and the road used by Bakai....

Third outpost on the river Molodova . . . where all the
roads from the Seim and Rylsk come together....

Fourth outpost on the upper Ochka [River]....

Fifth outpost on the Oka near the ... ford, fifteen versts
from Orel....

Sixth outpost above Oleshan....

Seventh outpost beyond the Oka....

Eighth outpost beyond the Oka....

xi. *Outposts from Meshchera*

First outpost on the Kargonaeva [River], and this river flows
into the Barysh River, and the Barysh River flows into the
Sura [River]....

Second outpost on the river Shoksha between the Sura and
Mokshanskii Forest....

Third outpost on the upper part of the river Lomova. . . .

Fourth outpost above the Vad....

xii. *Outposts from Shatsk*

First outpost at the Lipovetskii Forest....

Second outpost on the Chelnava [River] at the mouth of the
Lamka [River]....

xiii. *Outposts from Riassk (now Riazhsk)*

First outpost ... on the Voronezh [River]...

Second outpost above the Lomova near the Nogaiskaia
Doroga....

Third outpost on the Riasa [River]....

EXTRACTS FROM DOCUMENTS DESCRIPTIVE OF FORTIFICATIONS
AGAINST THE CRIMEAN AND NOGAI TATARS IN 1637–1647[3]

i. *1637. Circular of Instructions of the Tsar to Perm Velikaia*

... Last year, in 1636 (7144), for protection against the invaders
we ordered a town (*gorod*) to be built on the open frontier (*na pole*)
... and according to our order the town of Kozlov was built on the
open frontier on the [river] Lesnoi Voronezh. . . . From Kozlov
toward Shatsk, between the rivers Polnyi Voronezh and Chelnova
(Chelnava), an earthen rampart twelve versts long was constructed.
Three earthen forts with towers ... were erected on this rampart.
At Kasimov Ford an earthen fort and a rampart 1400 feet (200
sazhen) long were constructed. In previous years the Crimean and
Nogai [Tatars] used to come by the Kalmiusskaia and Iziumskaia
Sakmy (Roads) and by the Muravskii Shliakh. . . . In accordance
with our order, an ostrog with a permanent garrison was built between Livny and Elets on the river [Bystraia] Sosna, at the mouth
of the river Chernava; also an ostrog was built on the same Sosna,
below Elets, at Talitskii Ford. . . .

In 1636 (7144) ... on the Tatar Road (Nogaiskaia Doroga) a town
was built in place of the former Orlovsk Fort (*gorodishche*). . . . On
the River Tsna, at the mouth of the River Lipovitsa, the town of
Tanbov (now Tambov) was built. . . . From Tanbov toward Kozlov
the earthen rampart was reinforced by a row of poles. Beyond
Shatsk toward the frontier two towns—Lomov Verkhnii and Lomov
Nizhnii—were erected on the river Lomova. . . .

[According to the recommendations of Fedor Sukhotin and a
clerk (*pod'iachei*), Evsei Iur'ev, which were accepted by the govern-
ment] for protection against invasion by enemies, the following
towns with permanent garrisons, ostrogs, and fortifications are to
be constructed: A town is to be built on the river [Tikhaia] Sosna,
on the Kalmiusskaia Sakma near the Ternovskii Forest. . . . Another
town is to be built also on the Kalmiusskaia Sakma along the upper
[Tikhaia] Sosna, at the mouth of the Userd River in place of Nizhnee Fort; above the mouth of the Userd from the sources of the
river [Tikhaia] Sosna toward the sources of the river Volui, where
there is an ostrog, a rampart fifteen versts long must be constructed.
At each end of the rampart there should be a small ostrog. Also on

[3] *Akty, sobrannye v bibliotekakh i arkhivakh rossiiskoi imperii arkheografiche-
skoiu ekspeditsieiu imperatorskoi akademii nauk* (4 vols., St. Petersburg, 1836),
III, 410–411, 449–450, IV, 30.

the Kalmiusskaia Sakma, on the river Olshanka, at the mouth of the small river Trostenka, near the Ternovskii Forest an ostrog with a permanent garrison is to be established. On the river Oskol near the Zhestovy Mountains there is to be a small ostrog with a permanent garrison. On five fords along the river [Tikhaia] Sosna stakes and poles of oak should be imbedded in water, and also along the [Tikhaia] Sosna in three places in the woods, on the river Oskol, and on the Fomichkin River bend, trees should be felled and an abatis made.

On the Iziumskaia Sakma near Iablonov Forest an ostrog with a permanent garrison should be established. An earthen rampart should be built from the sources of the Kholka across the steppe to the small river Korocha. At both ends of the rampart—near the ostrog on the Korocha and on the small Kholka—small ostrogs are to be built.

A town with a permanent garrison is to be built on the Muravskii Shliakh by the Vorskla at the Karpov outpost. From this town a wall with forts should be built toward Belgorod as far as the small Viazenitsa.

ii. *1641. The Tsar's message to Prince Peter Pozharskii, the military commander (voevoda) of Odoev*

... As soon as you receive this message, order ... the construction of a barrier 140 feet in depth made of felled trees, instead of pits, from the River Vyrka to the River Sosenna. From the River Sosenna to the Peremyzhskaia and Kozelskaia abatis ... erect such earthen fortifications as you may find necessary. Along the abatis extending from the large Borovensk ostrog to the small Borovensk ostrog there used to be a moat, and between the abatis and the moat stood a double row of poles. ... Order the abatis to be reinforced, clear the moat, and strengthen the poles.

iii. *1647. Tsar's message*

...We ordered a town (*gorod*) with a permanent garrison to be built on the river Oskol, at the mouth of the Bel Kolodez, for protection against invasion by the Tatars. From this town across the Kalmiusskaia Sakma (Road) an earthen rampart, with permanent earthen fortifications along the rampart, should be constructed.

162   THE URGE TO THE SEA

OUTPOSTS ON THE SOUTHERN FRONTIER (1571–1642)–FROM THE
DOCUMENTS BY BELIAEV AND BAGALEI

i. *Frontier outposts (according to Beliaev[4])*

From the front-line towns, at a distance of four or five days' journey, sometimes nearer, outposts were established in the steppe, and these in turn were placed at distances from each other of one or, rarely, two days' journey. These outposts were in constant communication with each other and composed a series of continuous lines athwart all the trails across the steppe used by the Tatars to invade Russia. They [the outposts] stretched in groups from the sources of the Sura to the Seim, and then from the Seim they turned toward the Vorskla and the Donets. The first, most eastern group lay in a convex line from the Barysh, a tributary of the Sura, to the Lomov, a tributary of the Tsna; the second group, from the Tsna to the Riasa, a tributary of the Voronezh; the third group, from the Riasa, along the Bystraia Sosna and its tributaries, to the sources of the Oka; the fourth, along the tributaries of the Seim; the fifth, from the Seim to the Sula, the Psiol, and the Vorskla; the sixth, along the tributaries of the Vorskla and the Donets to the mouth of the Aidar. Before 1571 there were, altogether, seventy-three outposts and they were officially divided into twelve groups. . . .[P. 13.]

In the same year [1640], May 11 [the military commander (*voevoda*)] Tolstoi arrived at Khotmyshskoe Gorodishche. He built there an ostrog of oak, 2345 feet (335 *sazhen*) in circumference, with seven towers, three with gates and four without gates. He constructed roofs over the towers, as well as shutes for throwing missiles, and embrasures for shooting. On the Muscovite side beyond the ostrog he dug a moat 14 feet (2 *sazhen*) deep. Toward the river Vorskla he built an underground passage 545 feet (75 *sazhen*) long and 21 feet (3 *sazhen*) wide. He armed the newly built ostrog with nine cannon, to which in 1641 were added six more sent from Moscow. . . . [P. 49.]

From the town of Userd up the Sosna River it is fifteen versts to the ostrog of Rozdornyi. The circumference of the latter is 420 feet (60 *sazhen*). Around the ostrog there is a moat 14 feet (2 *sazhen*) wide. . . . Beyond the moat there is a double row of poles with crosspieces. . . . There are two copper cannon. . . . [P. 50.]

[4] I. Beliaev, "O storozhevoi, stanichnoi, i polevoi sluzhbe na pol'skoi ukraine moskovskago gosudarstva do tsaria Alekseia Mikhailovicha," *Chteniia . . . pri moskovskom universitete*, No. 4 (1846), pp. 5–86.

From the town of Userd beyond the River Userd from the ...
Ilovskii Forest there are earthen ramparts and a moat. Beyond the
moat there are three rows of poles with crosspieces. On the earthen
ramparts there are five earthen towers ... and the sixth tower is
made of oak with eight walls and stands on the hill. ... This tower
is 42 feet (6 *sazhen*) high to the top. Its diameter is 38 1/2 feet (5 1/2
sazhen). ... Through this tower pass the gates. Altogether, in 1641
and 1642 this rampart was made 9583 feet (1369 *sazhen*) long, not
counting space for towers. ...
... Across the ford there is a palisade of oak in the water ... and
on both banks holes conceal sharpened poles. ... [P. 52.]

ii. *Description of the towns of the Belgorod line of 1668 (after
Bagalei*[5])

Belgorod. One wooden fortress (*gorod*) is built like a stockade
with a parapet and has ten towers. ... The circumference of the
fortress is 4552 feet (650 1/4 *sazhen*). Inside it there are two wells
with good water. Leading from this fortress and ostrog there is
another fortification toward the river Donets: two walls constructed of earth and crowned with a palisade of oak. Two gates
lead through these walls. Along the river Donets there is a third
wall, a stockade without a parapet. At the bridge across the river
Donets there is a tower with a gate. The circumference, including
the three walls, gates, and towers, is 9499 feet (1357 *sazhen*). ...
[P. 54.]
On the Belgorod line, between Belgorod and Bolkhovets [on
one side], and along the Severnyi Donets in the direction of Nezhe-
golsk on another side, according to the inspection and description
by a Belgorodian, Peter Nechaev, made in the current year, the
earthen rampart and the palisade of oak in many places are in a
dilapidated condition. The timbers are rotten ... and in some
places the rampart has collapsed. ... In the summer they cut the
grass near the rampart and burn it. From the Belgorod fortress
toward Akhtyrsk, and on the other side of Belgorod toward Korotoiak and Uryv, the earthen rampart, the palisade of oak, the abatis,
and the turrets made of logs are in good condition. [Pp. 56–57.]

[5] D. I. Bagalei, *Materialy dlia istorii kolonizatsii i byta stepnoi okrainy moskov-
skogo gosudarstva v XVI–XVIII stoletii* (Kharkov, 1886), pp. 54, 56.

Appendix 4 ⚄ Seventeenth-Century Descriptions of Portages and Ostrogs, and River and Land Transportation in Siberia

A LIST OF [WESTERN] SIBERIAN TOWNS AND BLOCKHOUSES (OSTROGS) [COMPILED NOT LATER THAN 1640][1]

CONCERNING the location of each town and ostrog, specifying the river above which the listed town or ostrog is situated and stating the distance between the towns or ostrogs, over both the winter and summer land routes, by horses and by sleighs (*narty*) to which dogs are harnessed, as well as the distance by the river routes, in large boats (*doshchaniki*) and in light craft (*strugi*).The list has been compiled from the information given by the serving men of Tobolsk and of other Siberian towns. [The list also includes information pertaining to the stage service:] what people do the driving, how far, and over which roads they drive. All this [information] is written down in this list, each item separately.

The town of Verkhoturie stands above the river Tura. Traveling in large boats from Verkhoturie to the ostrog of Turinsk by the water route, it takes three days' sailing down the Tura to reach the mouth of the Tagil River. From the mouth of the Tagil River to the ostrog of Turinsk one travels two and one-half days (*pol-3 dni*). In lighter craft the journey from Verkhoturie to the ostrog of Turinsk may be made in four days. The return journey from the ostrog of Turinsk to Verkhoturie in large boats upstream takes nine days; in lighter craft, five days. On horses, via the summer and winter land routes, the journey to the ostrog of Turinsk takes four days, and traveling posthaste it may be made in three.

The ostrozhek (small blockhouse) of Tagil is in the County (*Uezd*) of Verkhoturie above the Tagil River. Traveling on horses, over the winter and summer land routes, the journey [from Verkhoturie] to the ostrozhek of Tagil takes one day; in large boats over the water route down the Tura, it takes three days to reach the Tagil River and three more days up the Tagil to reach the ostrozhek.

---

[1] A. Titov, *Sibir' v XVII veke. Sbornik starinnykh russkikh statei o Sibiri i prilezhashchikh k nei zemliakh* (Moscow, 1890), pp. 9–22. Oleg Maslenikov assisted in the translation of this document.

[165]

The ostrozhek of Nev'ia is in the County of Verkhoturie above the Nev'ia River. Traveling on horses, over the winter and summer land routes, the journey from Verkhoturie to the ostrozhek of Nev'ia takes three days. No water route is used from Verkhoturie to Nev'ia.

The journey from Verkhoturie to Pelym over the winter and summer land route takes five days. No one goes in boats by water from Verkhoturie to Pelym.

Messengers sent on urgent government business from the Siberian towns—Tobolsk, Tiumen, or the ostrog of Turinsk—to the Sovereign at Moscow, either in the fall or before the road is closed (po poslednemu puti), go by the following route. From Verkhoturie they travel by way of the Chiusovaia (now Chusovaia) [River] and the ostrogs of the Stroganovs. One man who hails from Solikamsk, traveling lightly, is sent forth from Verkhoturie to hire carts, vessels, and oarsmen. The boats and oarsmen obtained in Solikamsk are brought along the Kama to the mouth of the Chiusovaia River, since there is no stage station (iam) along the Chiusovaia and the Stroganovs will not furnish carts, boats, or oarsmen. Going from Verkhoturie to the Chiusovaia, people with luggage travel three days by the land route to reach the end of the portage; from the end of the portage it takes three days' sailing down the Chiusovaia to reach the Kama. Traveling in carts and boats, the oarsmen being obtainable with the boats in Solikamsk, the journey from the mouth of the Chusovaia [sic] River to Laishev is made in eight days; from Laishev to Kazan is another thirty versts' journey overland. With a load, the journey from Verkhoturie to Solikamsk over the summer land route consumes from eight to ten days or a fortnight, or even longer; traveling light and fast, the journey may be made in five or six days. Traveling over the winter road, the distance may be covered in five or six days, and traveling thus posthaste, four days. The journey down the Kama from Solikamsk [to the mouth of the Kama] can, in light craft, be made in ten days, and from [the mouth of] the Kama sailing up the Volga it takes another five days to reach Kazan. Traveling posthaste on horses over the winter route, the journey from Verkhoturie to Moscow via Ustiug Velikii takes three weeks. The messengers who come from Kazan do not ride to Verkhoturie by way of the ostrogs of the Stroganovs or the Chiusovaia portage, since, there being no stage station established at the Chiusovaia, they have no place to hire carts. Volunteer (okhotniki) drivers drive from Verkhoturie along four roads: to Solikamsk, to the Chiusovaia River, to the ostrog of Turinsk, and to Pelym.

The ostrog of Turinsk stands above the Tura River. From the ostrog of Turinsk to Tiumen, it takes two and one-half days' traveling in large boats (*doshchaniki* and *lodii*) down the Tura to reach the mouth of the Nitsa River; from the mouth of the Nitsa to Tiumen, still traveling along the Tura, there is another one and one-half days' journey. In light craft the journey from the ostrog of Turinsk to Tiumen may be made in two days. The return journey from Tiumen to the ostrog of Turinsk along the Tura River upstream may be negotiated in nine days in the heavier vessels, and in lighter craft, in six. Traveling on horses over the winter and summer land routes, the journey from the ostrog of Turinsk to Tiumen may be made in three days. Traveling in the direction of Pelym, it takes three days over the summer land routes with horses to reach the village of Tabarinsk of the County of Pelym. From the village of Tabarinsk it takes five more days of driving to Pelym. [In all,] it takes eight days of driving to reach Pelym [from the ostrog of Turinsk]. The journey from the village of Tabarinsk to Pelym may be made over the water route up the Tavda River; sailing in large boats, this journey may be completed in seven days, and in small boats, in four days. No water route is used between the ostrog of Turinsk and the village of Tabarinsk. Volunteer stage drivers drive from the ostrog of Turinsk to the village of Tabarinsk. The tribute-paying Voguls of Pelym drive stages from the village of Tabarinsk to Pelym for all who are sent on state business.

The town of Pelym stands above the Tavda River. The length of time required to reach Verkhoturie and the ostrozhek [*sic*] of Turinsk [therefrom] over the winter and the summer land routes by horses, and over the water routes, has already been described above. The tribute-paying Voguls of Pelym engage in transportation service from yurt to yurt along the three routes from Pelym: to Verkhoturie, to the ostrog of Turinsk, and to Tiumen.

The Chiubarovo Village (*sloboda*) is situated above the Nitsa River in the County of Turinsk. It has a small ostrog. From the ostrog of Turinsk, traveling by horses over the winter and summer land routes, it takes one day to reach the village. Owing to the distance, the water route from the ostrog of Turinsk to Chiubarovo is not used as a means of communication.

The town of Tiumen stands above the Tura River. Traveling along the summer route on horses, it takes seven days to reach

Tobolsk from Tiumen; traveling over the winter route, the same journey may be made in five days; sailing over the water route in large boats down the Tura River, it takes three days to reach the Tobol River; then four [more] days along the Tobol to reach the Irtysh; thence it is only one more verst along the Irtysh to Tobolsk. Thus, in all, it takes a week to reach Tobolsk from Tiumen in large boats. In lighter craft the journey may be made in four days. The return voyage from Tobolsk to Tiumen takes, in larger boats, ten days, and in lighter craft, six. From Tiumen to Pelym, over the water route, down the Tura to the mouth of the Tobol . . . Tiumen volunteer coachmen drive stages from Tiumen along three roads: to Tobolsk, to Pelym, and to the ostrog of Turinsk. From Tiumen, messengers are sent to Ufa with news on government business. It is a three weeks' journey by horses from Tiumen to Ufa. [The travelers] take carts from one yurt to another from the dependent (*zakhrebetnye*) and tribute-paying Tatars. In winter the journey to Ufa may be made on skis in five weeks.

The town of Tobolsk stands above the Irtysh River. The town of Tara may be reached from Tobolsk on horses by the winter route in two weeks' time, and traveling posthaste, in ten days. The journey may be made in three weeks along the summer route by poor roads, unless one goes through the tribute-paying rural districts (*volosts*). The journey from Tobolsk to Tara, traveling in large boats along the water route up the Irtysh River, the way the bread supplies are sent with serving men, takes three days to reach the mouth of the Vagai River; from the mouth of the Vagai, twelve more days to the mouth of the Ishim; and from the mouth of the Ishim to the town of Tara along the Irtysh, two weeks more. In all, it takes four weeks and a day to reach Tara from Tobolsk via the water route. Messengers on government affairs, on light craft to Tara . . . take ten days, and posthaste, eight.

Traveling in large boats up the Irtysh, the way serving men of Tobolsk and of other Siberian towns of the Tobolsk Administrative Region (*Rozriad*) go for salt, takes four weeks and three days to reach the Iamysh Salt Lake from Tara. The return trip down the Irtysh takes two weeks, and from Tara to Tobolsk, ten days.

To insure the protection of the Sovereign's tribute-paying rural districts, small blockhouses are established throughout the counties of Tobolsk and Tara.

The small blockhouse of Vagai stands above the Vagai River. The distance thence to Tobolsk along the winter and summer land routes is a single day's travel by horses; three days' travel in large boats by the water route up the Irtysh; and two days' travel in lighter craft [along the same route].

The small blockhouse of Kaurdat stands above a lake. The distance to it from Tobolsk over the winter route is four days' travel by horses, while by the summer land route it is six days' travel; and by the water route up the Irtysh, ten days' travel in large boats, and in light craft, posthaste, three days.

The small blockhouse of Tebendin stands above the Irtysh River. The distance to it from Tobolsk over the winter and summer land routes is five days' travel by horses; by water it is one week's travel in large boats up the Irtysh, and three days' travel in lighter craft.

The small blockhouse of Ishim Ustie stands above a lake. The distance to it from Tobolosk by the winter route is six days' journey on horses, and by the summer route, ten; the distance over the water route is a fortnight's journey up the Irtysh in large boats, and five days' fast travel in lighter craft.

The small blockhouse of Tarkhansk stands above the Tobol River. The distance to it from Tobolsk is four days' travel by horses over the winter route, and over the summer land route, five days; by the water route up the Tobol River it is a seven-day journey in large boats and a five-day voyage in lighter craft.

And when the serving men are sent from Tobolsk to these small blockhouses on government business or at news of the approach of [hostile] military forces, the dependent and tribute-paying Tatars of Tobolsk transport them.

Traveling in large boats from Tobolsk to Berezov, via the water route, when serving men are sent from Tobolsk with the government grain, one sails for nine days down the Irtysh to its confluence with the Ob', down the Ob' for ten more days, then by way of a branch (*protok*) of the Ob' it takes another half day (½ *dnishche*) to reach the River Sob' [*sic*], and one-half day more sailing down the Sob' [*sic*] [to Berezov]. The distance from Tobolsk to Berezov via the winter route is a week's journey by horses to the mouth of the Irtysh, with dependent and tribute-paying Tatars driving stages from village to village.

The Sovereign's tribute-paying Ostiaks of Surgut County drive sleighs with dogs from the mouth of the Irtysh as far as the Sotnikov Yurts in four days. The Ostiaks of Prince Dmitrii Alachev drive from the Sotnikov Yurts to Berezov in five days. When they send the serving men on government business from Tobolsk to Surgut by the winter route, the dependent Tatars of Tobolsk drive stages for them from Aremzinsk Village to Tobolsk. The journey takes one day. The tribute-paying Ostiaks of Tobolsk cover the distance from Aremzinsk Village to the mouth of the Irtysh in six days. From the mouth of the Irtysh the tribute-paying Ostiaks of Surgut County drive sleighs with dogs. In all, the journey from Tobolsk to Surgut by horses and sleighs with dogs takes two weeks. The journey over the water route, used for sending serving men with the government grain supplies down the Irtysh in large boats, takes nine days to the mouth of the Irtysh, and from the mouth of the Irtysh up the river Irtysh [sic] to Surgut, ten days more. In all, the journey from Tobolsk to Surgut via the water route consumes two weeks and five days, while in lighter craft, posthaste, it may be made in two weeks.

The distance from Tobolsk to Babasan Village, en route to the town of Pelym, over the winter route is two days' travel by horses, the dependent Tatars of Tobolsk doing the driving. From Babasan Village tribute-paying Ostiaks of Tobolsk drive to Pelym County in four days. Tribute-paying Voguls of Pelym County drive from Pelym County [boundary] to Pelym in five days. In all, the distance from Tobolsk to Pelym via the winter route is eleven days' travel by horses, and traveling posthaste it takes nine days. By the water route up the Tobol and Tavda rivers it is a three weeks' journey. It takes nine days' travel by horses to reach Tabarinsk Village in Pelym County, driving over the summer land route. No one goes by the land route by horses from Tabarinsk Village to Pelym.

The dependent Tatars of Tobolsk drive the stage from Tobolsk for the Sovereign's military commanders (*voevodas*), officers, and others who travel from Moscow to Siberian towns and ostrogs. They drive along the four roads: to Tiumen, to Berezov, to Tara and to Pelym. The serving Tatars of Tobolsk aid them in their driving, since their children, brothers, and nephews also live in dependence [upon the government].

The town of Tara stands above the Agirka River. From Tara news messengers are dispatched to the town of Tomsk. Going from Tara to Tomsk by horses over the summer land route, one travels two weeks through Tara County to Terenin Village. From Terenin Village to the town of Tomsk also takes two weeks. Messengers with news are also sent from Tara to the ostrog of Narym. The distance from Tara to Narym County over the summer land route is three weeks' travel by horses through the black forests. The Tara tribute-paying Tatars do the driving to the town of Tomsk and to the ostrog of Narym. There is neither a winter route nor a water route from Tara to the town of Tomsk and to the ostrog of Narym. There are no other stage routes from the town of Tara.

The town of Berezov stands above the Vagulka River. Government serving men are sent on state business to Obdor. Traveling in light craft from Berezov to Obdor over the water route down the Ob', the journey may be made in four days; nine days are consumed in travel over the winter route by sleighs with dogs, the Sovereign's tribute-paying Ostiaks doing the driving.

The winter quarters (*zimov'e*) of Obdor stands above the Pului River. The distance between the winter quarters of Obdor and the town of Mangazeia over the water route is three week's travel in large sailboats (*kochi*) under favorable wind. The return trip takes the same length of time. There is no travel to Mangazeia in winter.

From the towns of Berezov and Tomsk, and from the ostrogs of Eniseisk and Krasnoiarsk, furs gathered as the Sovereign's tribute (*iasak*) are sent to Moscow across the Ural Mountains (Kamen'). Going from Berezov to Russia, it takes four days of navigating up the Ob' [*sic*] in light boats to reach the mountains; thence overland over the portages (*voloki*), two weeks more; from the portages down the Usa River it takes ten days to reach the Pechora River; down the Pechora to the Izhma River, three days; up the Izhma to Izhma Village of Pustoozersk County, two days. Itinerants (*guliashchie liudi*) are hired as sailors from Berezov to Izhma Village, and they are remunerated at Berezov with funds out of the Sovereign's treasury.

The patrimonial estate (*votchina*) of Prince Dmitrii Alachev is also located in Berezov County above the Ob' River.

Mention of distances from there to Berezov and Tobolsk via the winter and the water routes and of the other places, to which the Ostiaks of Prince Dmitrii Alachev carry communications, has been made above.

The town of Mangazeia stands above the Taz River. Driving over the winter route, it takes three weeks to reach Turukhansk from Mangazeia en route to the Eniseisk ostrog, though traveling posthaste the trip may be made in one week. It takes one [more] week to reach the Inbatsk winter quarters from Turukhansk; and from the Inbatsk winter quarters it is six days' travel to the Podkamennaia Tunguska River. Various serving men from Mangazeia when sent on government business to the Podkamennaia Tunguska

River are driven by Russian coachmen on sleighs with dogs. The fare for transportation is collected from the merchants and entrepreneurs (*promyshlennye liudi*).

The Sovereign's tribute-paying Ostiaks make the journey from the Podkamennaia Tunguska River to the Eniseisk ostrog by sleighs with dogs in three weeks. If the water route is used from Mangazeia to the Eniseisk ostrog, it takes two days of sailing up the Taz River in large craft to reach the River Volochaika; then six days upstream to the portage. The portage is half a verst long. At the portage they do not carry large boats; but they drag light craft (*kaiuki* and *strugi*) across to another river also called the Volochaika. It takes two days to reach the Turukhan River. It takes six more days sailing down that river to reach the Turukhansk winter quarters. From Turukhansk they sail up the Enisei to the Zakamennoe-tribute winter quarters, a journey of three weeks. From Zakamennoe to the Eniseisk ostrog it takes two more weeks of sailing up the Enisei. In all, it takes eight weeks by water to reach the Eniseisk ostrog from Mangazeia.

How they send the serving men from Mangazeia to the great Lena River below the Turukhan [River] to collect the Sovereign's tribute [is listed] below. . . .

A LIST OF EASTERN SIBERIAN PORTAGES AND BLOCKHOUSES (OSTROGS) IN 1668[2]

FROM Tobolsk down the Irtysh, passing Dem'iansk, one travels to the Samarovsk stage station (*iam*), then to the mouth of the Irtysh River—a half-day's journey. From the mouth of the Irtysh up the Ob' River it is about nine days' journey to Surgut; from Surgut, using the same river, they travel three or four weeks to Narym; from Narym there is a day's journey to the mouth of the Ket'; and up the Ket' River to the ostrog of Ketsk they travel eight or nine days. From the ostrog of Ketsk to the Makovsk winter quarters (*zimov'e*) along the same Ket' they travel six or seven weeks, and from the Makovsk winter quarters to the ostrog of Eniseisk across the portage there is a land journey lasting two days.

From the ostrog of Eniseisk up the Enisei River it is two day's journey to the mouth of the Tunguska River. Along the Tunguska River upstream, there is a journey twelve weeks long to the ostrog of Nizhnii Bratsk. Then [one travels] along the river [upstream] and over the rapids; above the mouth of the Ilim [the upper part of the Tunguska] is called the Angara. From the ostrog of Nishnii

[2] Titov, *op. cit.*, pp. 30–36.

Bratsk [at] the mouth of the Oka River up the Angara River it is two weeks' travel to the ostrog of Balagansk. And from the Balagansk ostrog to the ostrog of Irkutsk they travel along the same river Angara about two weeks. And from the ostrog of Irkutsk up the Angara River they reach Lake Baikal in one week. There is a town on this Angara River. They cross Lake Baikal by sail to [the mouth of the] Selenga River in about three days, and go up the Selenga to the new ostrog of Selenginsk. From Lake Baikal to the mouth of the Khilka is a journey of thirteen days, and up the Khilka from its mouth to the ostrog of Irgensk is a journey of fourteen days. And from the Irgensk ostrog to the Ingoda River by lakes and portages is a day's journey.

And from the portage down the Ingoda and Shilka rivers they go by boats (*doplyvaiut*) to the ostrog of Nerchinsk at the mouth of the Nercha River in three days. In this ostrog at the present time Larion Tolbuzin, a lesser noble ("boiar son") of Tobolsk, lives with serving men. From the ostrog of Nerchinsk to the mouth of the Arkhunia (now Argun') three days of river travel are required. In this place the rivers Shilka and Arkhunia come together, and from this place begins a river called the Amur. The Arkhunia River flows from the great Lake Salar, a lake where there is an abundance of fish. Near this lake the Chinese savages, the men of Targachin, wander, and they live on fish. Following the Amur River there is a one-day journey to the small Chinese town of Lapkaev, but the town is deserted by the Chinese people, who fear the Russians.

From the ostrog of Eniseisk there is a journey of six weeks. . . . From the ostrog of Ilimsk there is a portage to the river Muka at a distance which may be covered in two days. Here stands a chapel. This chapel was built in fulfillment of the vows of the Russian merchants. From the chapel down the Kuta and Lena rivers, passing the mouths of the Kirenga, the Chiuchiui, the Vitim, and the Olekma rivers, there is a journey of two weeks on a large boat to the ostrog of Iakutsk. From the ostrog of Iakutsk down the Lena River one reaches the sea in three weeks. And between the Lena and Kirenga rivers there are a monastery and a church, and between the monastery and the church is a distance of three versts.

From the ostrog of Iakutsk to the ford across the Aldan River is a journey of one week by land. From [this] ford one travels four weeks to the winter quarters of Verkhoiansk, which is situated on the Iana River. From the Verkhoiansk winter quarters to the Zashiversk winter quarters one travels three weeks, and the latter

stands above the river Indigirka. It takes about four weeks to travel
from the Zashiversk winter quarters to the Alazeevo winter quarters, and the latter are above the Alazeia River. From the Alazeevo
winter quarters one travels to the Serednee winter quarters on the
Kolyma River in one week, and at the sources of this river there
is a winter quarters called Verkhnee. One gets to this winter quarters from Serednee, using sleighs, in three weeks. At the mouth of
the same river [Kolyma] there is also a winter quarters, called
Nizhnee, and to this from the Serednee winter quarters it is a journey of about five weeks. In all these winter quarters there live the
serving men from the Iakutsk ostrog to gather the Sovereign's fur
tribute (*iasak*). These rivers, on which are the winter quarters, are
visited by Russian merchants coming to trade by sea on large craft
(*kochi*), and they reach the sea from Iakutsk by going down the Lena.

From the Lena River up the Olekma, passing the mouth of the
Niukria, to the mouth of the Tugir, one travels on a large boat
without load about five weeks; with a load, it takes all summer.
Along the Tugir River is a ten days' journey to the above-mentioned
Daurian town of Lapkaev. The portage here goes through swamps
and lakes and rivers, and is very difficult because one has to go on
foot through these rivers, lakes, and swamps.

From this little town of Lapkaev one travels a week down the
Amur River, passing the mouth of the Kamar River, to the mouth
of the Zeia River. From the mouth of the Zeia down the Amur
River to the mouth of the river Shingal [Sungari?] is also a journey
of one week. At the mouth of the river Shingal there is a forest,
and in this forest there is a Chinese outpost. China extends from
the Shingal beyond the Amur River all the way to the sea. The
Naul flows into the Shingal, the river Korga flows into the Naul,
and on the Korga there is a Chinese town of Mungut. From the
Shingal to this town the journey takes two weeks. In this town there
are stationed twenty or thirty or forty Chinese soldiers for protection against Russian serving men. From this town there is a portage
to the Chinese Kingdom, and these people [the garrison] ride on
horses across this portage in ten days if posthaste, or in a month if
they travel with supplies.

From the mouth of the Shingal River down the Amur River there
is a journey of four days to the mouth of the Ushura. From the
Ushura [Ussuri?] down the Amur there is a journey of one week to
the mouth of the Khamun. Along all these rivers are settlements
of the Daurian people, and in many places they have built small

towns. They raise summer crops of various kinds of grain, and apples, pears, watermelons and other melons, and cucumbers. You can grow every kind of Russian vegetable along the River Amur. From the mouth of the Khamun down the Amur to the seacoast and to the land of the Giliaks is a journey of two weeks. The Giliaks live near the sea, and do not raise crops but live on fish. You cannot travel to the Chinese Kingdom by this sea on account of the ice, but there is a passage to the Nipponese Kingdom (Japan). There are gold and silver and precious stones in the Nipponese Kingdom, and silk is also produced.

From the ostrog of Eniseisk to the ostrog of Krasnoiarsk the land journey takes ten days, while travel by water up the River Enisei might take three weeks. From the ostrog of Eniseisk down the river Enisei, passing the mouths of the rivers Podkamennaia Tunguska, Elogui, and Nizhniaia Tunguska, it is a journey of ten days to the Turukhansk winter quarters in small vessels. On the river Podkamennaia Tunguska a winter quarters is established where the serving men from Eniseisk live to collect the Sovereign's fur tribute. From Turukhansk one travels two weeks along the Enisei River to the sea.

From Narym to the town of Tomsk up the rivers Ob' and Tom the journey takes ten days. From the town of Tomsk to the ostrog of Kuznetsk it is a journey of ten days up the Tom River. From the town of Tomsk down the Tom River to the Ob' and up the Ob' River to the mouths of the Biia and Katun' one travels on a large boat for ten weeks, and at the mouths of both of these rivers there are evergreen forests. This place is suitable for the erection of a Great Sovereign's town or ostrog because the fields are good for agriculture. There is an abundance of various animals, both sables and foxes, and there are small rivers with beavers, so the Great Sovereign will receive a large profit. The River Biia flows from Lake Teletskoe, which can be crossed on a small craft in five days. Many natives wander near these places who do not deliver the tribute to the Great Sovereign. And they say that one travels from the mouths of the Biia and the Katun' across the steppe to the Chinese Kingdom in two months. There is actually a trail between the Kontaishin and Mungalsk [Mongolian?] settlements (*ulusy*), but the distance to the mountains is not known. From Tomsk one travels to the Mungalsk settlements in a month and a half, to the Kontaishin [Kontaisha?] settlements in two months; and from the Kontaishin settlements to the town of Tangut in two months.

Appendix 5 ⚓ A List of the More Important Monasteries in Their Relation to the River Systems and the Ostrogs

A. MONASTERIES OF THE NOVGOROD REGION[1]

River system	Name	Date of founding
(See App. 1)	Iurievskii m.	1030
	Antoniev m.	1106
	Dukhov c.	1162
	Khutynskii Varlaamskii m.	1192
	Zverin Pokrovskii c.	1130
Region of A. Volga, xxiv,	Skovorodskii m.	1355 or before
xxv, xxvii–xxix; D.	Kirilov m.	Mentioned in the 12th century
Western Dvina, xi–		
xviii; E. Velikaia, ii, iii;	Panteleimonov m.	12th century
F. Shelon', i	Desiatin c.	1327
	Klopskii Troitskii m.	14th century
	Viazhitskii m.	1411
	Savvo-Visherskii m.	14th century
	Syrkov c.	1548
	Derevenitskii m.	14th century

[1] Abbreviations here used are m. for monastery and c. for convent. The word "pustyn'" may be best translated as "retreat." For references in regard to the Novgorod region see: A. Rado, *Guide Book to the Soviet Union* (New York, 1928), p. 337; I. Pushkarev, *Opisanie rossiiskoi imperii* (St. Petersburg, 1844), I:1, 28; I. Privol'ev, "Khutynskii monastyr'," *Istoricheskii vestnik* (St. Petersburg), XLIX (1892), 455; A. G. Slezkinskii, "Khutynskii monastyr'," *ibid.*, XCIV (1903), 926; A. G. Slezkinskii, "Savvo-Visherskii monastyr'," *ibid.*, LXXXVI (1901), 270; *Dopolneniia k aktam istoricheskim* (12 vols., St. Petersburg, 1846–1872; hereafter cited as *D.A.I.*), IX, 203; I. F. Tiumenev, "Po puti iz Variag v Greki," *Istoricheskii vestnik*, LII (1893), 156. Russian chronicles mention about fifty more monasteries around Novgorod: *Polnoe sobranie russkikh letopisei* (24 vols., St. Petersburg, 1846–1914; hereafter cited as *P.S.R.L.*), III, 5–253 *passim*, IV, 12–140 *passim*. In 1386 the Novgorodians for strategic reasons burned twenty-four monasteries: *P.S.R.L.*, IV, 94.

B. MONASTERIES OF THE TIKHVIN REGION[2]

A. Volga xxx	Uspenskii Tikhvinskii m.	16th century
	Dymskii Antoniev m.	12th century
	Troitsko-Zelenskii m.	16th century
	Besednyi Nikolaevskii m.	16th century
	Vaselievskii m.	Mentioned in the 16th century

C. MONASTERIES OF THE BELOOZERO REGION[3]

A. Volga xxxii, xxxiii	Kirilov Novoozerskii m.	1517
	Nilosarskaia pustyn'	15th century
	Kirilov Beloozerskii m.	1397
	Ferapontov m.	14th century
A. Volga xxxii	Borisoglebskii m.	Mentioned in 1615
	Voskresenskii c.	Mentioned in 16₄7
A. Volga xxxi–xxxvii	Goritskii m.	Mentioned in 1488
	Kamennyi m.	Mentioned in 1488

D. MONASTERIES OF THE CHEREPOVETS REGION[4]

A. Volga xxxi–xxxvii	Cherepovskii Voskresenskii m.	Chartered in 1432
	Vyksenskaia pustyn'	Mentioned in the 16th century
	Troitskii Ust'-Shekhonskii m.	Mentioned in 1477
	Nikitskii m.	Mentioned in 1477

E. MONASTERIES OF THE USTIUZHNA REGION[5]

| A. Volga xxviii–xxx | Nikolaevskii Modenskii m. | Very ancient |

F. MONASTERIES OF THE BOROVICHI REGION[6]

| A. Volga xxvii, xxviii | Dukhovskii m. | 1345 |

---

[2] Pushkarev, *op. cit.*, I:1, 30–31; *D.A.I.*, I, 119, 126, 220; Tiumenev, *op. cit.*, pp. 145–152; "Tikhvinskaia systema," *Entsiklopedicheskii slovar'* (hereafter cited as *Entsik. slovar'*), XXXIII:1, 278–279.

[3] Pushkarev, *op. cit.*, I:1, 6, 32; I. F. Tiumenev, "Poezdka v Nilovu-Sorskuiu pustyn'," *Istoricheskii vestnik*, LXXIV (1896), 228; N. V-ko, "Monashestvo," *Entsik. slovar'*, XIX:2, 726; *D.A.I.*, II, 64, III, 126; *P.S.R.L.*, VI, 238; Komitet severa, *Ocherki po istorii kolonizatsii severa* (St. Petersburg, 1922), p. 14; Kirilov Beloozerskii m. "was one of the most important strategic points in the northern part of Russia": D. R., "Kirilo-Beloozerskii monastyr'," *Entsik. slovar'*, XV:1, 113.

[4] V. S. Ikonnikov, *Opyt russkoi istoriografii* (2 vols. in 4 books, Kiev, 1891–1908), II:1, 895; Pushkarev, *op. cit.*, I:1, 33; *D.A.I.*, I, 220, 358.

[5] Pushkarev, *op. cit.*, I:1, 33; A. Shchekatov, *Geograficheskii slovar' rossiiskago gosudarstva* (7 vols., Moscow, 1801–1809), IV, 636.

[6] Pushkarev, *op. cit.*, I:1, 33–35.

G. MONASTERIES OF THE ST. PETERSBURG AND OLONETS REGIONS[7]

A. Volga xxx	Konevskii m.	1398
	Lialikinskii m.	Mentioned in 1573
	Nikolskii m.	Mentioned in 1573
	Valaamskii m.	Mentioned in 1597
A. Volga xxxii	Aleksandro-Svirskii Troitskii m.	1506
	Klimetskii m.	15th century
	Paleostrovskii m.	12th century
A. Volga iii	Spasskii m.	14th century
	Syrinskii m.	Mentioned in 1647

H. MONASTERIES OF THE MOSCOW REGION[8]

A. Volga xi	Iosifov Volokolamskii m.	1479
	Voznesenskii m.	1572 or before

I. MONASTERIES OF THE KOSTROMA REGION[9]

A. Volga xxxviii–xli	Ipatievskii Troitskii m.	Mentioned in 1535
	Vozdvizhenskii m.	Mentioned in 1654
A. Volga xlii	Makar'evo-Unzhenskii m.	15th century

J. MONASTERIES OF THE ARKHANGELSK REGION[10]

J. Northern Dvina i–xxiv	Arkhangelskii m.	15th century
	Nikolaevskii Karelskii m.	15th century or before
	Pertominskii m.	1599
	Antoniev Siiskii m.	1520
	Chukchenemskii m.	15th century
J. Northern Dvina i–xxiv; I. Onega vii	Ivanovskii c.	
	Pokrovskii m.	
I. Onega vii	Emetskii Blagoveshchenskii m.	
	Emetskii Predtechenskii c.	

[7] K. V. Kudriashov, *Russkii istoricheskii atlas* (Moscow-Leningrad, 1928), table VII; Arkheograficheskaia Kommissiia, *Akty istoricheskie* (5 vols., St. Petersburg, 1841–1842, index, 1843; hereafter cited as *A.I.*), I, 349, V, 386; *D.A.I.*, I, 66, 235–236, III, 130; *P.S.R.L.*, III, 233; A. F. Marks, *Bol'shoi vsemirnyi nastol'nyi atlas Marksa* (St. Petersburg, 1904–1905), table 20; Ikonnikov, *op. cit.*, II:1, 894.

[8] *P.S.R.L.*, IV, 152; Rado, *op. cit.*, p. 109; *D.A.I.*, I, 364; Komitet severa, *op. cit.*, p. 40.

[9] *D.A.I.*, III, 364; Komitet severa, *op. cit.*, p. 14; *P.S.R.L.*, V, 149.

[10] Pushkarev, *op. cit.*, I:2, 26–28, 30, 32; Marks, *op. cit.*, table 16; *A.I.*, I, 428, III, 82, IV, 56; Komitet severa, *op. cit.*, pp. 37, 46.

K. MONASTERIES OF THE SHENKURSK REGION[11]

	Troitskii m.	1637
	Bogoslovskii m.	1450
	Troitskaia pustyn'	1590
	Predtechenskaia pustyn'	1654
	Makarievskaia pustyn'	1667
	Nikolaevskaia pustyn'	17th century
	Preobrazhenskii m.	
J. Northern Dvina iii;	Troitskii m.	
I. Onega vii	Uspenskii m.	
	Vvedenskii m.	17th century
	Voznesenskii m.	(second half)
	Nikolaevskii m.	
	Voskresenskii m.	
	Spasskaia pustyn' na Boru	
	Nikolaevskaia pustyn'	1503
	Nikolaevskii m.	1576
	Zosimo-Savvatieva pustyn'	1574

L. MONASTERIES OF THE ONEGA REGION[12]

	Krestnyi m.	1656
I. Onega i–vii	Solovetskii m.	14th century (first third)
	Oshevenskii m.	1453

M. MONASTERIES OF THE PINEGA REGION[13]

	Ust'-Shchelinskaia pustyn'	?
J. Northern Dvina xxiv	Krasnogorskii m.	1606
	Arkhangelskii m.	17th century

[11] Pushkarev, op. cit., I:2, 33–34; D.A.I., I, 34–35, IX, 206; "Troitskie monastyri," Entsik. slovar', XXXIII:2, 874–877.

[12] Pushkarev, op. cit., I:2, 35–36; N. L., "Solovetskii monastyr'," Entsik. slovar', XXX:2, 782–784; "Kirilov Aleksandro Oshevenskii monastyr'," Entsik. slovar', XV:1, 114; A.I., III, 72; D.A.I., V, 344; Komitet severa, op. cit., p. 40.

[13] Pushkarev, op. cit., I:2, 37; Kudriashov, op. cit., table VII.

N. MONASTERIES OF THE VOLOGDA REGION[14]

A. Volga xxxiv, xxxvii	Troitskii Kaisarov m.	1147
	Dukhov or Spaso-Kamennyi m.	16th century
	Uspenskii or Gornyi c.	Mentioned in 1647
	Synzhemskii m.	14th–15th centuries
	Pelshemskii m.	14th–15th centuries
	Rabaganskii m.	14th–15th centuries
	Spaso-Prilutskii m.	1371
	Siamskii Rozhdestvenskii m.	1524
	Kushtskii m.	14th–15th centuries
	Verkolskii m.	14th–15th centuries
	Zaonikievskaia pustyn'	1588
	Il'inskii m.	Mentioned in 1648
	Vologodskii Pesochnyi m.	Mentioned in 1615

O. MONASTERIES OF THE GRIAZOVETS REGION[15]

A. Volga xxxviii	Pavlov Obnorskii m.	1414
	Arseniev m.	1530
	Korniliev Komelskii m.	1515

P. MONASTERIES OF THE KADNIKOV REGION[16]

A. Volga xxxvii	Glushitskii m.	1402
	Lopatov m.	15th century
	Semigorodskaia pustyn'	15th century
	Dunikalova pustyn'	1679

Q. MONASTERIES OF THE SOLVYCHEGODSK REGION[17]

J. Northern Dvina xxii, xxiii	Kariazhemskii Nikolaevskii m.	1535
	Soiginskii m.	1540
	Vvedenskii m.	Mentioned in 1682
	Vymskii Arkhangelskii m.	?

R. MONASTERIES OF THE USTIUG REGION[18]

A. Volga xxxvii–xlvi	Arkhangelskii m.	1216
	Ioannovskii c.	13th–14th centuries
	Troitskii Gliadenskii m.	1190
	Iankovskaia pustyn'	1654

[14] Ikonnikov, *op. cit.*, II:1, 201, n. 6; Shchekatov, *op. cit.*, I, 978; Pushkarev, *op. cit.*, I:4, 95, 99–105; *D.A.I.*, III, 126; *A.I.*, I, 380, III, 60; *P.S.R.L.*, VI, 48.

[15] Pushkarev, *op. cit.*, I:4, 104–105; A. V. Kruglov, "Poezdka v Kornilievo-Komelskii monastyr'," *Istoricheskii vestnik*, LXX (1897), 216.

[16] Pushkarev, *op. cit.*, I:4, 106–108.

[17] Pushkarev, *op. cit.*, I:4, 110; *D.A.I.*, X, 406; Kudriashov, *op. cit.*, table VII.

[18] Pushkarev, *op. cit.*, I:4, 114, 117; "Arkhangelskie monastyri," *Entsik. slovar'*, II:1, 212; *D.A.I.*, IV, 38, X, 211.

S. MONASTERIES OF THE TOTMA REGION[19]

J. Northern Dvina iii   Spaso-Sumorin m.   1554

T. MONASTERIES OF THE TOBOLSK REGION[20]

A. Volga liv-lvii
Tobolskii Znamenskii m.	1587
Zosimy i Savvatiia m.	1601
Abalatskii m.	17th century
Uspenskii c.	17th century
Mezhdugorskii m.	1653

U. MONASTERIES OF THE VERKHOTURIE REGION[21]

A. Volga liv–lvii
Nikolaevskii m.	17th century
Pokrovskii c.	1604

V. MONASTERIES OF THE TURINSK REGION[22]

A. Volga lv, lvii
Nikolaevskii m.	17th century
Pokrovskii c.	1604

W. MONASTERIES OF THE TIUMEN REGION[23]

A. Volga lv, lvii
Troitskii m.	1616
Il'inskii c.	1622

X. MONASTERIES OF THE TOMSK REGION[24]

L. Ob' i–xi
Uspenskii m.	?
Kazanskoi Bozh'ei Materi m.	1663

Y. MONASTERIES OF THE TARA REGION[25]

L. Ob' i–xi   Spasskii m.   1624

---

[19] Pushkarev, *op. cit.*, I:4, 111.

[20] N. Abramov, "Materialy dlia istorii khristianskogo prosveshcheniia Sibiri," *Zhurnal ministerstva narodnago prosveshcheniia*, LXXXI (1854), 27, 30–31; *Sibirskaia sovetskaia entsiklopediia* (3 vols., Novosibirsk, 1929–1932), III, 506; Shchekatov, *op. cit.*, I, 7.

[21] Abramov, *op. cit.*, p. 18; *Sibirskaia sovetskaia entsiklopediia*, III, 504; J. E. Fischer, *Sibirskaia istoriia* (St. Petersburg, 1774), pp. 231, 304–305.

[22] Abramov, *op. cit.*, pp. 18, 23; *Sibirskaia sovetskaia entsiklopediia*, III, 506; Fischer, *op. cit.*, p. 305; V. K. Andrievich, *Istoriia Sibiri* (5 vols., St. Petersburg, Irkutsk, Tomsk, Odessa, 1887–1889), I, 183.

[23] Abramov, *op. cit.*, p. 23; *Sibirskaia sovetskaia entsiklopediia*, III, 506; Shchekatov, *op. cit.*, VI, 370; Fischer, *op. cit.*, p. 192.

[24] Abramov, *op. cit.*, pp. 24, 31; Fischer, *op. cit.*, p. 304; *Entsik. slovar'*, XXXIII: 2, 491.

[25] Abramov, *op. cit.*, p. 24; Fischer, *op. cit.*, p. 304.

Z. MONASTERIES OF THE ENISEISK REGION[26]

M. Enisei i–ix
$\begin{cases}\text{Rozhdestvenskii c.} & 1623 \\ \text{Spasskii m.} & 1644\end{cases}$

AA. MONASTERIES OF THE ISETSK REGION[27]

A. Volga lv, lvii
$\begin{cases}\text{Dalmatov-Uspenskii m.} & 1644 \\ \text{Rafailovskii Troitskii m.} & 1651\end{cases}$

BB. MONASTERIES OF THE BEREZOV REGION[28]

L. Ob' i–xi   Troitskii m.   1656

CC. MONASTERIES OF THE TURUKHANSK REGION[29]

M. Enisei i   Troitskii m.   1660

DD. MONASTERIES OF THE KRASNOIARSK REGION[30]

M. Enisei i–ix   Vvedenskii m.   1646

EE. MONASTERIES OF THE KUZNETSK REGION[31]

L. Ob' i–xi   Khristorozhdestvenskii m.   1648

FF. MONASTERIES OF THE KIRENSK REGION[32]

M. Enisei vii   Troitskii m.   1663

GG. MONASTERIES OF THE IAKUTSK REGION[33]

N. Lena i–x   Spasskii m.   1659

HH. MONASTERIES OF THE IRKUTSK REGION[34]

M. Enisei v
$\begin{cases}\text{Voznesenskii m.} & 1672 \\ \text{Znamenskii c.} & 1693 \\ \text{Posolskii Preobrazhenskii m.} & 1681\end{cases}$

---

[26] Abramov, *op. cit.*, pp. 24, 29; Andrievich, *op. cit.*, I, 182; Shchekatov, *op. cit.*, II, 420.

[27] Abramov, *op. cit.*, pp. 29, 31; Fischer, *op. cit.*, pp. 396–397; Shchekatov, *op. cit.*, VI, 368.

[28] Abramov, *op. cit.*, p. 31; *Sibirskaia sovetskaia entsiklopediia*, III, 506.

[29] Abramov, *op. cit.*, p. 31; *Sibirskaia sovetskaia entsiklopediia*, III, 506; Shchekatov, *op. cit.*, VI, 370.

[30] Abramov, *op. cit.*, p. 29.

[31] *Loc. cit.*

[32] Abramov, *op. cit.*, p. 31; Shchekatov, *op. cit.*, III, 478.

[33] Abramov, *op. cit.*, p. 31; *Sibirskaia sovetskaia entsiklopediia*, III, 506–507.

[34] Abramov, *op. cit.*, pp. 33–34; *Sibirskaia sovetskaia entsiklopediia*, III, 506; Shchekatov, *op. cit.*, II, 805.

II. MONASTERIES OF THE SELENGINSK REGION[35]

M. Enisei v   Troitskii m.   1681

JJ. MONASTERIES OF THE ALBAZIN REGION[36]

Q. Amur i–v   Spasskii m.   1671

KK. MONASTERIES OF THE BRATSK REGION[37]

N. Lena i–x   Spasskii m.   17th century

LL. MONASTERIES OF THE NEVIANSK REGION[38]

A. Volga lv   Vvedenskii m.   17th century
A. Volga lvii   Rozhdestvenskii m.   17th century

---

[35] Abramov, *op. cit.*, p. 36; *Sibirskaia sovetskaia entsiklopediia*, III, 507; Shchekatov, *op. cit.*, V, 865.

[36] F. Shperk, "Rossiia Dal'nego Vostoka," *Zapiski imperatorskogo russkogo geograficheskogo obshchestva*, XIV (1885), 60.

[37] Shchekatov, *op. cit.*, I, 548.

[38] A. Dmitriev, "K poluvekovoi godovshchine smerti Petra Andreevicha Slovtsova," *Permskii krai*, II (1893), 293; Fischer, *op. cit.*, p. 304; Andrievich, *op. cit.*, I, 182.

Appendix 6 ⚹ A List of Important Siberian Ostrogs

A. OSTROGS OF THE TOBOLSK REGION

River system	Name	Date of founding
(See App. 1)		
L. Ob' i–xi	Abatskii[1]	17th century
L. Ob' i–xi	Achinskii[2]	1621
L. Ob' viii	Belskii[3]	1668
K. Pechora v, vi	Berezov[4]	1593
L. Ob' i–xi	Ialutorovskii[5]	1630
L. Ob' i–xi	Isetskii[6]	1650
L. Ob' i–xi	Ishimskii[7]	1630 (approx.)
L. Ob' viii	Ketsk[8]	1597
L. Ob' i–xi	Korkinskii[9]	17th century
L. Ob' i–xi	Kuznetsk[10]	1618
L. Ob' viii	Makovsk[11]	1618
L. Ob' i–xi	Meleskii[12]	1621
L. Ob' xi	Mangazeia[13]	1610

[1] S. V. Bakhrushin, *Ocherki po istorii kolonizatsii Sibiri v XVI i XVII vv.* (Moscow, 1927–1928), p. 173.

[2] *D.A.I.*, V, 420, VI, 316–319, VII, 341, VIII, 45.

[3] *D.A.I.*, VI, 314–315, 354.

[4] G. F. Mueller, *Istoriia Sibiri* (Moscow-Leningrad, 1937), pp. 346, 350, 358; Bakhrushin, *op. cit.*, pp. 62–63, 73–76; V. I. Ogorodnikov, *Ocherk istorii Sibiri* (3 vols. in 2 parts, Irkutsk, Vladivostok, 1920, 1924), II, 37.

[5] Ogorodnikov, *op. cit.*, II, 36.

[6] I. E. Fischer, *Sibirskaia istoriia* (St. Petersburg, 1774), p. 396.

[7] Ogorodnikov, *op. cit.*, II, 36.

[8] Fischer, *op. cit.*, p. 196; Ogorodnikov, *op. cit.*, II, 39, 45; Mueller, *op. cit.*, pp. 302–304, 412–415.

[9] Bakhrushin, *op. cit.*, p. 173.

[10] Mueller, *op. cit.*, pp. 451–454; Fischer, *op. cit.*, p. 215; D.A.I., VI, 324–325, VII, 49, 50.

[11] Bakhrushin, *op. cit.*, p. 160.

[12] Fischer, *op. cit.*, pp. 279–280.

[13] Mueller, *op. cit.*, pp. 394, 395; Ogorodnikov, *op. cit.*, II, 38, 45; Fischer, *op. cit.*, p. 206; Bakhrushin, *op. cit.*, pp. 151–152; P. N. Butsinskii, *Mangazeia i Mangazeiskii uezd (1601–1645)* (Kharkov, 1893), *passim*.

L. Ob' i–xi	Narym[14]	1596
K. Pechora vii	Obdorsk[15]	1596
A. Volga liv	Pelym[16]	1593
L. Ob' i–xi	Surgut[17]	1593
L. Ob' i–xi	Tara[18]	1594
L. Ob' i–xi	Tarkhansk[19]	1630 (approx.)
L. Ob' i–xi	Tebendinsk[20]	1630 (approx.)
A. Volga liv–lvii,		
L. Ob' i–xi	Tobolsk[21]	1587
L. Ob' i–xi	Tomsk[22]	1604
A. Volga lvii	Turinsk[23]	1600
L. Ob' xi	Turukhansk[24]	1607
A. Volga lvii	Verkhoturie[25]	1598

B. OSTROGS OF THE ENISEISK REGION

M. Enisei i–ix	Abakansk[26]	1676
M. Enisei v, vi	Balagansk[27]	1654
M. Enisei v	Barguzin[28]	1648
M. Enisei v, vi	Bratsk[29]	1631
M. Enisei vii	Chichuiskii[30]	1650 (approx.)

[14] Fischer, *op. cit.*, p. 196; Ogorodnikov, *op. cit.*, II, 45; Bakhrushin, *op. cit.*, p. 112; P. N. Butsinskii, *K istorii Sibiri: Surgut, Narym i Ketsk do 1645 g.* (Kharkov, 1893), pp. 16–24.

[15] Ogorodnikov, *op. cit.*, II, 37; Bakhrushin, *op. cit.*, p. 75.

[16] Mueller, *op. cit.*, pp. 346–354; Ogorodnikov, *op. cit.*, II, 35–36.

[17] Butsinskii, *K istorii Sibiri . . .* , pp. 1–16; Fischer, *op. cit.*, p. 178; Ogorodnikov, *op. cit.*, II, 38.

[18] Mueller, *op. cit.*, pp. 354–361; Fischer, *op. cit.*, p. 180; Ogorodnikov, *op. cit.*, II, 34.

[19] Ogorodnikov, *op. cit.*, II, 36.

[20] *Loc. cit.*

[21] *Sibirskiia letopisi* (St. Petersburg, 1907), pp. 42, 257; Mueller, *op. cit.*, pp. 274–275; Fischer, *op. cit.*, p. 169; Ogorodnikov, op. cit., II, 34.

[22] Mueller, *op. cit.*, p. 812; Fischer, *op. cit.*, p. 209; Ogorodnikov, *op. cit.*, II, 39.

[23] Mueller, *op. cit.*, pp. 383–385; Fischer, *op. cit.*, p. 203; Ogorodnikov, *op. cit.*, II, 36.

[24] Bakhrushin, *op. cit.*, p. 114; Fischer, *op. cit.*, p. 237.

[25] Mueller, *op. cit.*, pp. 375–377; Fischer, *op. cit.*, p. 201; Ogorodnikov, *op. cit.*, II, 36.

[26] *D.A.I.*, VII, 334.

[27] *D.A.I.*, IV, 55; Ogorodnikov, *op. cit.*, II, 65.

[28] Bakhrushin, *op. cit.*, pp. 110, 137, 138; Ogorodnikov, *op. cit.*, II, 70.

[29] Bakhrushin, *op. cit.*, pp. 137, 161; Fischer, *op. cit.*, p. 350; Ogorodnikov, *op. cit.*, II, 64.

[30] Bakhrushin, *op. cit.*, p. 128.

M. Enisei v	Eravninsk[31]	Before 1675
M. Enisei i–ix	Eniseisk[32]	1619
M. Enisei vi	Ilimsk[33]	1630
L. Ob' i–x	Inbatsk[34]	1607
M. Enisei v	Irgensk[35]	1652–1653
M. Enisei i–ix	Irkutsk[36]	1652
M. Enisei v	Itankinsk (Itantsinsk)[37]	Before 1682
M. Enisei i–ix	Krasnoiarsk[38]	1629
M. Enisei i–ix	Kansk[39]	1628
M. Enisei v	Kabansk[40]	1680–1690
M. Enisei v	Kiakhta[41]	1727
M. Enisei viii	Nizhne-Viliuisk[42]	1634
M. Enisei v	Nizhne-Udinsk[43]	1647
M. Enisei v, vi	Rybnoi[44]	1628
M. Enisei v	Selenginsk[45]	1667
M. Enisei v	Telembinsk[46]	1658
M. Enisei v, vi	Tunkinskii[47]	?
M. Enisei vi	Ust'-Kut[48]	1631
M. Enisei v	Ust'-Prorva[49]	1652

[31] Bakhrushin, op. cit., pp. 110, 139.

[32] Fischer, op. cit., p. 277; Ogorodnikov, op. cit., II, 45; Bakhrushin, op. cit., p. 160.

[33] Fischer, op. cit., p. 354; Ogorodnikov, op. cit., II, 64; D.A.I., III, 303–304.

[34] A. Shchekatov, Geograficheskii slovar' rossiiskago gosudarstva (7 vols., Moscow, 1801–1809), II, 757; K. V. Kudriashov, Russkii istoricheskii atlas (Moscow-Leningrad, 1928), table ix.

[35] F. Shperk, "Rossiia Dal'niago Vostoka," Zapiski russkago geograficheskago obshchestva (St. Petersburg, 1885, pp. 1–503), XIV, 57; Ogorodnikov, op. cit., II, 72.

[36] Fischer, op. cit., p. 557; Bakhrushin, op. cit., p. 161; Ogorodnikov, op. cit., II, 65.

[37] D.A.I., IX, 210; Shchekatov, op. cit., V, 863.

[38] Fischer, op. cit., p. 282; Ogorodnikov, op. cit., II, 45; Bakhrushin, op. cit., p. 161.

[39] Fischer, op. cit., p. 400; Ogorodnikov, op. cit., II, 45.

[40] Shchekatov, op. cit., V, 863.

[41] Shchekatov, op. cit., III, 1044.

[42] Kudriashov, op. cit., table ix.

[43] Ogorodnikov, op. cit., II, 66.

[44] D.A.I., VIII, 176; Fischer, op. cit., p. 343.

[45] Bakhrushin, op. cit., p. 167; Ogorodnikov, op. cit., II, 73.

[46] Bakhrushin, op. cit., p. 139; Ogorodnikov, op. cit., II, 73.

[47] Shchekatov, op. cit., II, 805.

[48] Fischer, op. cit., p. 355.

[49] Ogorodnikov, op. cit., II, 72.

M. Enisei v	Ust'-Strelochnyi[50]	1650
M. Enisei v	Verkhne-Angarsk[51]	1647
M. Enisei v	Verkhne-Udinsk[52]	1647
M. Enisei viii	Verkhne-Viliuisk[53]	1634

C. OSTROGS OF THE IAKUTSK REGION

N. Lena vi	Amginsk[54]	1633
P. Kolyma ii	Anadyrsk[55]	1649
N. Lena i–x	Bauntovsk[56]	Before 1674
N. Lena viii–ix	Butalsk[57]	1637
N. Lena vi, vii	Dolonsk[58]	1679
N. Lena i–x	Iakutsk[59]	1632
N. Lena i–x	Kirensk[60]	1630
P. Kolyma ii	Nizhne-Kolymsk[61]	1644
N. Lena iv, v	Olekminsk[62]	1636
N. Lena ix	Okhotsk[63]	1648
P. Kolyma i	Penzhinsk[64]	1679–1680
N. Lena vi, vii	Selenbinsk[65]	1679
P. Kolyma i, ii	Sredne-Kolymsk[66]	1644
N. Lena iv, v	Tugirsk[67]	1647–1648
N. Lena i–x	Tutursk[68]	1631
N. Lena vi–viii	Ust'-Aldansk[69]	Before 1639

[50] Ogorodnikov, op. cit., II, 87.
[51] Ogorodnikov, op. cit., II, 69.
[52] Ogorodnikov, op. cit., II, 73.
[53] Shchekatov, op. cit., I, 822.
[54] Bakhrushin, op. cit., p. 162.
[55] Bakhrushin, op. cit., pp. 132, 165.
[56] D.A.I., VI, 367.
[57] Bakhrushin, op. cit., p. 163.
[58] Bakhrushin, op. cit., p. 136.
[59] Fischer, op. cit., p. 352; Bakhrushin, op. cit., pp. 162, 164; Ogorodnikov, op. cit., II, 49.
[60] Kudriashov, op. cit., table IX; Shchekatov, op. cit., III, 477.
[61] L. S. Berg, Istoriia geograficheskogo oznakomleniia s iakutskim kraem (Leningrad, 1927), p. 8.
[62] Fischer, op. cit., p. 372; Ogorodnikov, op. cit., II, 49.
[63] Bakhrushin, op. cit., p. 140; D.A.I., III, 331, 398, 400.
[64] D.A.I., VIII, 176.
[65] Bakhrushin, op. cit., pp. 133–134.
[66] Berg, op. cit., p. 8; Shchekatov, op. cit., V, 1142.
[67] D.A.I., III, 173, 261, IV, 89, 94.
[68] Fischer, op. cit., pp. 357–358.
[69] D.A.I., II, 232.

N. Lena viii, ix	Ust'-Maisk[70]	Before 1661
N. Lena viii	Ust'-Uliisk[71]	1639
O. Iana i, ii	Verkhoiansk[72]	1638
N. Lena i–x	Verkholensk[73]	1642
N. Lena vi, vii	Verkhozeiskoe[74]	1681
P. Kolyma ii	Verkhne-Kolymsk[75]	17th century (second half)
O. Iana ii	Zashiversk[76]	1639
N. Lena i–x	Zhigansk[77]	1632

D. OSTROGS OF THE NERCHINSK REGION

Q. Amur i–v	Achansk[78]	1651
Q. Amur i–v	Albazin[79]	1665
Q. Amur i–v	Argunsk[80]	1655
Q. Amur i–v	Chita[81]	End of 17th century
Q. Amur i–v	Kumarsk[82]	1652
Q. Amur i–v	Kosogirskii[83]	1655
Q. Amur i–v	Nemilenskoe[84]	1682
Q. Amur i–v	Nerchinsk[85]	1653–1654
Q. Amur i–v	Ust'-Dukichinskii[86]	1682

[70] *D.A.I.*, IV, 247, VI, 404.
[71] Shperk, *op. cit.*, p. 34.
[72] Kudriashov, *op. cit.*, table IX.
[73] Ogorodnikov, *op. cit.*, II, 66; Shchekatov, *op. cit.*, II, 805.
[74] *D.A.I.*, VII, 368.
[75] Berg, *op. cit.*, p. 8; Shchekatov, *op. cit.*, V, 282–283.
[76] Kudriashov, *op. cit.*, table IX; *D.A.I.*, V, 337–339.
[77] Bakhrushin, *op. cit.*, p. 162.
[78] Snperk, *op. cit.*, p. 67; Ogorodnikov, *op. cit.*, II, 90.
[79] Shperk, *op. cit.*, pp. 41, 59; Bakhrushin, *op. cit.*, p. 167.
[80] Shperk, *op. cit.*, p. 54.
[81] *Bol'shaia sov. entsik.*, LXI, 665.
[82] Shperk, *op. cit.*, pp. 49, 52, 55.
[83] Shperk, *op. cit.*, p. 55.
[84] Shperk, *op. cit.*, p. 64.
[85] Shperk, *op. cit.*, p. 57; Ogorodnikov, *op. cit.*, II, 72.
[86] Shperk, *op. cit.*, p. 64.

E. OSTROGS OF THE PETROPAVLOVSK REGION

R. Bol'shaia	Bol'sheretskii[87]	1703
R. Kamchatka	Nizhne-Kamchatsk[88]	1703
R. Oliutora	Oliutorskii[89]	1714
	Petropavlovsk[90]	1740
R. Tigil	Tigilsk[91]	1775
R. Kamchatka	Verkhne-Kamchatsk[92]	1697

F. OSTROGS OF THE OKHOTSK REGION

R. Ud	Udsk[93]	1680
R. Taui	Ust'-Tausk[94]	?

[87] Shchekatov, *op. cit.*, I, 513.

[88] Shchekatov, *op. cit.*, IV, 577.

[89] A native ostrog, several times attacked and finally captured by the Russians in 1714. S. V. Bakhrushin, "Istoricheskie sud'by Iakutii," *Iakutiia* (Leningrad, 1927), p. 283 (9).

[90] Shchekatov, *op. cit.*, IV, 1135.

[91] Shchekatov, *op. cit.*, VI, 193.

[92] Ogorodnikov, *op. cit.*, II, 106.

[93] *D.A.I.*, III, 83; Ogorodnikov, *op. cit.*, II, 50–51.

[94] Kudriashov, *op. cit.*, table IX.

INDEX

ABBREVIATIONS

c., convent   o., ostrog
l., lake   p., portage
m., monastery   r., river
            v., village

Index

[Prepared with the assistance of Martine Emert and Allene Johnson]

Abakansk o., 186
Abalatskii m., 182
Abatskii o., 185
Achansk o., 189
Achinsk o., 185
Achmet, Khan of the Golden Horde (1480), 62, 65
Agirka r., 170
Aidar r., 58, 61, 162
Aidarskaia, outpost, 156
Akhtyrka, on fortified line, 64
Akhtyrsk, 163
Akutan Pass, 88
Alaska, 88
Alazeevo o., 174
Alazeia r., 79, 174
Albazin o., 189
Aldan r., 78, 82–83, 149–50
Aldanskii p., 149
Aleksandro-Svirskii Troitskii m., 179
Aleutian Islands, 88
Alexander, Prince of Novgorod (Nevskii), 25–26, 31, 44
Amazar r.–Niugzi r.p., 149
Amginsk o., 78, 188
Amur r., 82–83, 173, 175; Amur system, 151; Amur r.–Enisei r., 151; Amur r.–Lena r., 151
Anadyr r., 79, 81; Anadyr r.–Aniui r.p., 151
Anadyrsk o., 79, 188
Anatolia, 2
Anegiske, see Onega
Angara r., 81, 172–73; see also Tunguska (Verkhniaia) r.
Aniui r.–Anadyr r.p., 151
Antoniev m. (Novgorod region), 177
Antoniev Siiskii m., 179
Arctic Ocean, 4, 8, 32, 39, 95–96
Aremzinsk v., 170
Argun' (Arkhunia) r., 83, 173
Argunsk o., 189

Arkhangelsk, 52–53; region, 179
Arkhangelskii m. (Arkhangelsk region), 179; (Pinega region), 180; (Usting region), 181
Arkhunia, see Argun'
Arseniev m., 181
Asia Minor, 2
Athabaska l., 3, 4; r., 3
Azov, Sea of, 58, 61, 64

Babasan v., 170
Bab'e l., on the Württemberg Canal system, 95
Baikal l., 81–83; Baikal l.–Shilka r. road, 83, 147, 173
Bailiff of the Portage (*Voloch'skyi Tiun*), 15, 31, 153
Bakaev shliakh, 60, 156
Bakhmutovskaia, southern frontier outpost, 156
Balagansk o., 81, 173, 186
Baltic–Caspian axis, 36; Moscow barred from, 41, 43
Barabinsk, on the Transsiberian, 101
Barancha r., 125
Barguzin r., 82
Barguzin (Barguzinsk) o., 82, 186
Barysh r., on the southern frontier, 159, 162
Bauntovsk o., 188
Belaia Kalitva r., 61
Belaia Vezha (Sarkel), 19, 65
Belgorod, 64, 163
Bel Kolodez r., 161
Beloe l., see Beloozero
Beloozero l., 26, 29–30, 39, 62, 117–18
Belskii o., 185
Belye Berega, outpost on the southern frontier, 157
Berda r.–Konskaia r.p., 132
Berestovaia r.–Severnyi Donets r.p., 126, 131

Berezina r.–Rutoveha r.p., 23; Berezina r.–Ushacha r.p., 23, 128, 132
Berezina, *small*, r., 23
Berezov o., 69, 169–71, 185
Berezovka r.–Nem r.p., 124, 142
Besednyi Nikolaevskii m., 178
Bezhitsy, 31–32, 42, 47
Biia r., 175
Bitiug r., 61
Black–Baltic Sea route, 16, 24; Russian expansion to, 54–66
Blagoveshchenskoe l., 93
Bludnaia r.–Iudoma r.p., 150
Bogoslovskii m. (Shenkursk region), 180
Boino l., 133
Bol'shaia Bereka r., 58, 112
Bol'sheretskii o., 190
Bolshoi Volochek p., 136
Bolshma r.–Pidma r.p., 119, 139
Bolva r., 109
Borisoglebskii m., 178
Boris, Prince of Tver (1445), 31
Boris Godunov, Tsar, 50
Borodava r., 118
Borodino, Battle of, 23
Borovaia r., 58, 61
Borovensk o., 161
Borovichi, 116
Bratsk o., 81, 186
Brianda (Brianta) r.–Niuemka r.p., 149; 83
Brosno l., 133
Bug, Zapadnyi, r., 127; Dnieper–Bug Canal, 127
Bukhinskii p., 124
Buriats, 81–82
Burpee, Lawrence J., 2–3
Butalsk o., 188
Buzha r.–Kliazma r.p., 112
Byk r., 58, 65
Bystraia r., 61
Bystraia Sosna r., 60, 61, 162

Canals: importance of, 89–103; Upper Volga Waterway, 92, 115; Tikhvin Waterway, 92–93, 116; Mariinsk system, 93–95, 117; Northern Catherina Canal, 95, 123; Ob'–Enisei Canal, 97, 145; Moscow–Volga, 99, 112–113; White Sea–Baltic Canal, 99; Tvertsa

Canal, 100; projected canals: Kama–Pechora, 95–97, 124; Volga–Don, 99–100, 65, 107
Canoemen, *see* Ushkuiniks
Captain's Bay (Dutch Harbor), 88
Carelen, *see* Karelia
Casimir, King of Poland-Lithuania (1480), 62
Caspian Sea, 4, 33, 35–36, 41; Caspian–Baltic trade route, 4, 33, 35; Caspian–Baltic axis, 36; Moscow barred from, 41
Catherine II, the Great, 22, 66
Chagoda r.–Volozhba r.p., 116
Chagodoshcha r., 116–17
Charandskoe l., 119
Charles XII (of Sweden), 52
Chaussées, land trails, 54
Chechuisk p., 75
Chelnova (Chelnava) r., 62, 160
Cherekha r.–Sudoma r.p., 136–37; Cherekha r.–Uza r.p., 43, 136–37
Cherepovskii Voskresenskii m., 178
Chereva r.–Voloshozero (Voloshevo) l.p., 138
Chernaia Kalitva r., 61
Chernava r., 160
Chernavsk, terminal of Kalmiusskaia Sakma, 61
Chernoruchenka r., 115
Cherta, continuous fortified line, 66
Chervlennaia r., 65
Chesha r.–Chizha r.p., 151
Cheshskaia Gulf, 151
Cheshskii p., 151
Chichiusk (Chichiuskii) o., 75, 186; *see* Chiuchiui
Chigla r., 61
China, fur trade with, 85
Chir r., 61
Chirka r., 29, 143
Chita o., 189
Chiuchiui r., 173; *see* Chichiusk
Chiusovaia (Chusovaia) r., 125, 144, 166
Chizha r.–Chesha r.p., 151
Chona r., 78, 148
Chudskoe l., 136
Chukchenemskii m., 179
Chulym r., crossed by the Transsiberian, 101
Church, first in Siberia, 86

Churchill r., 3
Churka r.–Titea r.p., 148
Chusovaia (Chiusovaia) r.–Pyshma r.p., 125, 144; Chusovaia r.–Iset r.p., 125, 144; Chusovaia Sylva r.–Zheravlia r.p., 125, 144
Chusovskoe l., 124
Clearwater r., 3
Columbia r., 3
Constantinople (Tsargorod), 11, 14, 19, 21
Copori, see Kopor'e
Coporie, see Kopor'e
"Country-beyond-the-Portage," see Zavolochie
Crimea, Crimean Peninsula, 54, 64
Crimean Tatars, 54; trails used by, 56–61; 64
Crusade, Fourth, 19
Cumberland l., 3

Dalmatov-Uspenskii m., 183
Dankov, see Donkov
Davy, Moret and, 2
Dederin (Dedrina), 47
Dedilov, 60, 61
Dedrina, see Dederin
Dem'iansk o., 172
Derevenitskii m., 177
Derzha r.–Ruza r.p., 32, 35, 110
Derzhkovskii p., 116
Desiatin c., 177
Desna r., 60, 108, 109; Desna r.–Iput' r.p., 131; Desna r.–Oster r.p., 131
Devlet-Girei, Khan of the Crimean Tatars (1571), 62, 63
Dezhnev, explorer, 79
Diocese, first in Siberia, 86
Diomede islands, 88
Disna r., 128, 132; Disna r.–Miadel l.p., 132
Dmitrov, 36
Dnieper r., 1, 5, 8, 13–14, 16, 18, 23, 28, 35–36, 42, 58, 60; Dnieper system, 127–32; Dnieper–Dniester, 127; Dnieper–Vistula, 127; Dnieper–Bug Canal, 127; Dnieper–Niemen, 127–28; Dnieper–Western Dvina, 42, 128–30; Dnieper–Volga, 42, 130–31; Dnieper–Dnieper, 131; Dnieper–Don, 131; Dnieper–Sea of Azov, 131–32;

Dnieper–Luchesa r.p., 23, 133; Dnieper r.–Vazuza r.p., 113, 130; Dnieper r.–Veritsa(?) r.p., 129, 133
Dolgoe l., 115, 118, 139; Dolgoe l.–Volotskoe l.p., 118, 139
Dolonsk o., 188
Don r., 36, 56, 58, 60–62, 64–66; Don system, 126; Don–Dnieper, 126; Don–Volga, 126; Don r.–Shat r.p., 108, 126
Donets r., 60–61, 64–66; Severnyi Donets r.–Berestovaia r.p., 126, 131; Severnyi Donets r.–Seim r.p., 126, 131; 163
Donkov (Dankov), 61, 63
Donskaia o., 65
Donskoi, see Ivanovich, Dmitri
Dorogobuzh, 23
Drisa r., 135
Drut' r.–Obol r.p., 129, 133; Drut' r.–Usvitsa r.p., 129, 132
Dryginskaia Doroga, 157
Dubna r., 113
Dukhov or Spaso-Kamennyi m., 181
Dukhov c. (Novgorod region), 177
Dukhovskii m. (Borovichi region), 178
Dunikalova pustyn', 181
Dutch Harbor (Captain's Bay), 88
Dvina r., see Northern Dvina, Western Dvina
Dvin'e l.–Kunia r.p., 134, 137
Dvinka r., 134
Dymskii Antoniev m., 178
Dzhurich r.–Severnaia Kel'tma r.p., 123, 141

Egypt, 2
Ekaterinburg (Sverdlovsk), 95, 100
Elan' r., 61
Elets r.–Sob' r.p., 29, 144
Elogui r., 145, 175
Eloguiskii p., 145
Elovka r., 124
Elsha r.–Votria r.p., 130, 133
Embakh r., 136
Emenets l., 114, 135; Emenets l.–Ozerishche l.p., 138
Emenka r., 135
Emetskii Blagoveshchenskii m., 179
Emetskii Predtechenskii c., 179
Emetskoe l., 29

Emtsa r.–Onega r.p., 29, 140
Enisei r., 73, 75, 145–48, 151, 175; Enisei system, 145–48; Enisei–Ob', 145–46; Enisei–Amur, 147; Enisei–Lena, 147–48, 151; Enisei r.–Piasina r.p., 148, 175
Eniseisk o., 73, 75, 78, 81, 83, 146, 171–72; 175, 187; Eniseisk people, 83
Entala r.–Vokhma r.p., 121, 141
Entrepreneurs (*Opytovshchiks*), 73
Epifan, 63, 158
Erakleia l.–Ingoda r.p., 147
Esaulovskaia-Aksai r., 65
Esthonia, 48, 50
Estland, *see* Esthonia
Eravinsk o., 187
Eurasia, natural pivot of, 36
Ezerishche l., 135

Ferapontov m., 178
Fertile Crescent, 2
Finland, 48–49, 53
Finland, Gulf of, 44–46, 92
Finns, 34
Fords, in the advance to Black Sea, 64; 157–62
Fortified Line of 1571, *see* Line of 1571
Fur trade, 8, 28, 67, 84–85, 88; expansion-exhaustion tempo, 30; Moscow, 41; Novogorod, 41; bootleg, 88; markets in Leipzig and in China, 85; statistics on Russian furs, 85–86; furs pay administrative expenses of Siberia, 86; *see also* Iasak

Galich Mountains, on the southern frontier, 157
Germans, Novgorod advances against, 20–21; Baltic Germans, 26, 44
Glubokoe, 23
Glushitskii m., 181
Gnezdovo, 16
Godunov, Tsar Boris, 50
Golden Horde, 41, 62
Gonam r., 82, 149
Goritskii m., 178
Goriun r., 93
Gor'kii, 99
Gornyi c. (Vologda region), 181
Gorodenskoe Gorodishche, on the southern frontier, 159

Govniukha r.–Ukhta r.p., 142, 143
Grachi o., 65
Gridnevo, 23
Gudanow, Boris; *see* Godunov, Boris
Gustavus Adolphus, Örebro (1617) speech, 47–49; Stockholm (1617) speech, 49–52; understood significance of rivers, 47–52
Gzhat' r., 23, 36, 113, 130; Gzhat' r.–Obsha (?) r.p., 113, 130; Gzhat' r.–Voria r.p., 23, 36, 113

Hanseatic League, 27
Hedeby, 14
History, course of Russian, 103–104
Hotynka r.–Luga r.p., 137
Hudson Bay, 3
Huron l., 3

Iablonnoi range, 82–83
Iablonov, 64
Iagodna, settlement on the southern frontier, 157
Iakovlevskii Forest, on the southern frontier, 158
Iakroma r.–Kliazma r.p., 113
Iakutsk o., 78, 81–83, 173–74, 188; military commanders of, 82–83
Ial-Mal peninsula, 29
Ialutorovskii o., 185
Iama (Jama), later called Iamburg, 45–47, 50
Iamanets l., 114
Iamburg, *see* Iama
Iamnoe l., 116
Iamysh Salt Lake, 168
Iana r., 79, 150, 173; Iana system, 150; Iana r.–Lena r.p., 150; Iana r.–Indigirka r.p., 150
Iankovskaia pustyn', 181
Iaroslavl, 38
Iasak, tribute in furs, 68, 73, 75, 84; 165–175 *passim; see* Fur trade
Iasino o., 116
Iasolda r.–Shara r.p., 127
Iatriia r., 30, 143–44; Iatriia r.–Shchugor r.p., 143–44
Iauza r.–Kliazma r.p., 111
Iavon r., 115
Iazholbitse v., 42
Iksha r., 99

Ilim r., 75, 81, 147; Ilim r.–Muka r.p., 81, 147
Ilimsk o., 75, 187
Il'inskii c. (Tiumen region), 182
Il'inskii m. (Vologda region), 181
Ilmen l., 1, 8, 13, 32, 44
Ilmer, see Ilmen
Ilovlia r., 65, 107, 126; Ilovlia r.–Kamyshinka r.p., 107, 126
Ilovskii Forest, on the southern frontier, 163
Ilych r.–Sosva r.p., 143–44
Inbatsk o., 187
Indigirka r., 79, 150; Indigirka r.–Iana r.p., 150
Ingoda r.–Erakleia l.p., 147, 173
Insar, 64
Ioannovskii c., 181
Iosifov Volokolamskii m., 179
Ipatievskii Troitskii m., 179
Iput' r.–Desna r.p., 131
Irgen l., 82, 147
Irgensk (Irgenskii) o., 147, 187
Irkut r., 81
Irkutsk o., 81, 173, 187
Irtysh r., 67, 69, 124–25, 168, 170
Iset r.–Chusovaia r.p., 125, 144
Isetskii o., 185
Ishimskii o., 185
Isna r., 62
Istochino l., 115
Istra r., 15, 32; Istra r.–Lama r.p., 111
Itankinsk (Itantsinsk) o., 187
Itantsinsk (Itankinsk) o., 187
Itkla r., 93
Iudoma r., 78, 150; Iudoma r.–Bludnaia r.p., 150; –Urak r.p., 150
Iudomskii Krest p., 150
Iug r., 120–22
Iugria, 30–31, 34
Iukagirs, 79
Iurievskii m. (Novgorod region), 177
Iuza r.–Sharzhenga r.p., 120, 141
Iuzhnaia Kel'tma r., 123
Iuzhnaia Myl'ia r.–Severnaia Myl'ia r.p., 142–43
Iuzhnaia Mylva r.–Severnaia Mylva r.p., 142–43
Ivan III, the Great (1469), 42–43, 62
Ivan IV, the Terrible, 43; Livonian War, 44–45

Ivangorod (Iwanogrod, Ivanogrod), 44–47, 49–51
Ivan'kovo r., on the Moscow–Volga Canal, 99
Ivanogrod, see Ivangorod
Ivanovich, Dmitri, Grand Prince of Moscow, hero of Kulikovo, 56
Ivanovskii c. (Arkhangelsk region), 179
Iwanogrod, see Ivangorod
Izhma r., and v., 142; 171
Izhora r., 26
Izium, 58; founded, 64
Iziumskaia Sakma, 58, 60, 65, 160, 161

Jama, see Iama

Kabansk o., 187
Kadiak (Kodiak), 88
Kakolna r., on the southern frontier, 158
Kalka r., 20
Kalmius r., 58, 61; Kalmius r.–Voch'ia r.p., 131
Kalmiusskaia Sakma, 56, 58, 160–61
Kaluga, on old fortified line, 62
Kama r., 29, 30, 67, 69, 121–25, 141; Kama r.–Uzhga r.p., 122; Kama-Vishera-Lozva p. route, 69
Kamar r., 174
Kamen', Ural Mountains, 171
Kamennyi Ford, 159; m., 178; p., 144
Kamshino l., 135
Kamyshinka r., 65; Kamyshinka r.–Ilovlia r.p., 107
Kan r., 75, 101
Kansk o., 75, 187
Kara, Gulf of, 151
Karachev, 159
Karbatka r., on the Württemberg Canal system, 95
Karelia (Karelian Lakes), 45, 51
Kargonaeva r., 159
Kariazhemskii Nikolaevskii m., 181
Karpov, outpost, 64, 161
Kas' r., 97, 145–46; Kas'–Ket' Canal, 97; Kas' r.–Ket' r.p., 145–46
Kashira, on old fortified line, 62
Kasimov Ford, 160
Kasplia l. and r., 13, 16, 22, 130
Katun' r., 175
Katym r.,–Zeia r.p., 149

Katynka r., 13, 16, 22–23, 130, 133;
Katynka r.–Krapivka r.p., 23, 130,
133
Kaurdat o., 169
Kavast r.–Paala r., 136
Kazan, 43, 62; Tatar Khanate of, 41, 166
Kazanskoi Bozh'ei Materi m. (Tomsk
region), 182
Kel'tma r., Iuzhnaia, 123; Severnaia,
123; Severnaia Kel'tma r.–Dzhurich
r.p., 141; Northern and Southern
Kel'tma, 95
Kem r., 145; Kem r.–Ket' r.p., 146
Kena r., 29, 138
Kenozero l., 29, 138
Kesadra r., 116; Kesadra r.–S'ezzha r.p.,
116
Keshemskoe l., 95
Ket' r., 72–73; 145–46, 172; Ket'–Kas'
Canal, 97; Ket' r.–Toma r.p., 145;
Ket' r.–Kas' r.p., 145–46; Ket' r.–
Enisei r.p., 145, 172
Ketsk o., 72–73, 172
Kexholm, 45–47, 50–51
Keza r.–S'ezzha r.p., 116, 138
Khabarov, E. P., explorer, 83
Khamun r., 174
Khatanga r.–Piasina r.p., 148
Khazars, 19
Khilka r., 82, 147, 173
Khimka r., 99
Khmelnitsa r.–Tutka r.p., 120, 140
Kholka r., 161
Khoper r., 61
Khotmyshskoe Gorodishche, 162
Khot'slavskii p., 116
Khristorozhdestvenskii m., 183
Khupta r.–Riasa r.p., 107, 126
Khutynskii Varlaamskii m., 177
Khvalin Sea, see Caspian Sea
Khvost r.–Vydra r.p., 130; 133
Kiakhta o., 187
Kichug r.–Maramitsa r.p., 121, 141
Kiev (or Kievan Russia), 3, 14, 24–25,
131; Kievan state, 11–24
Kirenga r., 75, 173
Kirensk o., 75, 188
Kirghiz tribes, 72
Kirilov m. (Novgorod region), 177
Kirilov Beloozerskii m., 178
Kirilov Novoozerskii m., 178

Kirtas r., 143
Kliazma r., 35–36, 38, 111–13; Kliazma
r.–Skhodnia r.p., 111; Kliazma r.–
Iauza r.p., 111; Kliazma r.–Buzha
r.p., 112; Kliazma r.–Vlena r.p., 113;
Kliazma r.–Iakroma r.p., 113
Klimetskii m., 179
Klopskii Troitskii m., 177
Kobelsha r., 157
Kobra r.–Lunia r.p., 122, 141
Kodiak (Kadiak), 88
Kokshenga r., 139–40; Kokshenga r.–
Sukhona r.p., 140
Koliazin, 46
Koloksha r.–Pleshcheevo l.p., 112
Kolomak r., 58, 156
Kolomna, 36, 38; seizure of, 38; cus-
toms duties, 38
Kolotsa r., 22
Kolotskii m., 23
Kolp' r.–Lid' r.p., 117
Kolpna r., 158
Kolyma r., 79, 150–51; Kolyma system,
150–51; Kolyma–Penzhina, 150; Ko-
lyma–Anadyr, 151
Kolva r., 29, 97, 124; see also Visherka
r., 29
Konevskii m., 179
Konskaia r.–Berda r.p., 132
Konskie Vody r., 58
Kontaishin, settlements, 175
Kopor'e, 47–52
Kopylov, explores Aldan r., 78
Korga r., 174
Korkinskii o., 185
Korniliev Komelskii m., 181
Korocha o., 64; r., 161
Korotkii Volok p., 118–19
Korotkoe l., 118
Korotoiak, 163
Korytna r., 158
Koryzha r., 157
Kosha r.–Volochnia r.p., 115
Kosogirskii o., 189
Kostroma r., 31, 38–39, 119–20, 140;
Kostroma r.–Tolshma r.p., 120, 140
Kovzha r., 29, 93, 117; Kovzha r.–Vyte-
gra r.p., 117; Kovzha r.–Beloe l., 29
Kozelsk, on old fortified line, 62
Kozelskaia abatis, 161
Kozlov, 64, 65, 160

Krapivka (or Lelevka) r., 16, 23, 130, 133; Krapivka r.–Katynka, 16, 23, 130, 133
Krasivaia Mecha r., 56
Krasnogorskii m., 180
Krasnoiarsk o., 78, 81–82, 171, 175, 187
Krestnyi m., 180
Krivoi Bor, outpost on the southern frontier, 157
Krugloe l.–Volochanka r.p., 146
Krupino l., 93
Krynka r.–Volch'ia r.p., 132
Kubenskoe l., 29–30, 118
Kuchum, Tatar Khan of Sibir, 68
Kudanga r.–Pyshcug r.p., 121, 141
Kulenga (Kulinga) r.–Nizhniaia Tunguska r.p., 147
Kulikovo, plain of, battlefield and portage, 56
Kuloi r., 29, 142; Kuloi r.–Pinega r.p., 29, 142
Kumarsk o., 189
Kunia r., 16, 134, 137; Kunia r.–Usviat r.p., 134, 137; Kunia r.–Dvin'e r.p., 134, 137
Kupa r., 147
Kuprino l., 16, 130
Kurgan, on the Transsiberian, 101
Kurile Islands, 88
Kurlak r., 61
Kursk, 63
Kushtskii m., 181
Kust, outpost on the southern frontier, 158
Kuta r., 147, 173
Kuzemkina Dubrova, outpost, 158
Kuznetsk o., 72, 185

Lache l., 118–19, 139; Lache l.–Vytegra r.p., 139
Ladoga (Nevo) l., 13, 26, 29, 44–46, 49–53, 116–17
Laduga l., see Ladoga l.
Lama r., 15, 32, 35, 111; Lama r.–Voloshna r.p., 111; Lama r.–Istra r.p., 111
Lapkaev, 173–74
Lebedino l., on the Tikhvin Waterway, 93
Lelevka (Krapivka) r., on Western Dvina–Dnieper route, 16, 130

Lena r., 75, 78–81, 83, 148–50, 173–74; Lena system, 148–50; Lena–Enisei, 148; Lena–Amur, 148–49; Lena–Ul'ia, 149; Lena–Okhota, 150; Lena r.–Iana r.p., 150
Leningrad (St. Petersburg), 36, 100; Leningrad–Moscow Railroad, 92, 100
Lenskii p., 147
Lesnoi Voronezh r., 160
Lezha r., 119–20, 140; Lezha r.–Obnora r.p., 119, 140; Lezha r.–Monza r.p., 120, 140
Lialikinskii m., 179
Lid' r.–Kolp' r.p., 117
Lijfland, see Livonia
Likhvin, on old fortified line, 62
Line, of 1571, 63–66, 155–59; (of 1637–47), 160–61; (of 1571–1642), 162–63
Lipovetskii Forest, 159
Lipovitsa r., 160
Lithuania (Lithuanians), 21–22, 41–42, 62; see also Niemen
Liubech Convention (1097), 17
Liubosha r., 158
Liuto l., 116; r., 116
Livna r., on the southern frontier, 157
Livny, 63, 160
Livonia (Livonian War), 44–45, 49
Lodenitsa, see Lodyzhnitsa
Lodyzhnitsa (or Lodenitsa), 16
Lomov r., 162; Nizhnii, 160; Verkhnii, 160; see Lomova
Lomova r., on the southern frontier, 159, 162; see Lomov
Lopasnia r., 35, 110; Lopasnia r.–Pakhra r.p., 35, 110
Lopatov m., 181
Lovat' r., 5, 8, 13, 16, 18, 28, 135, 137–38; Lovat' system, 137–38; Lovat'–Volga, 137; Lovat'–Western Dvina, 28, 137; Lovat' r.–Usmen l.p., 18, 135, 137
Lower Tunguska r., see Tunguska r.
Lozva r., 69, 124, 144; Lozva r.–Vishera r.p., 124, 144
Lozvinsk o., 69
Luchanskoe l.–Otolovo l.p., 133; Luchanskoe l.–Zhadenie l.p., 133, 137
Luchesa r., 23, 129; Luchesa l.–Dnieper r.p., 23, 129; Luchesa r.–Dnieper r.p., 23, 129, 133

Luga r., 44, 137; Luga r.–Hotynka r.p., 137; Luga r.–Soba r.p., 137
Lunia r., 122, 141; Lunia r.–Kobra r.p., 122, 141
Luza r., 122

Mackenzie r., 3
Maia r., 78, 83, 149–50
Makar'evo-Unzhenskii m., 179
Makarievskaia pustyn', 180
Makovsk o., 73, 145, 172, 185
Malaia Nerl' r., 112
Malyi Volochek p., 136
Manchus, 84
Mangazeia, 72–73, 75, 171, 185
Maramitsa r.–Kichug r.p., 121, 141
Mariinsk System, of canals, 93
Matko l., 99
Mecha r., 60, 62, 157
Mechoshnaia o., protects portage from the Volga to the Don, 65
Medvezhia Gora, on railway paralleling the White Sea–Baltic Canal, 100
Meleskii o., 185
Merchik r., 60
Merl' r., 60
Meshchera, southern frontier town, 155
Mesopotamia, 2; Russian, see Mezhdurieche
Mestilov Gates, 159
Mezen, Gulf of, 151
Mezen r., 29, 143
Mezha r., 130
Mezhdugorskii m., 182
Mezhduriechie, Russian Mesopotamia, 35
Mezhevaia Utka r.–Rezh(?) r.p., 125, 144
Mezhvoloch'e l., 116
Miadel l., 128; Miadel l.–Disna r.p., 132
Miadelka r., 128
Minsk, Russian armies fail to meet at, 22
Mississippi r., 3
Mius r., 132
Modlona r., 118
Mokoshevichi, outpost, 157
Moksha r., 62
Mokshanskii Forest, 159

Molochnye Vody r., 58
Molodova r., 159
Mologa r., 32, 39, 92, 116–17
Moloma r., 121
Molosno l., 135
Monasteries, 4; in the struggle between Moscow and Novgorod, 39; list of, 177–84; Novgorod region, 177; Tikhvin region, 178; Beloozero region, 178; Cherepovets region, 178; Ustiuzhna region, 178; Borovichi region, 178; St. Petersburg-Olenets regions, 179; Moscow region, 179; Kostroma region, 179; Arkhangelsk region, 179; Shenkursk region, 180; Onega region, 180; Pinega region, 180; Vologda region, 181; Griazovets region, 181; Kadnikov region, 181; Solvychegodsk region, 181; Ustiug region, 181; Totma region, 182; Tobolsk region, 182; Verkhoturie region, 182; Turinsk region, 182; Tuimen region, 182; Tomsk region, 182; Tara region, 182; Eniseisk region, 183; Isetsk region, 183; Berezov region, 183; Turukhansk region, 183; Krasnoiarsk region, 183; Kirensk region, 183; Iakutsk region, 183; Irkutsk region, 183; Selenginsk region, 184; Albazin region, 184; Bratsk region, 184; Neviansk region, 184; first in Siberia, 86; see by monasteries, ostrogs
Monza r.–Lezha r.p., 120, 140; Monza r.–Shuia r.p., 120, 140
Moret and Davy, 2
Moscow, 3, 5, 15, 33; pivot of Eurasian empire, 35–88; crossroads of waterways and trunk lines, 36; capital, 35–36; domination of upper and middle Volga, 36, 38; domination of Caspian–Baltic axis, 41–54; silk and fur trade, 41; struggle with Novgorod, 33, 38–43; fur tribute, 84; China trade, 85; raids by Moscow into Siberia, 84; expansion to world empire, 54–88; expansion to Black Sea, 54–66, 155–163; expansion to Pacific, 66–88; port of five seas, 97; Moscow–Volga Canal, 97–99; Moscow–St. Petersburg (Leningrad) Railroad, 100

Moskva (Moscow) r., 15, 18, 23, 32, 35–36, 38, 99, 110–11; Moskva r.–Protva r.p., 23, 35, 110–11; Nizhnii Novgorod route, 36, 38
Mozh r., 60
Mozhaisk, 23; seizure of by Moscow, 38; customs duties at, 38
Mshaga r., 44, 137
Msta r., 15, 28, 32, 38, 92, 115–16; Msta system, 115–16; Msta r.–Volga r.p., 115–16, 138; Msta r.–Pechenevo l.p., 116, 138; Msta r.–Tvertsa r.p., 32
Mstino l., 92; Mstino l.–Tsna r.p., 115, 138
Mstislav (first son of Vladimir Monomakh), 17
Mstislavoviches, family of princes, 17
Mtsensk, outpost, 60, 64, 158
Muka r., 147, 173; Muka r.–Ilim r.p., 147
Mukhovets r.–Pina r.p., 127
Mungalsk (Mongolian) settlements, 175
Mungut, Chinese town, 174
Muravskii Shliakh, 56–61, 63, 65, 156–58, 160
Mutnaia r.–Zelenaia r.p., 29, 151
Myl'ia r., Iuzhnaia Myl'ia, 142–43; Severnaia Myl'ia, 142–43
Mylva r., Iushnaia Mylva, 142–43; Severnaia Mylva, 142–42
Mzha r., 156

Naharina p., 2
Napoleon's march to Moscow, 22, 100
Narfwen, see Narva
Narfweske r., see Narova r.
Narfwiske r., see Narova r.
Naroch l., 128, 132; r., 128, 132
Narova r., 44, 49–51
Narva, 44–45, 49–51, 53; Battle of, 52
Narviske r., see Narova r.
Narwen, see Narva
Narym o., 72, 170–71, 175, 186
Nasva r., 135–36; Nasva r.–Usha r.p., 138; Nasva r.–Velikaia r.p., 136
Naul r., 174
Navolok l., at portage between the Keza and the S'ezzha, 116
Neiva (or Rezh?) r.–Mezhevaia Utka r.p., 125, 144

Nelson r., 3
Nem' r., 29, 123–24; Nem' r.–Berezovka r.p., 124, 142
Nema (Nem' or Nef) r., 123–24
Nemilenskoe o., 189
Nepriadva r., 56, 158
Nercha r., 82, 173
Nerchinsk o., 82–83, 189; Treaty of, 83
Nerl' r., Bolshaia, 112; Malaia Nerl' r.–Solma r.p., 112
Neruch r., 109, 158
Neva, 13, 25–26; Prince Alexander of Novgorod defeats Swedes on the, 44; gives Russians direct access to Baltic, 45–46; in Swedish hands, 51–52; in Russian hands, 53
Nevel l., 135
Nev'ia o., 166; r., 166
Nevo l., see Ladoga l.
Newland (also Nyland), 50
New Mariinsk Canal, 93
Nicholas I, instructs building of Moscow–St. Petersburg Railroad, 100
Niemen r., ancient axis of Lithuania, 8
Nienshants, site of St. Petersburg (Leningrad), 45–46, 52–53
Nikitskii m. (Cherepovets region), 178
Nikolaevskaia pustyn' (Shenkursk region), 180
Nikolaevskii m. (Shenkursk region), 180
Nikolaevskii m. (Turinsk region), 182
Nikolaevskii m. (Verkhoturie region), 182
Nikolaevskii Karelskii m., 179
Nikolaevskii Modenskii m., 178
Nikolskii m., 179
Nilosarskaia pustyn', 178
Nipissing l., 3
Nitsa r., 125
Niuemka r.–Brianda (Brianta) r.p., 149
Niugzi (Niugchi, Niunzi, Niunchi, Niuga, Niuzia) r.–Amazar r.p., 149; Urka (Ura, Ui) r.p., 148
Niukhcha, 53
Niukria r., 174
Nizhne-Kamchatsk o., 190
Nizhne-Kolymsk o., 79, 188
Nizhne-Udinsk o., 82, 187
Nizhne-Viliuisk o., 187

Nizhnee o., 174
Nizhnii Bratsk o., 172
Nizhnii Novgorod, 36, 38; acquired by Moscow, 38–39; beginning of old fortified line, 62
Nizhniaia Tunguska r., *see* Tunguska
Nogai country, the, 64
Nogai Tatars, 54, 58–61
Nogaiskaia Doroga, 56, 60–61, 65, 159
Normans, in the commercial domain of Constantinople, 19
North America, Russian expansion in, 88
Northern Catherina Canal (Severo-Ekaterininskii), 95
Northern Dvina, 39, 43, 93–94, 140–42; country, 43; system of canals, 93–94; system of rivers, 140–42; Northern Dvina–Onega, 140; Northern Dvina–Voloshka, 140; Northern Dvina–Northern Dvina, 140–41; Northern Dvina–Pechora, 142; Northern Dvina–White Sea, 142
Northern Kel'tma r., 95; *see* Kel'tma r.
Nosva r., 135
Nöteborg, *see* Oreshek
Noteburg, *see* Oreshek
Novgorod, 3; region, 14; boundaries of, 15, 20; gateway to Europe and the Urals, 25–34; colonizing center, 26; river boatmen of, 27; on verge of hunger, 28, 31–32; districts of, 28; trappers of, 30; Ilmen region, 31, 33; fur empire of, 34; sphere of influence, 34, 38; canoemen or braves of, 39; relations and struggle with Moscow, 41–42; in Swedish hands, 46–47, 51; grain for, 54; raids by, 84
Novo-Arkhangelsk (Sitka) o., 88
Novo-Bogoroditsk o., 65
Novonikolaevsk, *see* Novosibirsk
Novosibirsk (Novonikalaevsk), on Transsiberian, 101
Novosil, outposts sent out from, 158
Novyi Torg, *see* Torzhok
Nydyb r.–Volosnitsa r.p., 122, 141
Nyen, *see* Neva
Nyland, *see* Newland
Nystadt, Treaty of, 22, 44, 53

Ob', Gulf of, 146, 151

Ob' r., 29–30, 67, 69, 72–73, 97, 124–25, 143–46, 169, 171, 175; Ob' system, 144–46; Ob'–Pechora, 143–44; Ob'–Volga, 124–25, 144; Ob'–Enisei, 145–46; Ob'–Enisei Canal, 97, 100, 145–46
Obdorsk o., 72, 171, 186
Obnora r.–Lezha r.p., 119, 140
Obol r., 135; Obol r.–Drut' r.p., 129, 133
Obsha r.–Gzhat' r.p., 113, 130
Odoev, on old fortified line, 62
Odrovo l., 135
Oemokon (Omolon) r., 150
Oginskii Canal, 127
Ognega, *see* Onego l.
Oka r., 32, 35–36, 38, 56, 60, 62, 64; 107–17 *passim*
Okhota r.–Urak r.p., 150
Okhotsk, Sea of, 78, 83; o., 188
Okhotskii p., 150
Okov, forest of, source of the Dnieper, 11
Olekma r., 78, 83, 148–49, 173–74
Olekminsk o., 78, 188
Oleshan, outpost, 159
Olgerd, Lithuanian Prince (1345–1377), 22
Olintorskii o., 190
Olshanka r., 161
Olshansk, 64
Olym r., 60–61
Om r., near the Transsiberian, 101
Omolon (Oemokon) r., 150
Omovzha r., 136
Omsk, on the Transsiberian, 101
Onega, Gulf of, 53, 99
Onega r., 29, 51, 118–19, 138–40; system, 138; Onega–Ladoga, 138; Onega–Volga, 139; Onega–Northern Dvina, 139; Onega r.–Enitsa r.p., 140
Onego l., 29–30, 51, 53, 117, 138–39; Onego l.–Vytegra r.p., 29–30, 51, 53
Onezhskoe l., *see* Onego l.
Opytovshchiks (entrepreneurs), 73
Orchik r., 58
Orel, town, 159
Orel' r., 58, 126
Orel'ka r., 58
Oreshek (Noteburg, Schlüsselburg) o., 44–47, 49–50, 53
Osered r., *see* Seret

Oshevenskii m., 180
Oskol r., 58, 60, 63–64, 126, 161; old town, 63; new town, 64
Oskolets r.–Seim r.p., 126, 131
Osma r.–Ugra r.p., 109, 131
Osokor o., 65
Oster r.–Desna r.p., 131
Ostiaks (government tribute-paying), 72, 169–71
Ostozh'e, landing place on Kama–Pechora route, 95
Ostrogs (in Siberia), 165–75, 185–90; monasteries in relation to, 177–84; built on the advance toward the Black Sea, 155–63; see Furs, Monasteries, Portages
Ostrogozhsk, 64
Osuga r., 115
Osviacha (Gorodok), 21
Otolovo l.–Luchanskoe l.p., 133
Ottawa r., 3
Outpost: Donets, 156; Putivl, 156–57; Rysk, 157; others, 157; Epifan, 158; Dedilov, 158; Novosil, 158; Mtsensk, 158; Orel and Karachev, 159; Meshchera, 159; Shatsk, 159; Riassk (Riazhsk), 159
Ozerishche l.–Emenets l.p., 135; Ozerishche l.–Odrovo l.p., 135

Paala r.–Kavast r.p., 136
Pacific Ocean, 2, 4, 8; expansion of Muscovite Russia to the Pacific, 66–88
Pakhnuttsova Doroga, 60, 63
Pakhra r., 35, 110; Pakhra r.–Lopasnia r.p., 35, 110; tributary of Moskva, 35
Paleostrovskii m., 179
Panteleimonov m., 177
Para r., 62
Pavlov Obnorskii m., 181
Pechenovo l.–Msta r.p., 116, 138
Pechora r., 29–31, 67, 124, 143–44; Pechora system, 143–44; Pechora–Mezen, 143; Pechora–Northern Dvina, 143; Pechora–Volga, 143; Pechora–Ob', 143–44
Pechorskii Volok, Pechora portage, 95, 124
Peibas l., see Peipus l.
Peipus l., 26, 50, 136

Pelenovo l., 116
Pelshemskii m., 181
Pelym o., 69, 160–70, 175, 186
Peno l.–Zhadenie l.p., 114, 133
Penzhina r.–Uiagan r.p., 150
Penzhinsk o., 188
Penzhinskii (or Penzhinsk) p., 150
Perechnaia r.–Sheksna r.p., 119, 139
Perekop, 58
Peremyzhskaia abatis, 161
Perevolochna p., 129
Perevolochnia r., 108; Perevolochnia r.–Pshevka r.p., 126
Perm, 31, 69
Perm Velikaia, instructions of Tsar to, 160
Pernava r., 136
Pes' r., 116
Peskovataia Tulucheeva (Podgornaia) r., 61
Peter I, the Great, 22; wins the Baltic coast, 44–45, 52–53; builds canals, 92, 99
Pertominskii m., 179
Petropavlovsk (in the Far East) o., 190
Petropavlovsk (on the Ishim), 101
Peza r., 29; Peza r.–Sake–Rubikha r.p., 143; Peza r.–Lake–Tsilma r.p., 143
Pezskii p., 143
Piasina p., 148; Piasina r.–Enisei r.p., 148; Piasina r.–Khatanga r.p., 148
Pidma r.–Bolshma r.p., 119, 139
Pil'va r.–Yk r.p., 123, 142
Pina r.–Mukhovets r.p., 127
Pinega r., 29; Pinega r.–Kuloi r.p., on Northern Dvina–White Sea route, 142
Pinezhskii p., 142
Pleshcheevo l.–Koloksha r.p., 112
Pnevitsy, outpost, 157
Pocha r., 138
Pochozero l., 138
Podgornaia r., see Peskovataia Tulucheeva r.
Podkamennaia Tunguska r., see Tunguska
Poairkov, Vasilii, explorer, 82–83; discovers Amur agricultural region, 83
Pokrovskii c. (Turinsk region), 182
Pokrovskii c. (Verkhoturie region), 182
Pokrovskii m. (Arkhangelsk region), 179

Pola r., 28, 33, 114–15, 133, 137; Pola r.–Runa r.p., 114, 137; Pola r.–Vydbino l.p., 133, 137
Poland (Poles), 22, 46, 52–53, 62; see also Lithuania
Polia r., 112
Polnyi Voronezh r., 160
Polotsk, region, 14; princes and role of, 18, 21, 26
Pontus, Sea of, see Black Sea
Porech'e, Russian army retreats to, 23
Porozovitsa r., 29, 93, 118, 140; Porozovitsa r.–Slavianka r., 118, 140
Portagers (Volochane), 20–21, 153–54
Portages (Voloki), and the important river systems, 107–51; in Siberia, especially, 165–75; monasteries in relation to, 177–84; on the road to the Black Sea, 155–63; Western Dvina–Dnieper, 155–64; sources of dispute, 15; basically important to Novgorod, 32–33; portages and portagers, 20–21, 153–54; see Monasteries, Ostrogs
Posolskii Preobrazhenskii m., 183
Povenets, on the route from the Baltic to the White Sea, 53, 99
Pozdyshka r., on the Württemberg Canal system, 95
Pra r., 112
Predtechenskaia pustyn', 180
Preobrazhenskii m. (Shenkursk region), 180
Pripet' r., 127
Pronia r., 107
Protva v., 23, 35, 110; Protva r.–Moskva r.p., 23, 35, 110
Psel r., 60
Pshevka r., 108; Pshevka r.–Perevolochnia r.p., 108, 126
Pshevskii Hill, on the southern frontier, 158
Psiol r., on the southern frontier, 156
Pskov, 43, 44
Pskovskoe l., 136
Ptich r.–Svisloch r.p., 128
Punema r., 119
Pupovo, landing place on Kama–Pechora route, 95
Pushnia r., 121
Putivl, important outpost in line of defense, 63, 156–57

Pyshchug r.–Kudanga r.p., 121, 141
Pyshma r., 101, 125, 144; Pyshma r.–Chusovaia r.p., 125, 144

Rabaganskii m., 181
Rafailovskii Troitskii m., 183
Railroads in relation to portages, 100–1, 103; Transsiberian, 100–1; Smolensk to Moscow, 100
Ranovaia r., 107
Resa r., 109
Reseta r.–Snezhat' r.p., 108
Ressa r., 109; Ressa r.–Volok r.p., 109, 131
Resseta r.–Snezhat' r.p., 108
Rezh r.–Mezhevaia Utka r.p., 125; 144
Riasa r., 107, 126; Riasa r.–Khupta r.p., 107, 126
Riassk, see Riazhsk
Riazan, on old fortified line, 62
Riazhsk (Riassk), 63, 159
Riga, 20
Roseta r.–Snezhat' r.p., 108
Rostislav Mstislavovich (sixth son of Mstislav), 17
Rostov, region of, 14, 20, 26, 33, 38
Rostovskoe l., 112
Rozdornyi o., 162
Rozhdestvenskii c. (Eniseisk region), 183
Rozhdestvenskii m. (Neviansk region), 184
Rozsokhi, outpost, 157
Rubikha r.–unknown lake–Peza r.p., 143
Rubikha r.–Lake–Peza r.p., 143
Rudnia, on Napoleon's line of march, 23
Runa r.–Pola r.p., 114, 137
Rurik, distributes the towns of Russia, 26
Rusa, Valdai Hills region, 43
Russia, Kievan, 13–24
Russian expansion into Asia, planned, 72
Russo-Turkish War (1768–1774), 22
Rutoveha r.–small Berezina r.p., 23
Ruza r., 15, 32, 110–11; Ruza r.–Derzha r.p., 110
Rybinsk, Russia's waterway center, 93, 99
Rybnoi o., 187

Rylsk, frontier town, 63, 159
Rzhev, Moscow–Rzhev Railway, 100

St. Petersburg, see Leningrad
Salar l., in Siberia, 173
Samara r., 58, 131–32
Samintsovo l., 115
Samoied tribes, pay tribute in furs, 72
Sarkel (Belaia Vezha), at portage from
  the Volga to the Don, 19, 65, 156
Sara r., 112; see Sarra r.
Sarra (Sara) r.–Solma r.p., 112
Saskatchewan r., in Canada, 3
Savinskii Ford, on the Donets, 156
Savinskaia, outpost on the Donets, 156
Savvo-Visherskii m., 177
Schleswig, portage of Slien-Treene, 14
Schlüsselburg, see Oreshek
Schugor r., 30; Shchugor r.–Iatriia r.p.,
  143–44; Shchugor r.–Vol'ia r.p., 143–
  44
Seim r., 58, 60, 126, 131, 157, 159, 162;
  Seim r.–Oskolets r.p., 126, 131; Seim
  r.–Severnyi Donets r.p., 126, 131
Selenbinsk o., 188
Selenga r., in Siberia, 82, 133, 147
Selenginsk o., in Siberia on the Selenga,
  82, 173, 187
Seliger l., in Valdai Portage region, 25,
  32, 114–15, 137; Seliger l.–Volotskoe
  l.p., 115, 137
Selim, Sultan, 65
Selizharovka r., Valdai Portage region,
  32, 114–15
Sementsov Ford, on the Mecha r., 157
Semigorodskaia pustyn', 181
Senno, portage of, 23
Serebrianka r.–Zheravlia r.p., 125, 144
Serednee o., 174
Seret (Osered) r., 61; Seret r.–Styr r.p.,
  127
Serezha r.–Zhelno l.p., 134, 137
Serpukhov, on old fortified line, 62
Sestra r., near the Vlena and Iakhroma-
  Kliazma portages, 113
Setka r.–Suran r.p., 122, 141
Severa, region in the Ukraine, 155
Severnaia Kel'tma r.–Dzhurich r.p.,
  123, 141
Severnaia Myl'ia r.–Iuzhnaia Myl'ia
  r.p., 142

Severnaia Mylva r.–Iuzhnaia Mylva
  r.p., 143
Severnyi Donets, see Donets
Severo-Ekaterininskii, Northern Cath-
  erina Canal, 95
Sevsk, terminal of Svinaia Doroga, 60
S'ezzha r.–Keza r.p., 116, 138
Shara r.–Iasolda r.p., 127
Sharzhenga r.–Iuza r.p., 120, 141
Shat' r.–Don r.p., 108, 126; Shat' r.–
  Volga r.p., 126
Shatsk, on the frontier, 62–63, 160
Shchukino v., on the Moscow-Volga
  Canal, 99
Shebalinov Ford, on the southern fron-
  tier, 156
Sheksna r., 30, 39, 117–19, 139; Sheksna
  r.–Perechnaia r.p., 119, 139
Shelon' r., system, 42–43, 137
Sheregodra l., 116; r., 116
Sheremet'ev, general of Peter I, 52
Shilenga r., Battle of, 43
Shilka r., 82–83, 147, 173
Shingal (Sungari) r., 174
Shomvukva r., 142
Shosha r., 15, 32, 35, 111; Shosha-Lama
  tributaries of Volga, 15, 32, 35
Shuia r., 120; Shuia r.–Monza r.p., 140
Shuiskii, Prince Vasilii Vasilievich, 43
Siamskii Rozhdestvenskii m., 181
Sias' r., see Siaz' r.
Siaz' r., on Tikhvin Waterway, 93, 116
Siberia, river system, 8; routes by land
  and sea to, 28–29; conquest of, 68–88;
  administrative costs paid by fur
  trade, 86; see also Monasteries, Por-
  tages, Rivers
Sibir, Kuchum's capital, taken by Yer-
  mak, 68
Siksha (modern Dasyksha) r.–Voloch-
  anka (modern Mati?) r.p., 149
Sitinets r., 116
Sitka (Novo-Arkhangelsk), 88
Sitno l., 116
Siverskoe l., on the Württemberg
  Canal system, 95
Skhodnia r., portages from, 35; Skhod-
  nia r.–Kliazma r.p., 111
Skopin-Shuiskii, makes treaty (1609)
  with Swedes, 46
Skovorodskii m., 177

Skverna r., on the southern frontier, 157
Slavianka r., 118; Slavianka r.–Poro-
zovitsa r.p., 118, 140
Slien, Gulf of, portage to Treene r., 14
Smolensk, ostrog, 5; strategic impor-
tance of, 16–24; princes of, 17; Trade
Codes of, 20, 28, 33, 42, 153–54; on
Western Dvina–Dnieper portage,
153–54
Snezhat' r.–Reseta r.p., 108, 131
Sob' r., 29, 144; Sob' r.–Elets r.p., 144
Soba r.–Luga r.p., 137
Sogozha r.–Toshna r.p., 119, 140
Soiginskii m., 181
Solikamsk, important town on Ural
frontier, 166
Solma r.–Sarra (Sara) r.p., 112; Solma
r.–Malaia Nerl' r.p., 112
Solovetskii m., 53, 180
Somina r., 116
Sominka r., on Tikhvin Waterway, 93
Somino l., on Tikhvin Waterway, 93,
112
Soroka, on the Stalin Canal, 99
Sosna r., frontier river, 108, 157–58
Sosva r., on the road to Siberia, 30;
Sosva r.–Ilych r.p., 143–44; Sosva r.–
Vol'ia r.p., 143–44
Southern Kel'tma r., Northern Cath-
erina Canal, 95; see Kel'tma r.
Sozh r., 131
Spaso-Kamennyi m., 181
Spaso-Prilutskii m., 181
Spaso-Sumorin m., 182
Spasskaia pustyn' na Boru, 180
Spasskii m. (Albazin region), 184
Spasskii m. (Bratsk region), 184
Spasskii m. (Eniseisk region), 183
Spasskii m. (Iakutsk region), 183
Spasskii m. (St. Petersburg-Olenets re-
gions), 179
Spasskii m. (Tara region), 182
Sredne-Kolymsk o., 188
Stalin Canal (White Sea–Baltic Canal),
97, 99
Stalingrad (Tsaritsyn), 65
Stanitsy, mobile patrols, 66
Stanovaia Riasa r., frontier r., 61, 157
Stanovoi ridge, on Okhotsk Sea–Lena
r. route, 83
Sterzh l., 114

Stolbovo, Peace of, between Sweden
and Russia, 47, 49
Storozhi, stationary guards, 66
Stroganovs, family of, 68–72
Stromilovo l., 115
Styr r.–Seret r.p., 127
Suda r., 117
Sudoma r.–Cherkha r.p., 136–37
Sukhona r., 29–30, 39, 118–20, 140; Suk-
hona r.–Kokshenga r.p., 140
Suleva r., on Nogaiskaia Doroga, 61
Sungari (Shingal) r., 174
Sura r.–Seim r.p., on the southern fron-
tier, 159, 162
Suran r.–Setka r.p., 122, 141
Surgut o., 72, 186
Suvela r., on Nogaiskaia Doroga, 61
Suzdal, 20, 33, 38; princes of, 38
Sverdlovsk (Ekaterinburg), 95, 100
Sviatogorskaia, on the southern fron-
tier, 156
Sviatoslav (third son of Iaroslav the
Great), 17
Sviatoslav (third son of Vladimir Mono-
makh), 17
Svid r., 118–19
Sviiazhsk o., 43
Svinaia Doroga, Tatar trail, 60, 157
Svisloch r.–Usha r.p., 128, 132; Svisloch
r.–Ptich r.p., 128
Sweden (Swedes), on the Neva, 25; in
the portage system, 44–54; see Gus-
tavus Adolphus
Svir' r., 28–29, 51, 53, 93, 117, 138–39;
Sweri, see Svir' r.
Sygva r., on Pechora–Ob' portage, 143
Sym r.–Tym r.p., 145–46
Synzhemskii m., 181
Syrinskii m., 179
Sysola r., 122–23, 141; Sysola r.–Volos-
nitsa r.p., 122, 141
Syrkov c., 177
Syz r.–Vesliana r.p., 123, 141

Tabarinsk v., 167
Tagil r., on portage route of the Volga–
Ob' systems, 125, 165
Tagil (or Tagilskii) Volok p., 125, 165
Taka River, see Takai
Takai (Taka) r., on the Nogaiskaia
Doroga, 61

Talitskii Ford, place of outpost, 157, 160

Tambov (Tanbov), on the fortified line in the south, 64–65, 160

Tangut, on the Chinese frontier, 175

Tara o., on the Irtysh, 69, 168

Tarbeev Brod, on the Voronezh, 61

Tarkhansk o., on the Tobol, 169, 186

Tatars (Tatar trails), 20, 25, 56–61, 72, 101

Tauia r., on the coast of Okhotsk, 78

Tavda r., in Siberia, 67, 69, 124, 167

Taz, Gulf of, 146

Taz r., 72–73, 146, 171

Tazovsk, see Mangazeia

Tebendin (Tebendinsk) o., 169, 186

Telekina r., on the Stalin Canal system, 99

Telekinskoe l., on the Stalin Canal system, 99

Telemba, on the Baikal-Shilka road, 83

Telembinsk o., 82, 187

Teletskoe l., 175

Terenin v., on the road from Tara to Tomsk, 170

Ternovskii Forest, near the Kalmiusskaia Sakma, 160

Tetera, see Shomvukva

Thannaim, see Niemen (?)

Tikhaia Sosna r., on the southern fortified line, 61, 160–61

Tikhvin p., 47, 93; Waterway, 92–93

Tikhvinka r., part of Tikhvin Waterway (Canal), 93; Tikhvinka r.–Valchina r.p., 116

Tim r., on the Muravskii Shliakh, 58

Time of Troubles, Swedes take advantage of, 46, 52

Titea r.–Churka r.p., 148

Tiumen o., in western Siberia, 69, 167–68

Tiun (pl. Tiuny), Bailiff of the Portage, 15, 20–21, 153–54

Tobol r., in western Siberia, 67, 69, 124–25, 168–71

Tobolsk o., 69, 75, 78, 186

Tobolskii Znamenskii m., 182

Tolshma r., 120; Tolshma r.–Kostroma r.p., 120, 140

Tom r., in western Siberia, 72, 175

Toma r.–Ket' r.p., 145

Tomsk o., in western Siberia, 72, 171, 175, 186

Tontora r., in the Lena-Amur portage route, 149

Topornia v., on the Württemberg Canal system, 95

Tor o., on the Velikii Tor r., 65

Toropa r., on the Lovat'-Western Dvina route, 16, 133–34

Toropets, key ostrog and seat of principality, 16, 21–22, 24, 42

Torzhok (Novyi Torg), key ostrog protecting Vyshnii Volochek portage, 5, 15, 20–21, 25, 27, 31–33, 42–43, 46, 54; see also Vyshnii Volochek

Toshna r.–Sogozha r.p., 119, 140

Totma, in Zavolochie, 39; see also Zavolochie

Transportation by river, in Siberia, 165–75; by land, 165–75

Transsiberian Railway, 100–1

Tre, a territory belonging to Novgorod

Treene r.–Gulf of Slien p., 14

Troitskaia pustyn', 180

Troitskii m. (Berezov region), 183

Troitskii m. (Kirensk region), 183

Troitskii m. (Selenginsk region), 184

Troitskii m. (Tiumen region), 182

Troitskii Gliadenskii m., 181

Troitskii Kaisarov m., 181

Troitskii m. (Shenkursk region), 180

Troitskii Ust'-Shekhonskii m., 178

Troitsko-Zelenskii m., 178

Trostenka r., on the Kalmiusskaia Sakma, 161

Trudy r., on the Volga–Don route, 108

Tsarevo-Borisov o., on the southern frontier, 64–65

Tsarevo-Zaimishche, on Napoleon's line of march, 23

Tsargorod, see Constantinople

Tsaritsa r., on the Volga–Don portage route, 65

Tsaritsyn (Stalingrad) on the Volga–Don portage route, 65

Tsilma r., 29; Tsilma r.–Lake-Peza r.p., 143

Tsna r., tributary of the Moksha-Oka, 62; Tsna r.–Mstino l., 115, 138; Tsna Canal, 92

Tsymla r., tributary of the Don, 61

Tugir p., in eastern Siberia, 83, 148–49, 174; r., 83, 148–49

Tugirsk o., in eastern Siberia, 83, 148–49, 188

Tula, on old southern fortified line, 58, 60–62, 65, 155

Tungus tribes, 75, 82

Tunguska r., in central Siberia, 73–74, 78, 147–48, 171–72; Nizhniaia (Lower) Tunguska, 73–74, 78, 147–48; Nizhniaia (Lower) Tunguska r.–Kulenga r.p., 73–74, 78, 147–48; Verkhniaia (Upper) Tunguska r., 73–74, 147; Podkamennaia Tunguska r., 73–74, 171–72, 175

Tungusskii p., between the Enisei and Lena rivers, 147

Tunkinskii o., in the Enisei basin, 187

Tura r., in western Siberia, 67, 69, 125, 165, 168

Turdeeva Mecha r., near the portage between the Upa and the Don, 158

Turinsk o., in western Siberia, 69, 165, 167, 186

Turmyshevskaia Doroga, on the Viazovna, 157

Turmyshskii Ford, on the southern frontier, 157

Turukhan r., a branch of the Enisei, 146, 171–72, 175, 186

Turukhansk o., on the Enisei, 75, 171–72, 175, 186

Tutka r.–Khmelnitsa r.p., 120, 140

Tutursk o., in the Lena system, 188

Tver, boundaries of, 15, 31–33, 43, 92

Tvertsa Canal, 92, 100; r., 15, 32, 115; Tvertsa r.–Msta r.p., 32

Tym r., in the Enisei-Ob' area, 60, 145–46; Tym r.–Sym r.p., 145–46

Ucha r., part of Moscow–Volga Canal system, 99

Uchur r., eastern Siberia, 82, 149

Ud r., in eastern Siberia, 82–83

Uda r., flows into Sea of Okhotsk, 60, 78

Udinsk o., later known as Nizhne-Udinsk, 82; see also Nizhne-Udinsk

Udraika r.–Usha r.p., 135, 138; Udraika r.–Velikaia r.p., 136

Udsk o., Okhotsk region, 78, 190

Udy r., see Uda r.

Uglich, men from, 38

Ugra r., 23, 62, 109, 131; Ugra r.–Osma r.p., 109, 131; Ugra r. tributaries–Viazma r.p., 23, 109; region through which Russian armies retreated before Napoleon, 23; battle of the, 62

Ui, with Niugzi forms the Turgirskii Volok, 148; see Tugirskii Volok

Uiagan r.–Penzhina r.p., 150

Ukhta r.–Govniukhva r.p., 142–43

Ukhtoma r., on the Volga–Onega portage route, 118

Ukhtomskii Volok, on the Volga–Onega portage route, 118

Ukraine, annexation of, 64

Ula r., on the Dnieper–Western Dvina portage route, 129

Ulia (or Ul'ia) r., 78

Ul'ia r., on the Lena–Ul'ia portage route, 78, 149

Ulla r., on the Dnieper–Western Dvina portage, 129

Umnak Pass, guarded by Unalaska Island of the Aleutian chain, 88

Unalaska Island, guards Umnak Pass, 88

Unimak Pass, guarded by Unalaska Island of the Aleutian chain, 88

Unzha r., on the Volga–Northern Dvina portage route, 120

Upa r., on the Volga–Don portage route, 56, 60, 62–63, 108, 158

Uperta r., on which an outpost at the Kamennyi Ford was located, 158

Upper Tunguska r., see Tunguska

Upper Volga Waterway, first and oldest of Russian canals, 92

Ura r.–Niugzi r.p., 149

Urak r.–Okhota r.p., 150

Ural Mountains (Kamen'), 29–30; country of, 34, 67, 171

Urka (Ura, Ui) r.–Niugzi (Niugchi, Niunzi, Niunchi, Niuga, Niuza) r.p., 148

Uryv, Belgorod fortification zone extends to, 163

Usa (ancient Sob'-Musa) r., 29, 128, 144

Userd r., and town, 160, 163

Usero, on the chief defense line of the south, 64

Usha r., 128, 132, 135; Usha r.–Svisloch r.p., 128, 132; Usha r.–Western Dvina r.p., 136; Usha r.–Nasva r.p., 135; Usha r.–Velikaia r.p., 135
Ushacha r.–Berezina r.p., 23, 128, 132
Ushcha r.–Udraika r.p., 135
Ushkuiniki (canoemen), see Novgorod
Ushura (Ussuri?) r., 174
Usmen l.–Lovat' r.p., 135, 137
Uspenskii or Gornyi c. (Vologda region), 181
Uspenskii m. (Shenkursk region), 180
Uspenskii Tikhvinskii m., 178
Uspenskii c. (Tobolsk region), 182
Uspenskii m. (Tomsk region), 182
Ussuri (Ushura?) r., branch of the Amur, 174
Ust'-Aldansk o., in the Lena region, 188
Ust'-Dukichinskii o., in the Amur region, 189
Ust'-Elovka, landing place on the Kama–Pechora route, 95
Ust'-Kut o., in the Enisei region, 187
Ust'-Maisk o., in the Lena region, 189
Ust'-Prorva o., in the Enisei region, 82, 187
Ust'-Shchelinskaia pustyn', 180
Ust'-Strelochnyi o., in the Enisei region, 83, 188
Ust'-Tausk o., in the Okhotsk region, 190
Ust'-Uliisk o., in the Lena region, 189
Ust'ia r., on the Onega–Northern Dvina portage route, 139
Ustiug, northern river center, 43; Velikii, 166
Usveia r., on the Dnieper–Western Dvina portage route, 129
Usviacha r., on the Western Dvina–Lovat' portage route, 134–35
Usviat r., on the Lovat'–Western Dvina route, 16, 134–35, 137; Usviat r.–Kunia r.p., 134, 137
Usvitsa r.–Drut' r.p., 129, 132
Utka, see Mezhevaia Utka
Uza r., tributary of the Shelon', 43; Uza r.–Cherekha r.p., 43, 136
Uzda r., on the Dnieper–Niemen portage route, 128
Uzhga r.–Kama r.p., 122, 141

Uzlovaia, railroad junction in the portage from the Oka to the Don, 56

Vad r., outpost on the southern frontier, 159
Vaga r., on the Onega–Northern Dvina route, 139–40
Vagai o. and r., on the route from Tobolsk to Tara, 168
Vagulka r., in western Siberia, 171
Vaigach Island, 29
Vakh r., on the Ob'–Enisei portage route, 145
Valaamskii m., 179
Valchina r., on the Tikhvin Waterway, 93; Valchina r.–Tikhvinka r.p., 116
Valdai Hills, grand portage of, 1–9; region of importance, 13, 30, 32, 36, 41–42, 44
Valdai l., in Valdai Hills region, 42
Valuiki o., on the southern frontier, 63
Varangians, 3, 11, 13, 14, 19
Varangian Sea, see Baltic Sea
Vaselievskii m., 178
Vazerinskoe l., on the Württemberg Canal system, 95
Vazuza r., 23, 36, 109, 113–14, 130–31; Vazuza r.–Dnieper r.p., 113, 130; Vazuza r.–Viazma r.p., 114, 131
Vel' r.–Voloshka r.p., 139
Velikaia r., 135–36; system, 136; Velikaia–Pernava, 136; Velikaia–Shelon', 136; Velikaia–Lovat', 136; Velikaia r.–Usha r.p., 136; Velikaia r.–Nasva r.p., 136; Velikaia r.–Udraika r.p., 136
Velikii Tor r., on the Muravskii Shliakh, 58, 65
Velikii Ustiug, see Ustiug
Velikoe l., on the Velikaia–Pernava portage route, 136
Veritsa r.–Dnieper r.p., 129, 133
Verkhne-Angarsk o., 82, 188
Verkhne-Kamchatsk, 190
Verkhne-Kolymsk o., 189
Verkhne-Udinsk o., 82, 188
Verkhne-Viliuisk o., 188
Verkhnee o., at the sources of the Kolyma, 174
Verkhoiansk o., on the Iana, 79, 173, 189

Verkholensk o., on the upper Lena, 82, 189

Verkhoturie o., important Ural center, 69, 165–66, 186

Verkhozeiskoe o., in the Lena region, 189

Verkolskii m., 181

Veska r., on the Volga–Volga portage route, 112

Vesliana r.–Syz r.p., 123, 141

Vetluga r., on the Volga–Northern Dvina portage, 121

Vezhki, outpost, 158

Viacheslav, Grand Prince of Smolensk (1054–1057), 17

Viatka, base of Ivan III, 43, 121–22

Viazenitsa r., on the southern frontier, 161

Viazhitskii m., 177

Viazma, 23, 109, 114, 130–31; Viazma r.–Vazuza r.p., 114, 130; Viazma r.–Ugra tributaries r.p., 23, 109, 131

Viazovna r., on the southern frontier, 157

Viborg, 45, 53

Viela r.–Kliazma r.p., 113

Vikings, 13–14

Viled' r.–Sysola r.p., 141

Viliia (Wilia) r., 128, 132

Viliui r., in central Siberia, 78

Viliuisk o., controls connection between the Lower Tunguska and the Chona, 78; p., 148; r., 148

Vioksa r., on the Volga–Volga portage route, 112

Virts l.–Pernava r.p., 136

Vishera r., 69; on the Kama–Pechora route, 95; Vishera r.–Lozva r.p., 124, 144

Visherka r., on the Kama–Pechora route, 29, 95, 124

Vitim r., in the Lake Baikal region, 82, 173

Vladimir, princely seat, 36; princes, 38

Vladimir Monomakh (Grand Prince of Smolensk, 1073–1078), 17

Vladychnia Kria, outpost at, 158

Vlena (Viela) r.–Kliazma r.p., 113

Vodla r., on the Onega–Ladoga portage route, 138

Vodlia r.–Kenozero l.p., 29

Vodolaga r., tributary of the Mozh-Donets-Don, 60

Vogulka r., on the Kama–Pechora route, 95; Vogulka r.–Volosnitsa r.p., 124, 143

Voguls, tribute-paying, 72, 167

Vokhma r.–Entala r.p., 121, 141

Vol l., on the Stalin Canal route, 99

Volch'ia r.–Kalmius r.p., 132; Volch'ia r.–Krynka r.p., 132

Volch'i Vody r., on the Muravskii Shliakh, 58, 61

Volga r., 1, 4, 5, 14, 16–18, 30–33, 35–36, 39, 65–66, 92; system, 107–25; Volga–Don, 107–8; Volga–Dnieper, 42, 108–9, 113–14; Volga–Volga, 109–13, 115, 117; Volga–Western Dvina, 114; Volga–Lovat', 114–15; Volga–Msta, 115–16; Volga–Ladoga, 116–17; Volga–Onega, 118–19; Volga–Northern Dvina, 118–24; Volga–Pechora, 124; Volga–Ob', 124–25; trade route, 33, 35–36; Upper Volga Waterway, 92; Volga–Don Canal, 99–100, 107

Vol'ia r., on Novgorod route to Siberia, 30; Vol'ia r.–Sosva r.p., 143

Volkov r., between Lake Ilmen and Lake Ladoga, 13, 26, 29, 45, 50–51, 92

Volochane, see Portagers

Volochaika, see Volochanka

Volochanka (Volochaika) r., 146; Volochanka r.–Krugloe l.p., 146; Volochanka r.– Volochanka r.p., 145–46; Volochanka (modern Mati?) r.–Siksha (the modern Dasyksha) r.p., 149, 172

Volochek, Bolshoi, p., 136; Malyi, p., 136; Vyshnii, p., 15, 115

Volochnia r.–Kosha r.p., 115

Volodskoe l.–Dolgoe l.p., 118

Vologda, a great center on the way to the north, 30–31, 39, 119, 133

Vologodskii Pesochnyi m., 181

Volok r.–Ressa r.p., 109, 131

Volok Lamskii, see Volokolamsk

Volokolamsk, 15, 31–32, 35, 42, 54; on Moscow–Rzhev Railway, 100; see also Novgorod

Volokoslavskii p., between the Chagoda and the Volozhba and between the Valchina and Tikhvinka, 116, 138
Volosha, see Volozhba
Voloshba (Volosha) r.–Chagoda r., 116, 138
Voloshevo l., 138; see Voloshozero
Voloshka r., 138–39; Voloshka r.–Vel' r.p., 139
Voloshna r.–Lama r.p., 111
Voloshozero l., 138; Voloshozero l.–Chereva r.p., 138
Volosnitsa r., 29; on the Kama–Pechora route, 95; 122, 124, 141, 143; Volosnitsa r.–Sysola r.p., 122, 141; Volosnitsa r.–Nydyb r.p., 122, 141; Volosnitsa r.–Vogulka r.p., 124, 143
Volotskoe l., 115, 118, 138; Volotskoe l.–Seliger l.p., 115, 137; Volotskoe l.–Dolgoe l.p., 118, 139
Volovo l., outpost at, 158
Volovo (?) (Znamenskoe), railroad junction near Kulikovo battlefield, 56
Volozhba (Volosha) r.–Chagoda r.p., 116
Volui o. and r., 160
Vop' r., on the Dnieper–Western Dvina route, 130
Vorgla r., on the southern frontier, 157
Voria r.–Gzhat' r.p., 23, 109
Voronezh o., 63–64; r., 61, 64, 107, 157
Vorskla r., 58, 60, 64, 162
Voskresenskii c. (Beloozero region), 178
Voskresenskii m. (Shenkursk region), 180
Votria r.–Elsha r.p., 130, 133
Votskaia Piatina (Wotskepetiniske country), 51
Vozdvizhenskii m., 179
Vozhanskoe l., on the Tikhvin Waterway, 93
Vozhe l., on the Volga–Onega portage route, 118–19
Voznesenskii m. (Irkutsk region), 183
Voznesenskii m. (Moscow region), 179
Voznesenskii m. (Shenkursk region), 180
Vselug l., on the Volga–Western Dvina portage route, 114
Vsevolod (fourth son of Iaroslav), 17

Vvedenskii m. (Krasnoiarsk region), 183
Vvedenskii m. (Neviansk region), 184
Vvedenskii m. (Shenkursk region), 180
Vvedenskii m. (Solvychegodsk region), 181
Vychegda r., 29, 95, 122–24, 141–42
Vydbino l.–Pola r.p., 133
Vydra r., 16, 130, 133; Vydra r.–Khvost r.p., 130, 133
Vyg l. and r., 99
Vyksenskaia pustyn', 178
Vym r., on the Northern Dvina–Pechora portage route, 142
Vymskii p., between the Govniukha and the Ukhta, 142
Vymskii Arkhangelskii m., 181
Vyrka r., on the southern frontier, 161
Vyshnii Volochek (Upper Little Portage), 32, 42, 92, 100, 115
Vytegra r.–Kovzha r.p., 117; Vytegra r.–Lache l.p., 139; Vytegra r.–Onego l.p., 29

Welock, see Volkhov
Western Dvina r., 1, 5, 8, 13, 16, 18, 35–36; system, 132–35; Western Dvina–Niemen, 132; Western Dvina–Dnieper, 42, 132–33; Western Dvina–Volga, 133; Western Dvina–Lovat', 28, 133–35; Western Dvina–Velikaia, 135; Western Dvina–Usha r.p., 136
White Sea, 4, 29, 95–96
White Sea–Baltic Canal (Stalin Canal), 97, 99
Wilia (Viliia) r., 128, 132
Winnipeg l. district portage, 2, 3; r., 2
Witovt, Lithuanian ruler, 22
Wolck, see Volkhov
Woods, Lake of the, 2
Wotskepetiniske country, see Votskaia Piatina
Württemberg Canals, 93–94

Yakutsk, see Iakutsk
Yenisei, see Enisei
Yeniseisk, see Eniseisk
Yermak, conquest of Siberia, 68–72; had "religious assistant," 86
Yk r.–Pil'va r.p., 123, 142

Zakamennoe o., on the Enisei, 172
Zaonikievskaia pustyn', 181
Zapadnyi Bug, r. on the Dnieper–Vistula portage route, 127
Zarachunskii Hill, an outpost in the south, 158
Zashiversk o., 79, 173–74; 189
Zavolochie, "Country-beyond-the-Portage," 26, 30–31, 35, 39
Zeia r., 82, 174; Zeia r.–Katym r.p., 149
Zelenaia r.–Mutnaia r.p., 29, 151
Zelenkov Ford, on the Mecha in the south, 157
Zhabka r., tributary of the Volga, 46
Zhadenie l.–Peno l.p., 114, 133; Zhadenie l.–Luchanskoe l.p., 133, 137
Zhadore (Zhadenie) l., on the Western Dvina–Lovat' portage route, 133
Zhelno l.–Serezha r.p., 134, 137

Zheravlia r.–Serebrianka r.p., 125, 144; Zheravlia r.–Chusovaia Sylva r.p., 125, 144
Zhestovy Mountains, in the south, 161
Zhigansk o., between Iakutsk and the Lena, 78, 189
Zhizdra r., on the Volga–Dnieper portage route, 108
Zhizhitsa r., on the Western Dvina–Lovat' portage route, 134
Zhizhitskoe l., on the Western Dvina–Lovat' portage route, 134
Zima, on the Transsiberian, 101
Znamenskii c. (Irkutsk region), 183
Zosimo-Savvatieva pustyn', 180
Zosimy i Savvatiia m., 182
Zusha r., on the southern frontier, 56, 60, 108, 158
Zverin Pokrovskii c., 177

DATE DUE

GAYLORD			PRINTED IN U.S.A